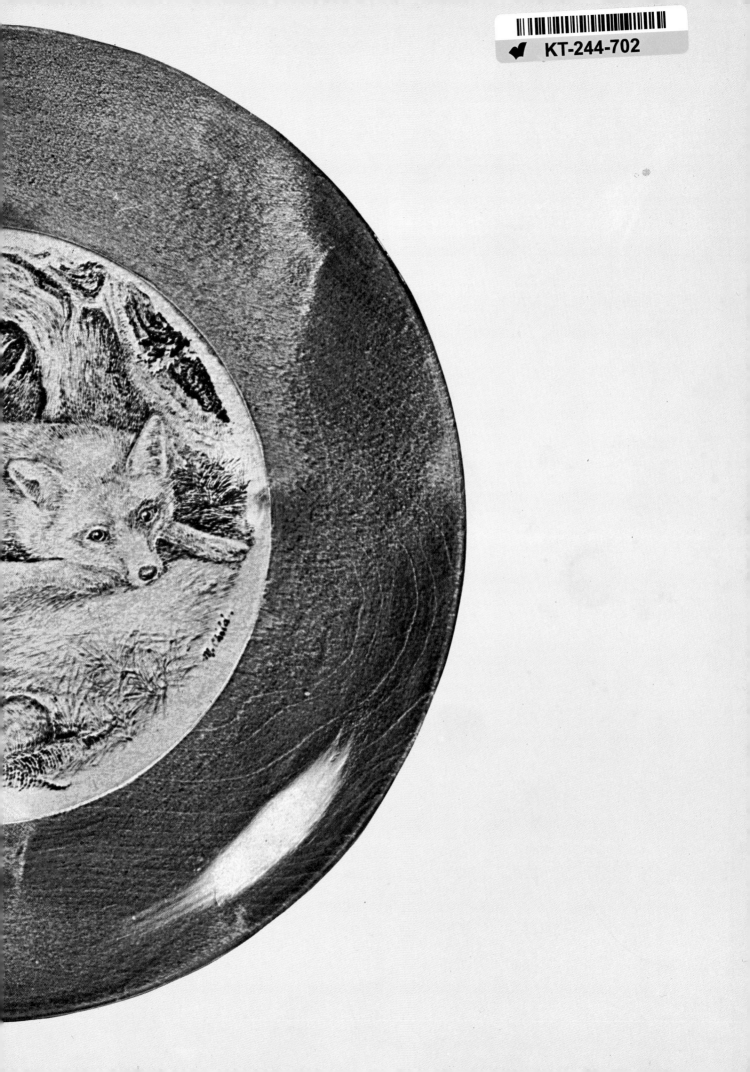

ideas for UNUSUAL HAND CRAFTS

Marshall Cavendish
London and New York

Edited by Susan Simmons.

Published by Marshall Cavendish Publications Limited,
58, Old Compton Street,
London, W1V 5PA.

© Marshall Cavendish Limited, 1972 and 1973.

This material first published by Marshall Cavendish Limited
in 1972 and 1973 in the partwork Golden Homes.

This volume first published 1975.

Printed in Great Britain by Carlisle Web Offset Ltd.

ISBN 0 85685 101 9

This edition not to be sold in the USA,
Canada or the Philippines.

Introduction

A hand craft is more than a hobby; using techniques that are often quite simple to master you can create something original and decorate your home. And with so many new and exciting materials available they have become more interesting and varied than ever before.

For instance, have you ever considered the use of polyester resin or concrete as decorative materials. Or how about making your own wallpaper, murals or even a set of chess pieces. All of these are described in detail along with glass engraving, pyrography or pokerwork, welding, brass rubbing, marquetry and many more unusual and traditional crafts.

Starting with the simpler skills and moving on to more advanced work — all designs and techniques are given clearly and concisely for the completion of every project.

Designed for men and for women, a whole host of new and original hand crafts are discovered for you to create beautiful and original articles within your home.

Contents

Mosaic table top

Mosaic is one of the most spectacular forms of decoration, with all the richness of jewellery on a far larger scale. But it is not at all difficult to do, and if you are prepared to devote a little time to it, you can achieve magnificent results with no prior experience of the art.

Mosaic panels can be made with almost any material: broken pieces of coloured glass, mirror or ceramic tile, interesting-coloured pebbles found on a beach, and even small glittering objects such as watch parts and chrome-plated nuts and washers. Anything will do provided it is small, hard and durable.

The mosaic described here, however, is made from special glass mosaic pieces bought from a hobby shop. Obviously, this is a more expensive way of doing it, but it has the major advantage that all the pieces are exactly the same thickness, so the finished mosaic has a level surface and can be used as a table-top. If you are planning to make a wall panel there is no need to restrict yourself in this way.

The brightest and best ready-made mosaic pieces are of glass and come from Italy and Scandinavia. Slightly cheaper ceramic mosaic pieces come from France and West Germany. Both types are sold by the square foot; about 2lb covers this area (metric equivalent: 1kg per 0.1sq m). Some colours, particularly red, gold and silver, are more expensive than others.

The mosaic illustrated was designed and made by the British stained glass and mosaic designer Michael Coles ARCA. A squared-up version of his design is shown in Fig.2 for you to copy if you like. If you stick to the size and shape of the original—18in. x 24in. or approximately 450 x 600mm—each square shown here will be 1½in. (38mm) across.

The finished panel is mounted on an extremely simple table base made of 50 x 50mm or 2in. x 2in. pine (see Fig.3). No knowledge of carpentry is needed to make this, and few tools. Its unusual construction also makes it very strong and rigid, so that it can be made in a larger size than described without loss of strength, though very large sizes should use 63 x 63mm (2½in. x 2½in.), or even 75 x 75mm (3in. x 3in.) timber.

Tools and materials

For the mosaic panel alone, you will need:
One piece of 19mm or ¾in. thick blockboard 24in. x 18in. or 600 x 450mm.

7ft 6in. (2.3m) of 30 x 60mm or 1¼in. x ¼in. pine for edging the mosaic panel. You can use metal or plastic edging if you prefer but you must edge it with something, because a mosaic panel has very sharp edges.

Below. *This striking design gives an idea of what you can achieve with mosaic if you use a little imagination.*

1

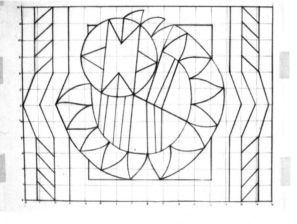

2

*Above: **Fig.1.*** *Arrange the pieces of mosaic in small containers to save time and trouble.*
Fig.2. *A squared-up plan of Michael Coles' original design for you to copy if you like.*
Fig.3. *The table frame: a very simple piece of construction, even for non-carpenters.*
Fig.4. *Mosaic-workers' tools: 'nippers', tweezers, spatula and small bricklayer's trowel.*
Fig.5. *Cutting a mosaic piece with the 'nippers'. Use only the point of the tool.*
Fig.6. *Building up the design. Only a small area should be worked at one time.*
Fig.7. *A close-up of the half-completed design, showing how the pieces are arranged.*
Fig.8. *Spreading the grout with a piece of wood. Most of it is wiped off afterwards.*
Large picture, right. *The finished table: an attractive and unusual piece of furniture.*

A small tin of pink wood primer.

9 sq ft (0.28sq m) of ready-made mosaic pieces from a hobby shop.

One pint or half a litre of special mosaic cement (Fixtite is a British example).

7lb or 3kg of ordinary tile grout.

A small amount of brown powder colour or any water-based paint.

A pair of 'mosaic nippers'—a special miniature tile-cutter for cutting mosaic pieces to shape. You can get these at the same shop as the mosaic. They are essential.

A pair of tweezers.

A palette knife.

A small pointed trowel, such as a bricklayer's dotter.

A thin wood strip about 6in. x 1½in. (150 x 38mm) with one end bevelled (ground off at an angle) to a chisel shape. This is for spreading grout on the finished mosaic. You could equally well use a wooden kitchen spatula.

Small panel pins ½in. or 13mm long for fixing the edging.

For the table base, you will need :

12ft (about 3.5m) of 50 x 50mm or 2in. x 2in. PAR (planed all round) pine.

2ft (600mm) of 25 x 25mm or 1in. x 1in. wood for battens to screw the table-top to.

Twelve 3in. (75mm) No. 8 screws.

Ten 1½in. (38mm) No. 8 screws.

Several sheets of sandpaper graduated from medium coarse to flour grade (the finest available).

Wood glue (any type).

A finish for the wood. The one described below uses teak oil, a small amount of polyurethane varnish and turpentine substitute.

Tenon or panel saw, screwdriver, bradawl, ruler and (if possible) a hand drill and a selection of twist bits.

Laying and finishing mosaic

The first thing to do is give the blockboard base on which the mosaic is to be laid a good coat of wood primer. This should be applied to both sides and the edges to keep the board from warping.

While the primer is drying, draw out the design for the mosaic on a sheet of paper the same size as the panel. If you are copying the design given here, first rule 1½in. (38mm) squares all over the paper in coloured ballpoint (use another colour for the design itself). Number the squares and transfer the design from Fig.2, one square at a time to ensure accuracy. Otherwise, draw your own design, keeping it bold and simple.

Now scribble all over the other side of the paper with the blackest and softest available pencil. When the primer on the baseboard is completely dry, pin the paper to it, making sure it is straight, and go over the design again (but not the grid) with a ballpoint, pressing fairly hard.

If this method doesn't transfer the design to the board as clearly as you would like, put carbon paper between the paper and the board and trace the design again.

Assemble as many saucers or small containers as you have colours of mosaic, and put pieces of one colour on each saucer.

A note about mosaic colours: even if you are planning to have one colour strongly pre-dominant, don't buy (say) 3sq ft of that colour. If the colour is off-white, buy 1sq ft of off-white, one of pure white and one of very pale beige, and mix them at random. This will make the plain surface much more lively, but basically the same colour. Variety is the essence of good mosaic work.

Ready-made mosaic pieces are usually square and much larger than you want, so practise cutting them to size and shape with the special 'nippers'. See Fig.5 for how to do this. Note that the cutting jaws of the tool are placed across only a small area. This will ensure a clean cut stretching out forwards from the jaws in an almost straight line. If you bridge the whole width of the mosaic piece with the jaws and then try to cut it, the result will generally be to break the piece into several irregular fragments.

It is a good idea to practise using the nippers until you can control their cut accurately. The cut and broken mosaic pieces will not be wasted; you can use them all in the design.

Never use the large mosaic pieces whole, even to make plain-coloured backgrounds. The effect is monotonous. Always cut the squares into several pieces; this will give the pleasantly irregular effect of a good mosaic.

Mosaic pieces are laid on small areas of the baseboard at a time, rather than being used to trace outlines right across the whole width. This is because mosaic adhesive dries rather fast (30 minutes) and is hard to remove when dry. If you have to stop in the middle of a section for more than a couple of minutes, always scrape off the wet adhesive or you will have to use a hammer and chisel later.

The best place to start on the design shown is one of the off-white petals of the central flower. First cut a few mosaic tiles in off-white and closely related colours into fairly small squares and rectangles, four or more per original square tile. Don't worry about the straightness of the sides of the squares.

Now spread a good thick, even layer of adhesive over the area of the petal only. Press the first pieces of mosaic into place to form a solid line around the edge of the petal. The outer edges of the pieces should follow the traced line exactly; the inner edges will then form a more irregular line. If you want to strengthen the outline of the petal, or any other outline, lay a second row of pieces just inside the first row and fitting against it as closely as possible. If not, fill in the centre of the area with rather irregular rows running across the area the short way. Press all pieces well down to give a level surface (but microscopic accuracy is not important, so don't worry about slight lumps).

The way a good mosaic is organized is shown in Fig.7. Note the careful balance between neat geometrical rows and complete randomness. If you can strike this balance, the finished mosaic will look pleasingly irregular but not messy. Try to get the pieces fitting together fairly closely to help this impression.

Continue to build the mosaic from the centre outwards, a small area at a time. When you get to the edge, trim the edge pieces carefully so that they do not stick out beyond the edge of the blockboard. If you don't do this, it will be difficult to make the edging strip sit straight.

Let the last batch of adhesive dry thoroughly (this will take more than an hour) and then turn the board upside down over a sheet of newspaper to shake off any loose fragments. If any pieces that were meant to be there fall off, they weren't properly fixed. Stick them back, pressing down well. Finish cleaning the mosaic with a soft cloth, but DON'T rub your bare hand over it. The pieces are sharp and will cut you.

It is now time to grout the mosaic, or fill the small gaps between the pieces and cover the sharp edges. Ordinary tile grout is quite suitable except for its staring white colour, which would spoil the subtlety of the mosaic. The colour can be toned down by adding a small amount of brown powder paint. Apart from this, follow the manufacturer's instructions for mixing.

Spread a very thin layer of the coloured grout on a sheet of paper to check its colour. It should be a very pale brown, not too dark.

Spread the grout all over the mosaic with the piece of wood or wooden spatula as if buttering a piece of bread (see Fig.8). Try to fill all the gaps between the pieces without coating the surface.

If any pieces do get covered up, wipe the grout off with a slightly damp cloth, then polish them with a dry cloth (watch your knuckles!) Then wait until the grout is dry on the surface, but not yet hard, and brush it with a soft brush to remove loose lumps. Allow the grout to harden for 24 hours, then polish the mosaic with clear furniture cream.

Finally, nail on the edging strip carefully with the panel pins. The bottom of the strip should be level with the bottom of the board and the top should cover the edge of the mosaic. You can mitre the corners of the edging if you know how; otherwise, cut two pieces to very slightly more than the length of the long sides plus twice the thickness of the edging, and nail them on so that they overlap the ends of the short edging pieces at both corners. Sand the end to the exact length.

Use an old nail (or a nail punch if you have one) to punch the ends of the panel pins slightly below the surface of the wood. Fill the dents thus formed with light-coloured plastic wood or special wood 'stopping', let this harden and sand it flat.

Finally, sand the edging strip all over with very fine or flour grade paper, and finish it as you prefer. One good method is described below.

The table frame

The table frame has eight main pieces : two long sides 24in. (600mm) long, two short sides 18in. (450mm) long and four vertical legs 12in. (300mm) long. All are of 50 x 50mm or 2in. x 2in. PAR timber, which has all its surfaces planed smooth to save you trouble. The planing reduces the actual width and thickness of the wood to $1\frac{3}{4}$in.-$1\frac{7}{8}$in.—a point to watch.

The length of all the pieces adds up to exactly 11ft or 3.3m, but you are strongly advised to buy a little more than this to allow for wastage.

In addition to the main pieces, there are two 12in. x 1in. x 1in. (300 x 25 x 25mm) battens, which are fastened to the inner surfaces of the two 18in. (450mm) top rails of the table frame, flush with their top surface. These provide something to pass screws through when mounting the mosaic panel on the frame, since it is impossible to screw through a mosaic from the top. Their exact size is unimportant ; so is the type of wood they are made of.

Mark out and cut the main frame pieces in the following manner. To cut a piece (say) 24in. long, first inspect the end of the wood to make sure it is cut straight and free from chips. If not, trim the damaged or crooked end. Then measure 24in. up the wood with your ruler and make a small pencil mark at this point. Use the ruler to draw a line all round the wood at right angles to its length. If you have done this correctly, the two ends of the line will meet exactly. A carpenter's try square is a great help if you have one, since it automatically creates a true right angle when laid along the wood.

Place a saw with its blade just on the far side of the pencil line, so as not to cut through the line. Cut the wood using moderate pressure and making sure that the blade runs straight. When nearly through the wood, reduce pressure drastically or you will tear the fibres as the blade emerges.

Don't mark the length of the next piece until you have cut the previous piece right off and inspected the cut end that removing it has left. You might need to trim this end slightly—hence the allowance for waste when buying the timber.

When all the pieces are cut to length, clean up their ends. A plane is a help if you have one, but keep turning the wood as you plane its end or the result will be crooked.

If no plane is available, use coarse sandpaper, then medium, then fine. The ends of the horizontal rails will be visible in the finished job, so finish them as well as you can. Round the edges and corners slightly with sandpaper.

The frame is glued and screwed together, using the longer screws of the two lengths you have bought. The horizontal rails should be drilled right through each end to make it easy to pass screws through them into the vertical legs. The holes *can* be drilled with a bradawl, but it will save you a lot of effort later if you make a larger hole with a real drill. The right sized drill bit to choose is one the same size as the shank (unthreaded part) of the screws you are using.

To find the right spot for drilling, measure the thickness of the wood, halve it and make a mark that distance from the end. Mark both sides of the wood as a double check. Drill one hole in each end of each horizontal piece (but not in any of the legs yet), both holes running the same way. Each drill hole should emerge through the mark on the other side.

It is now time to start assembling the frame. Consult Fig.3 to see how it goes together. The first step is to attach the two shorter rails to their legs. Put one leg down on the floor and lay a rail on top of it in the exact position it will occupy, with its end flush with the leg's outer edge and its top edge flush with the top of the leg. Prop up the other end of the rail with another leg to keep it level, then poke a bradawl through the pre-drilled hole in the rail to mark where the screw will go into the leg.

Lift off the rail and make a bradawl hole about 1in. (25mm) deep through the mark you have made on the leg. This will make it much easier to insert the screw (and also, curiously enough, much harder to pull it out without unscrewing it). Then mark the adjacent surfaces of the joint with a number so that you can assemble them correctly later.

When you have done this with all four legs, spread a reasonable, but not excessive, amount of glue on the surfaces to be joined and screw them together. A little soap or vegetable oil on the screws makes them easier to turn. Check that the legs are exactly at right angles to the rails with a try square, set square or hardback book cover pressed into the corner. Adjust if necessary, wipe off excessive glue with a damp cloth, and leave to dry.

The longer rails fit below the shorter ones. Prop the two rail-and-leg units on end with the rails on the inside, facing each other. Put the longer rails on the legs just below the shorter rails and mark the legs with a bradawl poked through the drilled holes as before. At the same time, mark a spot on the underside of the longer rails centrally below the place where the shorter rails cross them, and drill through this with the large drill so that you can screw the longer rails to the shorter rails as well as to the legs. Replace the longer rail in position and mark the shorter rails through the drillhole with your bradawl.

Now glue and screw the entire main frame together. Measure the diagonal distance both ways across the frame from leg to leg. The two measurements should be exactly the same if the frame is square. If they are not, straighten the frame before the glue dries by pulling it, so as to bend the screws a little. Leave it to dry.

Finally, glue and screw the two battens to the inside of the shorter rails level with the top, drilling large holes in the battens and small bradawl holes in the rails as before. Also drill two or three holes through the battens the other way (i.e. at right angles) for the top mounting screws. The outermost holes of these should be about 1in. (25mm) from the end of the batten so as to get a wide grip on the top, but the exact placing or number of the others is unimportant. The frame is now complete.

Turn the mosaic panel upside down, place the frame on it exactly in position and screw through the battens to the blockboard backing. This completes assembly.

The pine of which the frame is made can be given an attractive satin finish by sanding carefully with flour grade paper, then painting with a 50/50 mixture of polyurethane varnish and turpentine substitute. Rub this down gently with more flour grade paper or very fine wire wool. If you can be bothered to, put on another coat and rub that down too. Then smear a thin coating of teak oil all over with a soft cloth. The finish is hard-wearing and stainproof.

The method for producing a mosaic table top can also be applied to walls. The mosaic fish mural shown below is made up of individually set tesserae. This, although difficult to execute, has the effect of making the background an integral part of the whole design. An easier method is described overleaf.

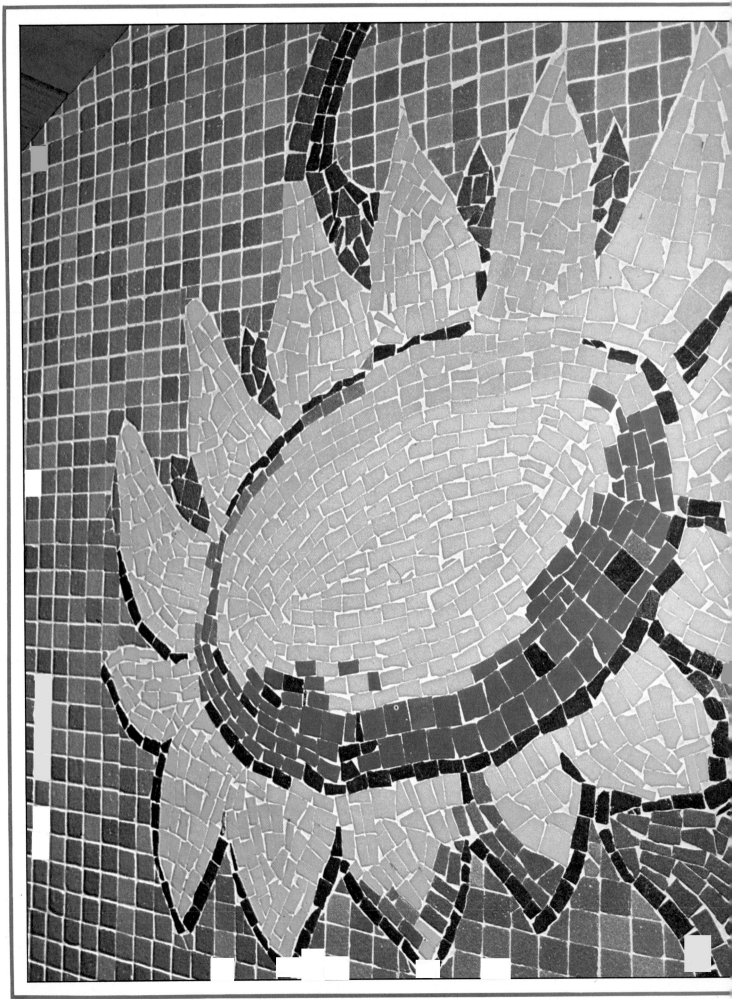

Mural in mosaic

A mural made with mosaic tiles can give your bathroom a rich appearance. With the vast range of colours and materials available, you can create a valuable addition to your home in a few days, at no great expense.

The method described in the former chapter for producing a mosaic pattern on a table top can just as easily be applied to walls. There are, however, two distinct disadvantages to this method of application when used to form a mural. One is the time it would take to apply a design, or even a random pattern, to a large surface. The other snag is that, unless you have previous experience of this method, you cannot really get a clear idea of what the finished picture will look like until all the pieces are in place. By this time the adhesive is rock hard, and there is little you can do to remedy any unwanted features.

The method of application described here not only avoids both of these problems, but is suitable for almost any surface and function, particularly for walls, floors and swimming pools. (Special additional techniques are needed

The mural shown in these photographs has been made by arranging individual mosaic tesserae to form the main design, with sheet mosaic for the background. This method has the advantage of cutting down the time involved in applying a design to a large area and is also suitable for almost any surface.

for large floor areas and swimming pools, and these will not be dealt with here.)

Mosaic tesserae

Tesserae (the small tiles used for mosaic designs) are not only sold loose, but also in 'sheets', mounted either on scrim or paper; usually there are nine sheets to a square metre. The scrim-mounted tesserae have a nylon scrim stuck with resin to their back surface; the scrim is not removed after application, but helps the adhesion of the mosaic. The paper-mounted tesserae have a sheet of paper stuck to the top surface with water soluble glue; after the mosaic is fixed, the paper is soaked off. In order to line up each sheet accurately, paper-faced mosaics have a $\frac{1}{4}$in. (6mm) margin round the edges. Face-mounted tesserae (those which have a sheet attached to the face) have their edges chamfered down towards the back, whereas back-mounted tesserae are square edged.

There is an enormous variety of tiles on the market suitable for mosaic work. They are sold in various shapes—round, oval, oblong, square, flat, rounded or concave. They can be made of vitrified glass, glazed or unglazed ceramic, or marble. Finishes also vary greatly, but generally only matt-finish vitrified ceramic or marble tiles are suitable for floors, as glass or glazed tiles will chip.

Designs

The way in which the sheets of tesserae are made up depends upon the supplier, but they can be bought either plain or patterned. The patterns vary from random mixtures of colours to formal arrangements such as the Greek Key pattern. Most suppliers will make up sheets to your own design, and the time taken, and the cost, depends on the intricacy of the pattern.

If you want to make up your own sheets of mosaic you will need a mosaic tray. This is a sheet of mild steel with thin raised divisions or guide lines, on to which you place the tesserae as you want them, right side up. When the tray is full you stick a sheet of brown sticky paper to the face of the tesserae, and the whole thing is then turned out to dry.

In the mural shown in the photographs, a motif has been used in conjunction with a made-up random background. Italian glass mosaic tesserae were used for both the motif and the background in this case, but ceramic tesserae could equally well have been used, depending on the required effect. The tesserae for the motif were bought loose by the pound (1sq.ft or 305mm sq. of mosaic tiles weighs about $2\frac{1}{4}$lb or 1kg), but the background was

NELSON HARGREAVES

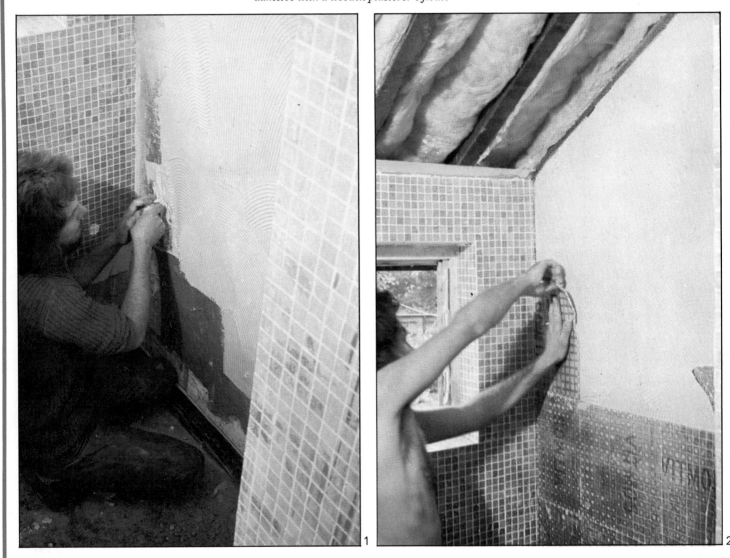

chosen from an imported range of three-colour random patterns.

Fixing

Mounting sheet mosaic is quite simple if you observe a few basic rules; the first of these is good preparation. The preparation and fixing method depend on the fixing surface, use and environment. Mosaic tesserae can be fixed to many different types of surface, and the fixing methods are basically the same as those used when fixing ordinary ceramic tiles. The important consideration is to choose an adhesive which is suitable for the fixing surface, and to the use to which the mosaic is going to be put. The atmosphere in kitchens and bathrooms is often damp, and direct wetness also occurs, particularly round showers.

The best fixing surface is cement-rendered clay brickwork. But it is also possible to fix mosaic tesserae to lightweight and aerated breeze blocks, plastered surfaces, building sheets and boards, old glazed tiles, painted surfaces and metal.

Fixing to brickwork and lightweight building blocks. The walls should be completed a minimum of four weeks prior to rendering. A 4:1 cement/sand mortar rendering should be applied ½in. (13mm) thick to the surface of the brickwork and left with a wood float finish for at least two weeks before fixing the mosaic.

A solid bedding technique is adopted when fixing the mosaic to the rendering. For this to be effective, each tessera must adhere fully to the adhesive. If any spaces are left behind the finished mosaic, expansion of air or moisture

trapped there could cause the tesserae to lift off.

Adhesives. There are several types and makes of adhesive suitable for fixing mosaic tesserae, but for brickwork applications, the British Ceramic Tile Council recommends CTF1, CTF2 or BAL-FLEX. All three are manufactured by Building Adhesives Ltd; CTF1 and CTF2 are both thin-bed adhesives, CTF2 is used where wet conditions or a damp atmosphere are likely to occur. BAL-FLEX is a flexible, water-based two-part material which can be used either as a thin-bed or a thick-bed adhesive up to ½in. (13mm) thick. It is particularly suitable for use with marble mosaic, where the thickness of the individual tesserae varies, or where background movement or vibration is likely to occur. When fully cured it is impervious to water. If you are in any doubt as to which type of adhesive to use,

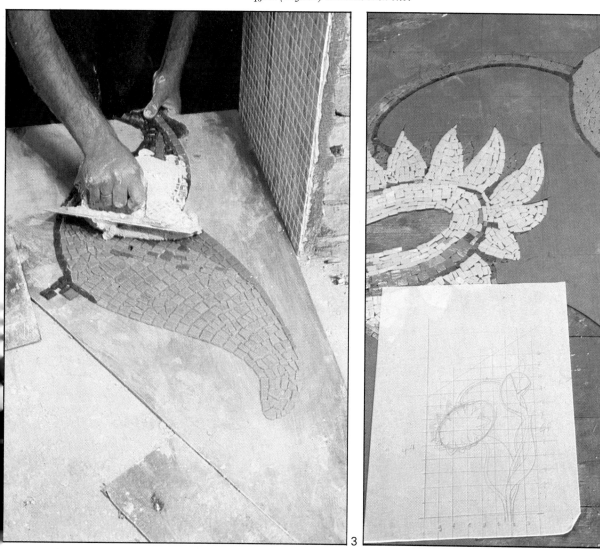

Fig. 3. The motif has been laid face down so that the chamfered backs can be filled with grouting. The surface is then wiped clean to remove the excess grouting.
Fig. 4. Working from a scale drawing, the individual mosaic tesserae are laid in place on the template, leaving gaps about $\frac{1}{16}$ in. (1.5mm) between each one.

3

4

ask your supplier.

Before fixing the tesserae, nail a batten below the proposed bottom edge of the mosaic. This will prevent the tesserae from sliding down the wall before the adhesive sets. The batten should be removed after you have finished fixing the mosaic.

Apply a screed of adhesive approximately $\frac{1}{8}$in. (3mm) thick to the rendering (Fig.1). This should be applied with a plasterer's laying-on trowel (experts sometimes use a mastic trowel with serrated edges, but this can leave air pockets when the mosaic is fixed). As the working time is approximately 20 minutes, it is inadvisable to spread more than one square metre at one time. Press the sheets of mosaic into position (Fig.2), and bed them down by beating them into the adhesive with a wooden

plasterer's float. The float should be slid, rather than lifted, off the mosaic.

Because it is difficult to fill the cracks between tesserae with chamfered backs after they are fitted, it is wise to pre-grout paper-faced mosaic just before fixing. Lay the sheets face down and fill the cracks with grouting (Fig.3). Remove any excess grout and lift the sheets into position. Once the sheets are in position and firmly bedded in, the paper can be soaked off, using a minimum of warm water. At the same time any traces of glue should also be removed. Grout once more, filling any gaps, and then wipe down the whole surface to remove any excess grout.

With nylon-backed mosaic, the scrim backing remains embedded in the adhesive, so grouting is done after the sheets of tesserae have been

fixed. Remove any surplus adhesive from the face before it sets. Allow twelve hours for the adhesive to dry then grout the joints as for ordinary ceramic tiling.

Making a mosaic mural

You can make up an intricate design similar to the unusual sunflower motif shown on page eleven, by following these instructions.

Make a scale drawing on paper, about 2in. to 1ft (50mm to 305mm) of the wall surface to which the mosaic is to be applied, and work out your design in colour. Use colours as near as possible to the tile manufacturer's colour charts. When you are satisfied with your design, divide it up into squares, again to scale, (6in. x 6in. or 150mm x 150mm full size is a handy size).

Lay out several sheets of expanded poly-

15

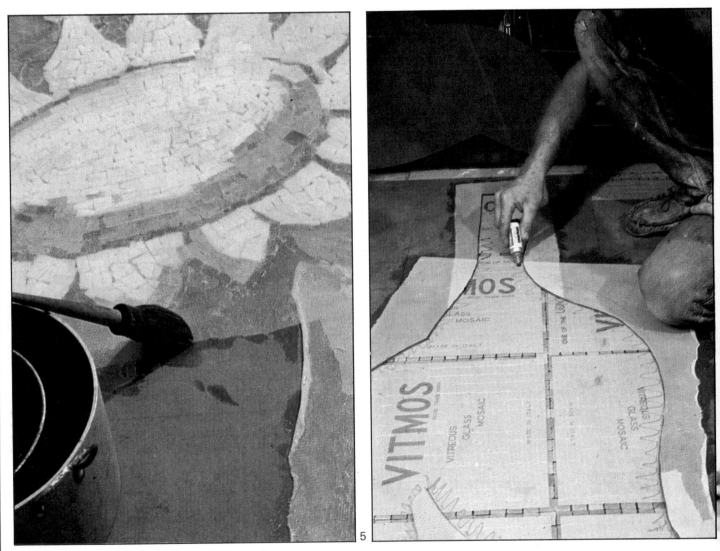

styrene wall lining, card or hardboard, on a table or the floor, according to the size of the finished mural. This board should be slightly thinner than the tesserae to be used. Transfer the design to this board, blowing it up to full size, then cut out the design using a handyman's knife such as a Stanley knife.

The template which is left can now be either stuck or pinned to a backing sheet of hardboard or similar materials, or the floor if it is smooth enough. The individual mosaic tesserae can now be cut, as shown in the previous chapter, and placed in position to form the pattern. Remember to leave gaps about $\frac{1}{16}$in. (1.5mm) wide between each tessera (Fig.4).

When you are happy with the layout, dip pieces of butter muslin in hot glue size, lightly wring each piece out, place it over the design

and press it on to the face of the tesserae using a sponge or brush to ensure adhesion (Fig.5). It is important that no excess glue dribbles down between the tesserae, as this will prevent the adhesive and grout from sticking. If the design is large it will be easier to apply the scrim in small sections; 18in. x 36in. or 0.5m x 1m is a manageable size.

When the glue has dried, use a handyman's knife to cut through the muslin round the edge of the design, and remove it from the backing sheet. If the design is very large, cut it up into smaller sections of about 18in. square and number each section before removing it. As you remove each section, transfer the numbers to the backing sheet. If glue has trickled down between the tesserae, and they stick to the backing sheet when you are removing the

design, just slide a paint scraper between the tesserae and the baseboard to ease them off.

To cut out the background, lay the sheets of background mosaic, cut to the full size of the wall or fixing surface, on to the backing sheet. Lay paper-faced mosaic paper-side up, and scrim-backed mosaic scrim-side up, but for scrim the template must be reversed beforehand. Place the inside shape of the design template over it and draw round it with a felt pen, shading in the waste section (Fig.6). The shape can now be cut out using mosaic nippers. Number each piece as before, and stack the pieces ready for fixing as described above.

If you plan your design carefully and take care over the preparation and application, a mosaic-covered wall can be an attractive feature of any room in your house.

Leaded lights and coloured glass

There are many hundred of thousands of houses, particularly British ones built before 1940, which have leaded windows. In really old houses, these may be formed of small squares of glass, but diamond-shaped pieces are more usual in newer buildings. Damage to a leaded window often causes the owner to throw it out and replace it with a sheet of uninteresting clear glass. The same applies to the coloured glass windows often found in Victorian and Edwardian houses. But here, instructions are given for the repair of leaded glass windows, and for making your own coloured-glass window panels. A coloured-glass window could add interest to any home—and the technique can be adapted to making fire screens and other items.

A leaded window depends for its strength on special channel-sectioned strips of lead into which the pieces of glass are slotted. These are called *calms* (pronounced either *cams* or *cames*) and are produced in a variety of different widths and channel thicknesses. The calms are cut into proper lengths and soldered together at each intersection so that the separate panels of glass are each fully surrounded by lead strip on all sides. The joins between glass and lead are then made waterproof with a special cement. The complete leaded window is remarkably rigid and quite weatherproof.

Materials

Lead calms can be bought through most glaziers; if they do not stock them, at least they should be able to tell you where you can get them. Two types are available. One has a flat surface, usually with a slightly beaded edge, and the other has a slightly convex surface. Both types are symmetrical in cross-section. The second type is stronger, and probably better suited to normal leaded window work, but it is less flexible than the flat type. For repair work, your choice will be governed by the type of calms originally used on the window.

The special cement used for sealing the glass to the lead can easily be made at home. Begin by mixing equal parts of plaster of paris and powdered whitening, and add to this one part of lamp black and about half a part of white lead. Now dissolve the mixture in boiled linseed oil until it takes on the consistency of very thick treacle, then stir in half a part of red lead. Finally, add turpentine or turps substitute slowly, stirring the mixture until it attains a thin, creamy consistency. This cement is inflammable; it is also poisonous because of the red and white lead in

it. It is best when handling it to wear gloves—and you must make sure you wash off any that gets on your skin and make certain that none contaminates food.

A polishing compound is used on the lead of the completed window to make it a decorative shiny black. This used to be done with black stove polish, and if you can still buy this in your area, use it. Otherwise, you can make up a suitable mixture by mixing vegetable black and turps substitute into a thick paste rather like shoe polish.

Tools

Making and repairing leaded windows is an old craft, and the tools required are simple. First, there is the glass cutter. If you are only working with glass having straight edges, a diamond cutter will suffice (this has a very small, cheap, industrial diamond and is not at all expensive). But if you are cutting curves, then a wheel cutter is the only type to use. For cutting the calms, you will need to buy a stripping knife. Cut the blade down so that it is about 2in. (50mm) long and quite stiff—the easiest way is to snap the blade approximately and then grind it to shape—and then re-sharpen the cut end. This rigid knife is an ideal tool for shearing through lead. A ½lb or 200g hammer is used for tacking against the glass on assembly (described below); its handle doubles as a tapper to force the glass into the channel of the calm. An oyster knife is used for prizing open and straightening the flanges of the calms. Use this exact type of knife if possible; otherwise use a knife with a large handle, very thick and rigid short blade, and a rather blunt edge on both sides. A flat piece of boxwood, sometimes called a *lathekin,* is needed for smoothing down the flanges. A parallel-sided palette knife or thin boxwood paper knife should be used under the flanges when they are pressed down so as to leave a small gap for the cement to be run in.

For minor repair work or making one or two small panels for windows, an ordinary soldering iron can be used. This may be either of the solid copper type requiring a flame for heating, or a largish electric one. But if you want to take up this work as a serious hobby, you should buy a gas soldering iron, which runs off the domestic supply or bottled propane gas. This type of iron is made with a circular-section copper bit set at right-angles to the handle, and is the easiest type of all to work with. The solder used in leadwork of this kind is the type known as tinman's solder. This should be bought, if possible, $\frac{1}{16}$in. or 1mm thick. Glaziers' suppliers sell these narrow strips. Use a tallow candle as flux.

If you are attempting stained-glass work, or

work involving the cutting of intricate shapes of glass, then you will need several pairs of special pliers called *grozers*. Two main types of grozing pliers are useful. The first has smooth, wide jaws and is used to snap off long, narrow strips of glass after they have been scored with a glass cutter. The second pair closes to a V-shape; it is used to chew the edge off a piece of glass where the amount to be removed is too small for the cutter to be effective. You can also use grozers to chew tight inside curves, bit by bit. Both types of grozers can be made from ordinary pliers by softening them in a fire and then grinding or filing their jaws. Alternatively, glaziers' suppliers may stock them, or be able to tell you where to find them.

Repairing a broken lead light

It is possible to make simple repairs to a leaded window when it is in place. You will, however, find it easier as well as safer to remove the *light* (this is the complete lead-framed assembly of glass) from its frame and work on a flat, clean workbench. If this cannot be done, and if it is also impossible to unscrew the window hinges, then consult Figs.12-16 to show you how to work on a window in place.

To remove the old light, proceed in exactly the same way as for the removal of a normal single pane of glass. The light will probably be secured with tacks and putty into a rebate in the window frame. Rake out the old putty, draw out the tacks with an ordinary pair of pliers, and then carefully ease out the light. You may find it necessary to hold a strip of wood along the inside edge of the lead and tap this lightly with a hammer in order to free the lead from the window frame.

The first operation in replacing a damaged pane is to turn back the flange of the lead calm on one side. Which side you choose depends on which is the most convenient side for you to work. Using either the oyster knife or the palette knife, gently insert the end of the blade between lead and glass at a point approximately in the centre of one side of the pane, and slide the knife back and forth with the handle as close to the glass as possible. This will slightly stretch the lead, and at the same time rake out the cement. Any attempt to open out the lead quickly, using the knife in the same way as you would use a screwdriver to open a can, will damage the lead. You must work gradually, progressively raising the handle of the knife on each pass so that the lead opens up smoothly.

You will find it impossible to open up the corners properly because of the soldered joints at the intersections of the calms. Turn the stripping knife so that the edge of the blade lies against the glass and the sharpened end points into the corner, then push the sharp end into the lead joint, cutting it more or less down the centre of the angle formed by the joined calms. Do this at all four corners of the piece, then continue opening up the leads until they are bent out at right angles.

If the damaged pane of glass is just cracked, you may have difficulty in removing the pieces, particularly if it is still more or less intact. Here, you may find it easier to score the broken pieces with the glass cutter, and then break out the glass in small bits. Hold the glass with pliers and twist them to break it. Guard against splinters breaking off from the edges as you twist, as these can fly into your face. Wearing a pair of lightweight goggles—as you should when grinding metal—is the best precaution.

Once all the old glass is out, make sure that the lead flanges of the calms are neatly bent straight out, then make a rubbing of the opening, using a piece of paper and the side of a pencil as shown in Fig.13. Cut a fresh piece of glass, using the rubbing as a pattern. You will find that even though you have cut into the calms at the corners, you will still have difficulty in opening the flanges right back at this point. To get the glass to fit, therefore, you must gently chip off

Using the basic techniques described here you can make an attractive coloured glass fire screen like the one shown below.

the pointed corners; this is done with the grozers as shown in Fig.14.

Hold the glass in one hand, take a grip of the pointed corner with the grozers, and squeeze them gently until a small piece breaks off the corner. Nibble gently at the glass bit by bit until you have removed enough. Once the corners have been rounded off in this manner, the new piece of glass should fit neatly into the leads. Note that this process of removing the corners of the glass is only necessary when you are replacing glass in an existing leaded panel and is not needed if you are assembling a panel from scratch as described below.

Hold the palette knife against the glass and gently rub the lead down on to it so that there is an even, parallel gap between lead and glass equal to the thickness of the knife. This should

be done with the boxwood piece, or lathekin, which should be rubbed along the lead to press it down to the blade of the knife. Again, work gently and progressively up and down the lead, moving the knife and the lathekin together. The joins in the calms, where you have cut into the thicker, soldered lead, may be hard to press down in this way. If you have any difficulty, gently tap the lead with the flat side of a hammer, supporting the other side of the glass with your hand.

Make sure that the gap between glass and lead flange is about $\frac{1}{16}$in. (1.5mm) and that it is quite even all the way round. For this type of repair, it is not necessary to re-solder the cut joins in the calms, particularly if you have made them on the inside of the window. Nor is it necessary to use special cement on the glass; an adequate repair can be completed simply by puttying the new piece. Mix up a small amount of linseed oil-based putty with lampblack to produce an evenly black compound, and press this into the crack between glass and lead all the way round on one side. Now do the same on the other side. The action of forcing the putty between glass and lead on the second side will push the glass to a more or less central position in the calm and give an equal thickness of putty on each side. Clean off excess putty with the palette knife.

Stained-glass work

The term 'stained-glass' is generally applied to any kind of coloured glass in leaded windows. It is, however, more properly clear or coloured glass into which coloured metallic oxides have been fired in a kiln. In this way, a piece of glass which is basically one colour can take on a number of different hues, and so form a portion of a transparent painting of the type found in church windows. Proper stained glass work of this kind is quite within the capabilities of a dedicated amateur who can afford the necessary equipment, and is described in specialist books on the subject.

A far easier technique for the average amateur is making a leaded window with ready-coloured glass. A panel of leaded coloured glass can be used in a hallway or bathroom window (where the daylight coming through will produce exciting effects) or can make an attractive and unusual firescreen as described here. The actual method of making up the leaded glass remains the same whatever its final purpose.

If you are going to make your own design, there are several points to watch. There are seven usual thicknesses of lead calm ranging from $\frac{5}{8}$in. (15mm) down to $\frac{1}{8}$in. (3mm), but the most easily obtainable sizes are probably $\frac{1}{2}$in. (13mm), $\frac{5}{16}$in. (7.5mm) and $\frac{1}{4}$in. (6mm). In drawing up your design, you must allow for the overall width of the lead strip, which has an important effect on the appearance of the panel, and also for the thickness of the calm core, normally about $\frac{1}{16}$in. (1.5mm), which controls the size of each piece of glass. For example, it is pointless to use a $\frac{1}{2}$in. (13mm) wide strip of glass between two $\frac{1}{2}$in. (13mm) calms; the glass will not be visible.

In any case, very small pieces of glass, or pieces with intricate shapes or sharp inside curves should be avoided. You *can* groze out

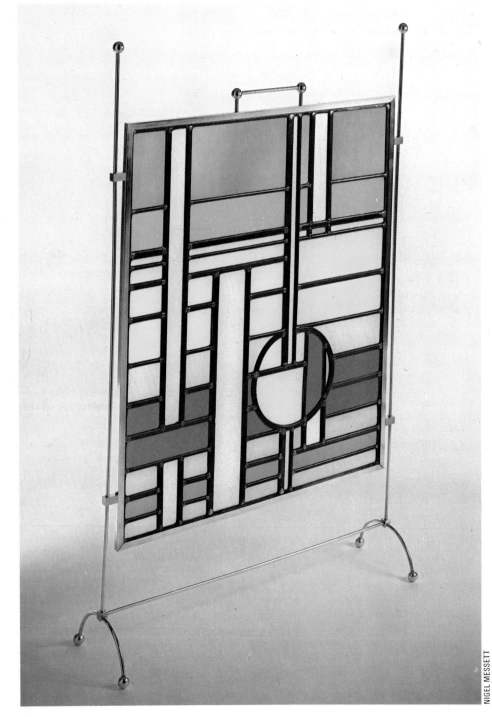

very small pieces with sharp inside curves that are too small to cut with the glass cutter, but there is a practical limit of about ½in. (13mm) internal radius. Internal angles (rather than curves) cannot be cut at all because the glass would almost certainly break. Where an internal angle is required in a glass piece of one colour, the shape must be made out of two pieces leaded together. It is also inadvisable to try to shape very narrow curved pieces of glass, since this requires great skill to avoid breakage.

Fig.1 shows a design for a coloured window or screen, which you can follow by scaling up the dimensions on to a large sheet of white paper. Alternatively, of course, you can design your own. First, find out what colours of glass are available in your area. This should give you some idea to start you off, and you can then make rough sketches until you arrive at a shape and combination of colours which pleases you. Scale this up to full size, following the instructions given below.

The cartoon

From your rough sketch, the next stage is to produce a full-sized working drawing sufficiently detailed to enable you to cut your glass to the exact size and shape you need. This drawing is called a *cartoon;* you can draw it on tracing paper or any white paper. Take particular care in enlarging the sketch to the cartoon stage, and mark all the lines with a thick pencil or felt-tipped pen that draws a line about $\frac{1}{16}$in. (1.5mm) wide. The thickness of this line represents the thickness of the central core of the calms. The actual cutting line of each piece of glass will then be on the near edge of the line next to it. Failure to allow for this, or any inaccuracy in cutting the glass to fit *inside* the lines, can produce an alarming change in the final size of the panel.

Cutting glass

Use a cutter with a new wheel and practice on odd scraps of glass to learn the right way to hold and use the tool. Exert enough pressure to score the surface of the glass without the wheel skidding across the surface. Don't press so hard that the wheel bites in and chips the surface of the glass. Lay the glass you are cutting from over the cartoon, and hold the cutter in such a way that you can make a clear, continuous stroke without faltering. Dipping the cutting wheel into paraffin before each cut lubricates the wheel and helps avoid chipping.

In making straight cuts on glass lying on the bench, always cut towards you, but stand slightly to one side so that your elbow will not hit your body as you move your arm. To cut a circle or a curved line, it is best to hold the cutter firmly and push it away from you, following the line on the cartoon. This is why a diamond is no use for cutting curves : the wheel is much more positive in its movement.

Cut out all the glass for your leaded panel at one go, ticking off each piece on the cartoon so as not to get confused over which pieces are cut and which are not. Lay the cut glass out on a piece of clear glass or hardboard as you cut it out until you have built up the whole picture. This way you can see what you are doing and correct any mistakes as they occur.

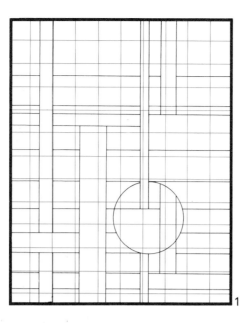

1

Fig. 1. The design for the firescreen panel shown on the page opposite. The squares are 2in. (50mm) and can be scaled up from this. *Figs. 2, 3 & 4.* Alternative suggestions for making attractive coloured glass panels. *Fig. 5.* (see over) The proper way to hold the wheel cutter for cutting the pieces of glass. *Fig.6.* How to cut the calm using the sharp edge of the knife. Press straight down through the lead and the flanges will not close up. *Fig.7.* Assemble the pieces systematically on the cartoon and mark each lead for cutting. See how the first corner of the design is squared up against two wood battens at right angles. The first pieces of coloured glass are being assembled on top of the cartoon. *Fig.8.* The circular detail is contained in one strip of lead bent round the glass. The pieces already fitted are held in place with short lengths of calm nailed to the bench top. *Fig.9.* Opening out the edge calm flanges. *Fig.10.* The complete design trued up square and ready for soldering the joints on one side. *Fig.11.* The gas soldering iron being used to solder up. A tallow candle is rubbed on each calm joint as flux. Complete one side at a time.

2

3

TRI-ART

4

5

7

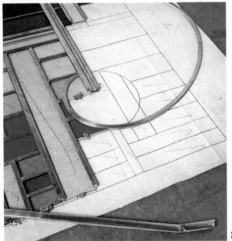

8

9

10

11

Preparations for work

Your work area should be clear and absolutely smooth—a sheet of plywood or hardboard laid on a work-bench will make an ideal surface. Pin the cartoon to this and tack two strips of wood about 1½in. x ½in. (40mm x 13mm) in cross-section, and slightly longer than the sides of the panel you are making, to two adjacent sides of the picture at right angles to each other. These strips act as stops to hold the panel steady as you build it up.

Measure up the total length of each size of calm you will require and add about 10 per cent to allow for inaccuracy and wastage. Stretch each length of calm slightly by holding one end in the vice and pulling gently on the other with a pair of pliers. This will straighten out any kinks

and twists.

Cut off a length of your thickest calm to make one side of the panel; take this measurement off the cartoon and add about ½in. (13mm) for safety. Place this piece of calm against one of the two laths you have tacked to the bench and cut another length of calm for the second side. There is no need to mitre the corners: they can just be butt jointed. The calm should be cut by pushing down on its face with the sharpened stripping knife. If the knife is sharp enough and you exert enough force, it will cut through the lead cleanly without closing up the channels. Support the lead on a wood block for cutting.

You are now ready to start assembly. Place the first piece of glass—the one which fits into the corner created by the two lengths of calm —firmly into place and make sure that it has slotted into the channels properly. Now take a length of calm and cut it to fit along the exposed side of this piece, butting against the first piece of calm at the end. Note that you must cut this length of calm shorter than the true length of the side of the piece of glass, so as to allow for the width of the flange of the lengths of calm it lies against. This stage is shown in Fig.7.

Keep adding pieces of glass and lengths of calm until they stretch all the way along one side. Make quite sure that the pieces of glass are properly inserted into their slots; you will have warning of any problems here by comparing the glass with the cartoon upon which it is superimposed. Tap the exposed edges of the glass pieces all along their length with the

wooden handle of the hammer to ensure that they are all a snug fit. To prevent the pieces from moving, cut a very short piece of calm about ½in. (13mm) long and slot it over the end of the last piece of glass. Then drive a short nail into the bench hard against the scrap piece of calm to hold it in place. These can later be removed as work proceeds.

You can now continue with the next row of glass pieces in the same manner. Lines which are supposed to be straight (as shown on the cartoon) should be represented by long, straight pieces of calm, and you must see that these lengths are in fact straight, and that any parallel lines are really parallel. Check this as you go, but there will also be a final check before soldering up.

Any curved pieces of glass, such as the circle shown in the design in the illustrations, must be framed in curved calm. This is easily formed by drawing the lead through the hands and gently pressing it in to shape. It bends very easily.

Once all the glass pieces are in place with their separating calms, you can cut and fit the final straight lengths of thick calm to the remaining two sides. Check the panel for squareness by measuring the sides and diagonals. An ideal way of ensuring that the edge calms are kept straight is to cut a long strip of plain glass, slot it into the open outer side of the calm and hold it down on the bench with tacks along the opposite edge. Make a final check to see that the pieces of calm in the design are laid straight and in their

20

proper position. The thickness of the glass is slightly less than the size of the gap between the calm flanges, so some movement can easily take place; it can also just as easily be corrected. The panel is now ready for soldering up. This must be done before removing it from the bench.

Soldering

Clean the end of the copper bit of your gas soldering iron. This must be absolutely bright and untarnished, or you will not be able to tin it properly. Light the gas and regulate the heat until the iron is at the correct temperature. Achieving and maintaining this exact temperature take a fair amount of practice. If the iron gets too hot, you will not be able to tin it, and furthermore, if it overheats in use you will burn away the lead calms instead of joining them.

Test for the proper heat during the tinning process by melting a little solder in a tin lid, letting it cool and rubbing the end of the iron on this as the bit heats up. When the solder starts to flow, you have reached the right temperature. A little powdered resin (rosin to some people) will help the solder to flow if scattered lightly over the solder in the tin lid before you start tinning the iron.

Once the copper bit is properly tinned—a smooth 'puddle' of tin should adhere evenly to the end—you are ready to solder. Rub the tallow candle over each calm joint. Now hold the thin stick of solder in one hand and the iron in the other. Melt off about $\frac{1}{8}$in. (1.5mm) of solder and quickly touch this on the calm joint.

With a little practice, you will find that each joint can be soldered in this way in a matter of seconds. Do not press the iron on to the calm—the lead will instantly dissolve. The technique is to touch the joint with the puddle of molten solder on the end of the iron—and it really should be just a touch—the heat of the iron passing into the lead calm through the molten solder.

When you have completed one side, the panel will be rigid enough to be removed from the bench and turned over. Solder the other side, then give both sides a good scrub with a dry stiff-bristled brush and you are now ready for the next stage—cementing.

Cementing

Cementing is rather a messy job, so spread old newspapers over your bench and wear an old apron to protect your clothes. It is advisable to wear thin plastic or rubber gloves, since the red and white lead in the cement is poisonous and could cause serious trouble if you have any open cuts on your hands. And after all that glass cutting, you will probably have one or two cuts.

Spread the cement all over the panel with a scrubbing brush, rubbing it in everywhere until every crevice is filled. Now spread whitening or plaster of paris all over the panel. This will speed up the drying of the cement. Turn the panel over and repeat the procedure for the other side. Leave the panel with both sides whitened for an hour or so, then brush off all the whitening with another scrubbing brush.

Any scum left on the glass can be wiped off with a cloth soaked in turpentine or turps substitute. Do this before the cement has time to set really hard, or it will be difficult to remove. Now leave the panel for a day or so for the cement to harden thoroughly.

To prevent your cement brush from setting solid, clean it immediately after use with turps substitute and then rinse it in hot water and detergent.

Complete the job by giving the panel another stiff brushing, this time with stove polish or the substitute described under the heading 'Materials'. This will shine up the lead calms, and also cover the cement joints with a protective coating.

Installing the panel

If your leaded glass panel is to go into a window frame, it can be fitted in precisely the same way as you would fit a normal one-piece clear glass window. Before this can be done, however, the open edges of the calms at the sides of the panel must be closed up by folding one edge over the other.

You may wish to use your panel as a decorative firescreen like the one on page 18. To do this, make a light framework of brass or aluminium into which the panel will fit. Alternatively, you could mount the panel in a plain wooden frame, or even in a decorative one made from picture-frame moulding. The panel needs to be lit from behind to look effective and so should be hung in front of a window or a light and not just placed on a wall like a picture.

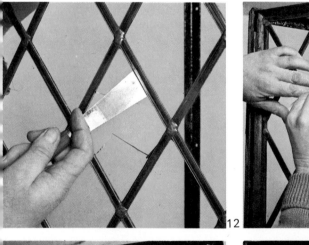
12

13

14

15

16

Fig.12. *Opening out the lead flanges around the broken piece of glass. You may have to cut the cracked section into smaller bits in order to remove them from the window using pliers.*
Fig.13. *With the lead flanges standing out at right-angles and the old glass removed, take a rubbing on a piece of paper and cut the new sheet of glass to suit this pattern.*
Fig.14. *Remove the points of the corners by grozing the glass with special grozing pliers.*
Fig.15. *Place the new piece of glass in the prepared opening and carefully rub down the flanges of the calms with a boxwood lathekin.*
Fig.16. *Seal both sides using linseed putty mixed with lamp-black. Clean off excess putty with a sharp knife and after it has hardened for a few days, polish it with black stove polish and shine the lead with a soft cloth.*

Bottle and glass cutting

The techniques of bottle and glass cutting can be put to a great many decorative uses around your home. You don't need a lot of sophisticated equipment to master the technique. Once you have learnt the basic skills, you'll be able to provide yourself with some useful, as well as beautiful, items for little or no cost.

The first part of this chapter deals with bottle cutting. Nowadays, there are a great many very striking bottles available. Bottles that once held wines, spirits or soft drinks can all be put to good decorative uses. Wine and spirit bottles should never be thrown away. With the aid of the bottle cutting technique, these will enliven your home with the sparkle and splendour of glass.

What to look for

Choosing exactly the right bottles to use depends on a number of factors. The first is the colour of the glass. What particular article you wish to make will have a bearing on what is the most suitable colour for the glass. If you intend to make an ashtray, it may be better to select a bottle in a dark coloured glass—either green or brown. On the other hand, should you wish to make drinking glasses, it may be better to choose clear glass bottles. It is true, however, that the colour of the glass you select is very largely a matter of personal preference.

The next consideration to bear in mind is that of shape. Look at a particular bottle. What shape does it suggest to you? It could—by just cutting off the narrow neck—become a very good looking and serviceable vase. This is especially true of those wine bottles which have a handle incorporated into the overall design. For objects like ashtrays, choose a bottle with a fairly wide base. Some bottles have a very wide base indeed —sometimes enough for such things as basins. Objects like drinking glasses are best made from conventionally shaped bottles.

Apart from colour and shape, the thickness of the glass is also important. Should you wish to make an ashtray, look for a bottle with a thick base. If the glass is too thin, the ashtray could easily get smashed or chipped. For making

Left. Bottle cutting is a rewarding hobby. Once the techniques have been mastered, a great many beautiful and useful items can be made to decorate the home.

drinking glasses, however, a bottle made of thin glass would be more suitable.

Try to avoid choosing those bottles with a lot of raised lettering on the glass. The lettering may well be in an awkward place. Cutting a line through the lettering will prove very tricky, especially for the beginner. Also, the finished work might look quite peculiar.

Once you have a good selection of suitable bottles, you'll need to get the right tools.

The tools

The first thing you'll need is a bottle cutter. These vary in price considerably, according to the quality and toughness of the materials, as well as the type of cutter used. Less expensive bottle cutters usually have a plastic frame. The blade looks like a small wheel, and is made of toughened tungsten steel. This less expensive bottle cutter is quite adequate for the beginner. Its one disadvantage is that the blade will wear out quite quickly, but these cost very little to replace. Also, because the construction of this bottle cutter is of plastic, it can easily get broken.

Higher up the price range, the models available are of a much more sturdy construction, usually having a steel or aluminium frame. With more expensive bottle cutters the blade is a small industrial diamond. This is far more hard wearing than tungsten steel. A good diamond blade should last virtually indefinitely.

The only other piece of equipment you'll need are some sheets of carborundum paper in two grades—fine and coarse. Now that you have the necessary equipment, you can begin to learn the bottle cutting technique proper.

The bottle cutting technique

The basic technique of bottle cutting is quite straightforward. Using the blade of the bottle cutter, carefully score a line in the exact place where you wish to break the glass. During this procedure, the bottle should be held firmly in place by the cutter's frame. Part of any bottle cutter is a small metal weight fixed to the end of a metal rod. Once the line has been scored around the outside of the bottle, the weight should be lowered into the bottle to the exact level of the line. Having made sure that the weight is in the correct position, you should give the inside of the bottle a number of firm, but gentle, taps. If you continue to do this, the glass should make a clean break along the scored line. Don't hit the glass too hard, or attempt to force it to break, if you do, the bottle is likely to shatter.

Now that the bottle has broken round the line, you'll need to smooth off the rough edge. This is where the carborundum paper should be used. First, take a sheet of coarse grade paper, wrap it round a small block of wood, and wet it slightly with ordinary tap water. Now, rub the rough edge·of the glass vigorously until most of the surface roughness has been worn down. If the finished article is to be a vase or an ashtray, the edge should be smooth enough after this stage. If you are making drinking glasses, however, a further smoothing down will be necessary. For this, a sheet of fine grade carborundum paper will be necessary. As with the coarse grade paper, it should be damped with water. Now all that remains is to give the edge of the glass a thorough rubbing down with the wetted fine grade carborundum paper.

Your glasses, vase or whatever is now ready for use. If you don't want to leave your finished work plain, you could add a trim.

Trimming

Trimming the edges of any glassware is usually done in brass, or brass finished plastic.

You can get brass coil at your DIY dealer. This coil is usually about $\frac{1}{8}$in. (3mm) wide, and should be stuck carefully around the edge of the glass—using an epoxy resin adhesive like Araldite.

An easier trimming alternative is gold or silver finished adhesive tape. This is very simple to put on—and the finished job looks just as effective as the coil method; but you can't wash it.

Saving your neck

Don't throw the neck of the bottle away. It can be put to very good decorative use. Smooth down the cut edge of the bottle's neck in the same way as described earlier in this chapter. When the edge is smooth, and clean of any loose particles of glass, stick the neck to an old unwanted saucer, using a contact adhesive such as Evostik. Plastic or paper flowers can be stuck around the base. These should be fixed onto wire for added firmness. Once the whole ornament has been assembled, you can spray it all over with an aerosol gloss paint. Alternatively, you could use a clear varnish spray.

A diverse assortment of bottle necks can be used in the making of a strikingly attractive, three dimensional, wall mural. Use a sheet of

chipboard or $\frac{3}{4}$in. (18mm) plywood. Emulsion paint the board in the colour of your choice. Once the paint has dried, arrange the bottle necks until you achieve an interesting and well balanced pattern. Now, stick the bottles onto the board, using a contact adhesive.

The glass cutting technique

Closely related to bottle cutting is the technique of glass cutting. When you buy a bottle cutter, you'll usually find that the blade is detachable and is attached to a wooden or plastic handle. You therefore have a perfectly servicable sheet glass cutter. Once you have learnt how to cut glass, you can put your new found skill to all manner of decorative uses—making trays, table tops and even glass wall murals.

Getting ready to cut

You should take care when cutting glass. Wrap your wrists in sticking plaster—or use proper wrist bands—to protect yourself against cuts from glass splinters.

A large, flat working surface will be needed to lay your sheet of glass down on. A thick blanket should be laid on the surface to protect it, and

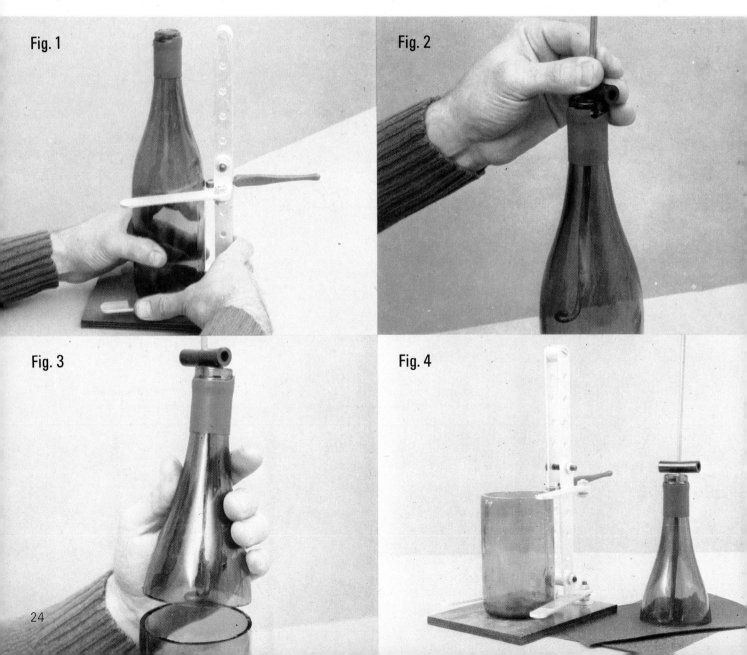

Fig. 1

Fig. 2

Fig. 3

Fig. 4

the glass, from getting scratched. If you intend to cut odd shapes make a template of stiff card. This should be the exact shape that you want, and must be approximately ⅛in. (3mm) smaller all round than the glass is to be.

Make sure it is possible to see the blade of your glass cutter as you are cutting. This will make mistakes far less likely.

If you want to cut a lot of glass, you'll find a wooden T-square very handy to guide the cutter along the marked line. A good ruler or steel tape will be necessary for accurate measuring. For marking the glass, you can use a felt tip pen, a chinagraph pencil or an ordinary crayon. Wax crayons are not suitable as the surface of the glass is too slippery for wax to make a good impression.

Cutting the glass

Once the glass has been correctly marked up, you can start the cutting proper. First, clean the glass with an ordinary window cleaner such as Windolene. Methylated spirits is an adequate alternative. The blade of the glass cutter should be lubricated by wiping it over with a piece of soft felt soaked in machine oil. When holding the cutter, the handle should rest between the first and second fingers—and your hand should always be clear of the glass. Score the surface of the glass along the line with the cutter. The cut should be made with a firm, continuous stroke. Move your arm along as you cut, and keep the rest of your body still. Do not try to recut, as there is a danger that the glass will break in an awkward place.

Having scored the line, the glass should be lifted slightly, and gently tapped from underneath, right along the outside edge of the score line. Put a small batten directly under the line. Place your hands on the surface of the glass—one on each side of the line. Gently press down **with your fingers until the glass breaks cleanly along the score line. It is advisable to wear gloves during this stage as protection.**

One of the best ideas for glass is glass painting. This comprises three or four sheets, fixed into a three sided wooden frame. A gap of approximately ¾in. (18mm) should be left between each sheet. Paint any image on the reverse side of each sheet of glass—using an oil or plastic based paint. The open side of the frame is the top. A fluorescent strip light should be fitted here. By doing this the painted images will be reflected outwards when the light is switched on.

The decorative appeal of glass is often underestimated. By mastering the bottle and glass cutting techniques you can produce some striking objects to beautify your home—at minimal cost. With a little imagination you will be able to add a lustrous originality to your home. With some inexpensive tools, and a bit of practice, you'll bring distinction to your decor with the sparkle of glass.

Figs.1 to 6. Here the six stages needed to make an attractive tumbler are shown. Fig.1. The first thing to do is to score the line round the outside of the bottle. To do this the bottle should be held firmly down on the base of the bottle cutter, and slowly rotated by hand until the line has been scored around the whole circumference. Fig.2. The line having been scored, a weight is lowered into the bottle to the level of the line. Gently tap the weight against the glass. Fig.3. After the glass has been tapped it should break cleanly around the line. Fig.4. Here the two halves of the bottle are shown. Figs.5 and 6. Smooth the edge off with carborundum paper. If you intend to use the glass for drinking an extra smoothing will be needed.

Fig. 5

Fig. 6

Concrete garden sculpture

Concrete can be beautiful, but because of its frequent unimaginative use in heavy construction work, we tend to regard it as one of the drabbest of building materials. This chapter helps dispel this view by exploring a little known aspect of this versatile material—its capacity to be cast into attractive sculptured forms to enhance your home and garden.

Mention concrete and most people immediately think of grey, lifeless slabs and equally lifeless multi-storey buildings. To some extent the view is a justified one. For a long time after concrete was introduced as a building material its use was unimaginative and wholly practical. Office blocks, bridges and silos—all these structures incorporated concrete in the most uninspiring way.

And yet concrete need not be unattractive. Good architects, in particular the French architect Le Corbusier, have shown that concrete buildings need not be the slab-sided, featureless structures they so commonly are. When properly reinforced, concrete can be cast into virtually any shape—a real advantage over 'natural' building materials.

Another criticism of concrete—that its colour and textures are lifeless—is also false. Raw concrete for heavy construction is usually dull and grey, but recently, textured and pigmented castings have been used increasingly for all purposes.

The use of concrete as a material for artists is also new, but as old prejudices die and new aspects of concrete become known, it becomes clear that this material is as versatile as it is strong.

Concrete sculptures for the home

Once you have accepted that concrete can be cast in attractive forms, don't be put off by the thought that to make a sculpture you have to be a skilled artist. Everybody has some artistic skill and in many ways sculpting is easier than painting. This is because you work in three dimensions, not two, and consequently the difficult job of proportioning the form is made at much easier. However, when designing a sculpture, don't be too ambitious at first, but concentrate on mastering the techniques of moulding and casting. Once you have learnt how to handle the materials, you can graduate

left. This highly original fish sculpture forms a striking feature of a garden pool and shows how concrete can be used in new and imaginative ways.

to more advanced work.

Gardens are the most suitable places to display your work, and the designs that you make should echo the overall appearance of the garden. A classical figure would look rather out of place in a vegetable garden, and a large and heavy sculpture would not suit most small gardens. Take a look at your garden and decide not only what form a sculpture should take, but also its most attractive location. This last consideration will depend largely on what special features your garden may possess. The stylised fish sculpture shown opposite would greatly enhance the side of a garden pool, a more abstract sculpture would be seen to advantage if it was set in an open space, such as a lawn.

Having assessed what form of sculpture would best suit your garden, draw up a design. Make quick sketches at first, concentrating on the basic form and outline. Don't incorporate too much detail as this will be largely obscured when the sculpture is cast. When you have made a design which pleases you, transfer it, full size, onto a large piece of stout paper.

Making an armature

The original model from which the mould is made is built up on a skeleton of heavy gauge wire called an armature. Very large models require an armature of welded mild steel.

To make the armature you must envisage the model as a three dimensional whole and work out the arrangement of a skeleton within this mass. Once the armature is complete, fix it onto a sheet of plywood.

Making the model

When you are confident that the armature reflects the shape you want to make, modelling can begin. If, on the other hand, you have any doubts about your design, you can save yourself much wasted time by first preparing a miniature model round a lighter armature. In making this miniature—referred to as a manequin—you can judge whether the basic shape, size and proportions are correct and, if necessary, modify the full size armature.

Materials for modelling will depend on the scale of the work. Larger models should be built up of a stiffish modelling clay which can be obtained from many artists' suppliers. Smaller models can be worked in plasticine.

The best technique to employ when working the modelling material is to apply large lumps to the armature, gradually building up the mass until the overall appearance matches your design. At this stage, work the material with your

Fig.1. To remove the plaster mould which surrounds the cast, chip it off with a chisel held at a shallow angle to the cast. When you reach the blue layer of dental plaster, work with more care, removing small sections.

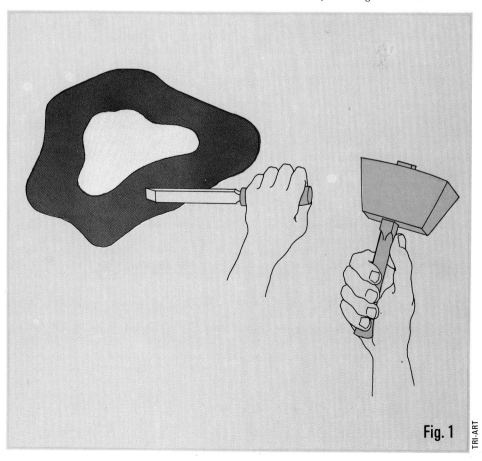

Fig. 1

TRI-ART

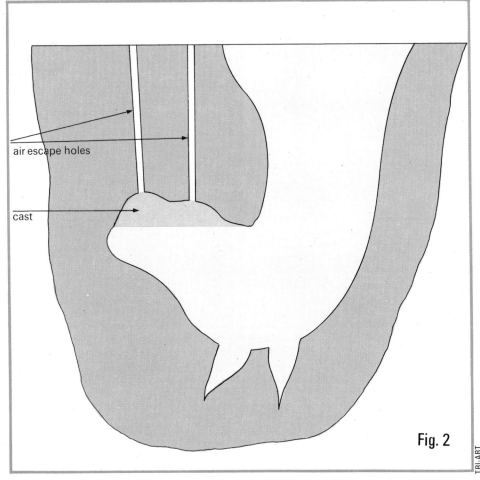

Fig. 2

Fig.2. Before pouring in the concrete mix, check that no air will be trapped in the mould and bore holes to points where this may occur.

hands and fingers only and build up the model from several points in rotation, rather than from one point outwards.

Once you have built up the basic form, finish the surface and add any details, using clay modelling tools. These tools, which can be obtained from most artists' suppliers, are made up of boxwood or hardwood and wire in various shapes and sizes. Most of these tools, however, can be improvised from ordinary household items—a teaspoon handle, for example, may be used in place of a spatula.

One thing to remember when working clay is that it must not be allowed to dry out. If, during the modelling stage, the work has to be left for any period, it should be covered first in damp cloths and then wrapped in a polythene sheet. When the model is finished, cover it until you have made up the plaster for casting.

Moulds

A few words about the different types of mould and moulding materials will be helpful at this point. Concrete can be cast from such diverse moulding materials as metal, wood, glass-fibre, rubber or plaster. The inflexible materials, such as wood and metal, can only be used for casting straight-sided objects. Sculpted castings have to be made from some malleable, paste-like material. Plaster, being cheap, easily obtainable and simple to work, is the ideal material for casting concrete.

Plaster moulds for casting concrete are of two basic types—piece moulds and waste moulds. Piece moulds, as their name implies, consist of two or more sections and are used for making

multiple runs, or work incorporating undercuts, or both. Waste moulds are made in two or more pieces, but are chipped away and thus destroyed when the concrete casting has set. They can only be used once, but are ideal for making an intricately worked casting, such as an ornamental sculpture.

Making a waste mould

Before mixing the plaster for the waste mould, the model must be prepared so that once the plaster has been applied and has set it can be removed, undamaged, in sections. For this you require paper-thin pieces of shim metal (non-rusting metals such as copper or zinc are best) which are cut to a trapezium shape, as shown in Fig.5. These shim pieces are set into the clay on an unbroken medial line right round the model, so that they divide it into two distinct halves. If your model incorporates any holes running through it, they must also be divided by shim pieces.

White pottery casting plaster, obtainable from plaster and some artists' suppliers is used for the bulk of the mould. You will also need a smaller quantity of fine dental plaster which can be obtained from some chemists' or dental suppliers. Both types of plaster are made up by mixing with water, the mix being roughly, by volume, eleven parts plaster to seven parts water.

If you are making a very large sculpture there

is a risk that, before you have completed the mould, some of the plaster will set prematurely. To prevent this, you must add a delayed setting agent, called size, to the plaster mix and, ideally, you should make up two or three mixes with different setting times, as follows.

Mix 1 : $\frac{1}{4}$ part water, plus $\frac{1}{20}$ part size-water plus plaster to within $\frac{1}{2}$in. (13mm) of water surface (setting time 5 minutes).

Mix 2 : $\frac{1}{2}$ part water plus $\frac{1}{15}$ part size-water plus plaster to within $\frac{1}{2}$in. (13mm) of water surface (setting time 15 minutes).

Mix 3 : $\frac{3}{4}$ part water plus $\frac{1}{10}$ part size-water plus plaster to within $\frac{1}{2}$in. (13mm) of water surface (setting time 20 minutes).

When making up the plaster mixes, work in a strict order of procedure. Prepare the dental plaster mix first and when it has been stirred to a creamy consistency, mix in a solution of Reckitt's Blue or blue ink. Apply this mix over the whole surface of the model to a depth of $\frac{1}{10}$in. (2.5mm), checking that you have covered any undercuts or surface ornamentation. As soon as the whole model has been covered, make up the bulk of the plaster mix. As pottery plaster is often lumpy, you should sieve it into the water and, when mixing it, use your hands only, taking care not to trap air within the mixture.

Apply the mix evenly over the first layer of dental plaster, to a depth of between 1$\frac{1}{2}$in. (38mm) and 3in. (75mm) depending on the size of the model. If the model is very large, you should reinforce the liquid plaster with pieces of jute or coarse hessian applied in layers as you build up the mould.

When the plaster has set, ease out the metal shims with a pair of pliers, then soak the whole mould with water. Aided by some judicious levering with a paint scraper or old knife, separate the mould sections and remove them from the model.

Any clay remaining in the mould should be removed and the interior washed out with the aid of a soft brush. Then the sections should be left to dry thoroughly—a process which may take several days.

When the mould is completely dry, two or three coats of shellac should be applied to the interior with a soft varnish brush. Dissolve shellac flakes, obtainable from a good quality decorators' colourman or varnish and polish suppliers, in equal parts, by volume, of methylated spirits. Allow the shellac to dry, then coat the interior of the mould with a parting agent. Traditionally, Russian tallow dissolved in paraffin is used. To make it, heat 1$\frac{1}{4}$ pints of paraffin to just below boiling point, then add $\frac{1}{2}$lb. of tallow and stir until it is dissolved. An alternative, but more expensive parting agent is linseed oil.

The mould sections should now be reassembled and held together by means of strong cord and rubber straps. When you are sure that the mould is firmly clamped together, turn it upside down and hold it in this position by setting it into a large lump of clay. To prevent air being trapped in the mould, bore holes to points where this may occur.

Making up a concrete mix

There is a wide range of concrete mixes suitable for casting; your choice will be

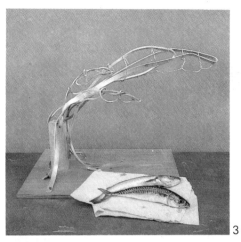

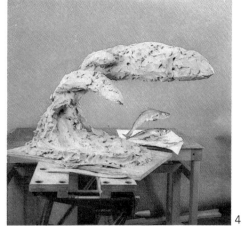

3

5

8

determined by the colour and texture you prefer and the specific use to which the mix is to be put. Below are listed two typical concrete mixes and the methods by which their texture and colour can be varied.

Concrete mix for thin sections

1 part cement
1¼ parts damp sand
3 parts ½in. (13mm) shingle
⅜ part water
plasticiser

Concrete mix for solid castings

1 part cement
1¼ parts damp sand
2 parts shingle
¼ part water
plasticiser

A natural stone finish can be achieved by substituting crushed stone aggregate for the aggregates listed in the mixes above. The stone aggregate should comprise 50% material over ¼in. (6mm) and 50% material under ¼in. (6mm) of which half should be sand less than ⅛in. (3mm).

Once the concrete has been mixed, pour it slowly into the upturned mould which should be vibrated. Vibrating the mould helps brings air to the surface of the concrete and ensures that the finished cast has a smooth surface.

If the casting is fairly large, it will require some form of reinforcement, ¼in. (6mm) thick steel rods or chicken wire, inserted into the concrete as the mould is filled, will satisfy this need.

When the concrete has been poured and

Fig.3. Build up the clay or plasticine model on a shaped wire armature.
Fig.4. Use a stiffish modelling clay for larger models and build it up from several points in rotation.
Fig.5. Set paper-thin pieces of shim metal on an unbroken medial line round the model.
Fig.6. Apply a thin mix of stained plaster to a depth of 1/10in. (2.5mm).
Fig.7. Then apply a mix of pottery casting plaster to a depth of 1½in.-3in. (38mm-76mm).
Fig.8. Allow the plaster to set, then ease out the shim pieces with a pair of pliers and separate the two mould sections.

tamped well down, it should be left to set. In normal conditions this will take from four to seven days and throughout this time the whole mould should be wrapped in polythene. This helps the concrete to cure evenly and prevents cracking.

Removing the plaster

After the concrete has set, the mould should be set right way up and the plaster chipped off with an old chisel. The bulk of the plaster can be removed in large chunks by striking the chisel held at a shallow angle to the mould. When you reach the blue layer of fine dental plaster proceed with more care, removing small sections at a time, otherwise you might damage the casting.

Once all the plaster has been removed, examine the casting for white stains. These stains, called efflorescence, can easily be removed by sponging them with 1:5 hydro-

chloric acid solution. Carry out this operation in the open air and wear rubber gloves and goggles, because this is a corrosive fluid. Once the stains have been removed, wash down the casting and the area surrounding it with cold water.

Further projects

Having erected the sculpture and seen how concrete can be used to such striking effect, you may wish to try your hand at other projects. The range of ornamental uses to which concrete can be put is extremely wide. As well as sculptures, you can make ornamental garden furniture, bird-baths and fountains. Using the basic knowledge and experience gained from making concrete garden sculptures, it is also possible to extend your scope to include more advanced projects such as decorative garden planters or even cast concrete garden furniture. Although these larger designs involve slightly more complicated techniques, such as the use of a piece mould (a mould composed of two or more pieces which can be taken apart and used again), they are not difficult to master and will enable you to enhance your home and garden at a fraction of the manufactured price — a good money-saving idea.

In fact so widespread is the use of concrete in all aspects of home construction and maintenance, that all DIY enthusiasts should be aquainted with its uses and properties. One thing is certain; once you have seen how attractively concrete can be worked, you will no longer regard it as a drab and uninteresting material.

Pebble polishing

Almost certainly, at some time or another, you will have collected pebbles from a beach while on holiday. When newly washed by the breaking waves, the eye-catching colours of these pebbles is hard to resist. However, they soon dry, and the colours fade quickly and look dull and uninspiring. Fortunately, it is quite a simple job to bring the colours back to life—as well as to give a permanent mirror finish to the surface of each pebble. Apart from the obvious use of polished pebbles in the making of jewellery, there are a variety of artistic uses to which they can be put—such as the creation of unusual wall decorations, or table surfaces.

Pebbles have been used for centuries as a raw material for making jewellery and decorative items for the home. Nowadays pebble polishing has been made easy by the range of equipment available to the beginner. You'll find that the pebbles and rocks—picked up from holiday beaches or in your garden—can be put to good use in decorating your home.

Polishing the pebbles

The best way of polishing beach pebbles is to use a tumbling machine. This consists of a

small barrel and two parallel rollers. These are turned by pulleys, and a rubber belt, driven by an electric motor. Tumbling machines are quite inexpensive, and can be bought from shops specialising in polished stone and pebble work, or handicraft shops.

First, place the pebbles in the barrel, and top it up with water. Once you have done this add one tablespoonful of coarse silicon carbide grit (80 grade) to the water. Secure the lid firmly to the barrel, which is placed on the rollers. The barrel is then turned on the rollers, at a speed of approximately one revolution per second, for the next seven days.

While this process is going on the pebbles roll, or 'tumble', against each other as the barrel turns. The silicon carbide grit gradually wears away all surface roughness.

Once this first stage is completed, remove the barrel from the rollers. You should wash the pebbles thoroughly in fresh water to remove all traces of the coarse silicon carbide.

The barrel will contain quite a lot of sludge at this stage. This should *not* be poured down the sink. If you do this you will run the risk of blocking the plumbing. Empty the sludge into a plastic bag. This can be thrown into the dustbin.

Rinse the barrel thoroughly to make sure that all traces of grit have been removed. Put the pebbles back into the barrel and top it up with clean water once more. Having done this, add one tablespoonful of medium silicon carbide grit (220 grade) to the water, and repeat the tumbling process for a further seven days.

During this second stage surface scratches caused by the coarse silicon carbide are removed from the pebbles. At the end of the second seven-day period you should remove the pebbles from the barrel and wash them carefully under running water. You should now clean the barrel thoroughly once more. Now, the entire process should be repeated for a third time—this time using fine silicon carbide (440 grade). This will give a smooth matt finish to each pebble.

After three weeks of continuous rotation inside the barrel, the pebbles should be absolutely smooth and ready to take their final polish. However, you must first remove all traces of silicon carbide grit from their surfaces and from the inside of the barrel. Carry out this third washing stage with great care. If you leave a single grain of silicon carbide on the pebbles, or on the inside of the barrel, you will fail to achieve a high polish during the final stage.

Once you are satisfied that you have cleaned everything carefully, place the pebbles back in the barrel. Top it up with clean water and add one teaspoonful of tin oxide or cerium oxide. Allow the pebbles to tumble inside the barrel for approximately twenty four hours. After this has been done the pebbles will be polished to a brilliance which will enhance their natural colours and beauty. You should now give the pebbles a final rinse under running water. This should leave you with a batch of sparkling pebbles which will never lose their lustre.

Left. Polished pebbles can be placed in jars to make beautiful ornaments for a desk, shelf or window sill. A very large pebble can easily be put to good use as a decorative paper weight.

The two main points to bear in mind for successful tumble polishing are:
1. Always load the barrel with pebbles of a similar hardness.
2. Include as wide a variety of pebble sizes as possible when filling the barrel.

It is easy to carry out a 'hardness test' when collecting your pebbles. Take a small penknife with you when searching a beach for likely specimens. As you pick up each pebble, scratch its surface with the blade of the knife. Put all those which cannot be scratched by the knife into one bag, and those which are easily scratched into another. If you keep the two batches separate when polishing, you shouldn't experience any trouble with pebbles of unequal hardness.

When out collecting pebbles, pick up very small ones as well as the large specimens. If you have a small machine, for use at home, the tumble polishing process will work best when the barrel is loaded with an assortment of pebbles ranging from the size of a pea to roughly the size of the top joint of your thumb. It is possible to buy larger commercial tumbling machines. These are more expensive than the small machines, but they may be worthwhile buying if you intend to take up pebble polishing as a regular hobby. Even in the larger machines—which can accommodate loads of up to 500 pebbles in the barrel—you'll need to load pebbles of various sizes into the barrel. With the larger machine the size of the pebbles could range between 1in. (25mm) and 2½in. (63mm) in diameter. The main point to remember is, whatever the size of your polishing machine, you should never load it with pebbles of a uniform size.

Once you have successfully polished the pebbles, you will be free to consider the range of decorative uses they can be put to around your home.

Making a paperweight

If you have the more expensive commercial tumbling machine it will be able to polish stones big enough to be used as paperweights on their own. However, these will be much too big for the inexpensive smaller tumbling machine. You can get a conversion kit which will transform an ordinary home power drill into a pebble polisher, on which single pebbles up to a diameter of approximately 3in. (75mm) can be polished. The silicon carbide used in the polishing process is supplied in the form of sanding discs, which are glued to a soft rubber backing pad. This moulds itself to the rounded surface of the pebble. The final polishing is carried out on a hard felt pad impregnated with polishing powder.

When choosing suitable pebbles for a paperweight, look for pebbles which have already been roughly worn to the correct shape by the abrasive action of waves and sand. One side of the pebble should be fairly flat, and the other domed. If you select a rounded pebble, you will need to spend considerable time during the coarse grinding stage in wearing down a flat base for the paperweight. Once the shape of the paperweight has been worked, and the polishing process is completed, a thin piece of green baize should be glued to the base. This will

protect tables and desk-tops from scratches. If you do this, it will be unnecessary to carry out the intermediate grinding and final polishing on the base as it will be covered by the baize.

Fish tanks and vases

Polished pebbles, of similar or different colours, will make beautiful additions to a tropical fish tank. They can even make the humblest goldfish bowl look quite exotic. The polish is not affected by water—in fact immersion in water actually adds to the already impressive sparkle. In large tanks the best effect is achieved by having several small groups of pebbles spaced with plants and sand.

A clear vase or, better still, one of those old-fashioned sweet jars with a ground-glass stopper, makes a delightful window ornament when filled with polished pebbles. Striking effects can be gained by grading the pebbles for colour and size when filling the container.

Below. A tumbling machine used in the pebble polishing process. Such machines can be fitted with one or two barrels. With two barrels, pebbles of two hardnesses can be polished.

NELSON HARGREAVES

Plant pots

You can attractively cover the surfaces of plant pots with polished pebbles. This will eliminate the need to spend a lot of money on ornamental pots for indoor plants. Ordinary unglazed earthenware pots will be quite sufficient, as all the necessary decoration will be provided by the pebbles. Coat the outside of the pot in plaster of Paris. The pebbles can then be embedded in this before it sets. Coarse sand should be sprinkled in the gaps between the pebbles to disguise the plaster. If you are covering several pots—to be used in the same window or plant display—choose pebbles of a roughly uniform size.

A similar treatment can be used to give a new lease of life to an uninspiring earthenware vase, jug or ornament picked up in a jumble sale or a junk shop. Half a dozen or so brightly polished pebbles glued to the surface with an epoxy resin adhesive, such as Araldite, will brighten up the dullest object.

Trinket boxes

Your smallest polished pebbles can be used to cover old and, perhaps battered, trinket boxes.

Again, these can also be glued on with an epoxy resin adhesive. A larger pebble will often prove suitable for use as an unusual handle, while four pebbles of equal size will provide legs for the box. Musical boxes, children's pencil boxes and the like are ideal for this kind of treatment.

Wall decoration

The main problem you'll come up against when attempting to cover large areas of wall with polished pebbles will be one of having enough pebbles to cover the whole area. Don't attempt such a project unless you are certain that you have enough pebbles—of the correct size—to complete the work.

It is best to cover small areas. Try a narrow border round a fireplace or serving hatch. The width of the border will depend on the number of suitable pebbles you have. However, it is important that you don't make the border too wide as there is a danger that such a border will look ugly and garish.

First, chip away the plaster from the area of the wall you plan to cover. Replaster the area and embed the pebbles into the new plaster before it sets. Wipe the pebbles clean with a damp cloth after the plaster has properly hardened.

Picture making

You can make delightful 'nature pictures' with polished pebbles, seashells, pieces of driftwood and other coastline debris that you find lying around when searching for pebbles on holiday beaches. You'll often find that the more out of the way stretches of coast offer the most fertile hunting grounds.

A piece of thick hardboard—cut to the required size—will provide a suitable backing board for your picture. The rough side of the hardboard should first be coated with an epoxy resin adhesive. Before the adhesive has dried, the whole surface should be sprinkled with sand to provide a perfect background for your beach finds. Shake off all the loose sand once the adhesive has dried. Now begin to work the design of your picture using the pebbles, shells and whatever. Anyone can make beautiful abstract designs. Pictures of fishes or seaside scenes require a little more artistic skill, but this need not be too difficult to master. For even better effects add driftwood, pieces of dried seaweed and cork to the basic design. A simple wooden frame will complete your pebble picture.

Table tops

Another good decorative use for polished pebbles is in the making of table tops. Occasional tables and coffee tables will benefit from the beautiful and original designs that can be produced in this way.

A piece of ¾in. (19mm) chipboard or plywood is the best material to use as a base for the table top. After cutting this to the required size it should be coated with a layer of cement (or plaster of Paris), or bitumen. Cement should be used if you want to achieve a light background to your pebble design. Bitumen, on the other hand, will give a dark grey or black background. The pebbles should be set into the bitumen, or cement, while it is still soft. Once it has set the

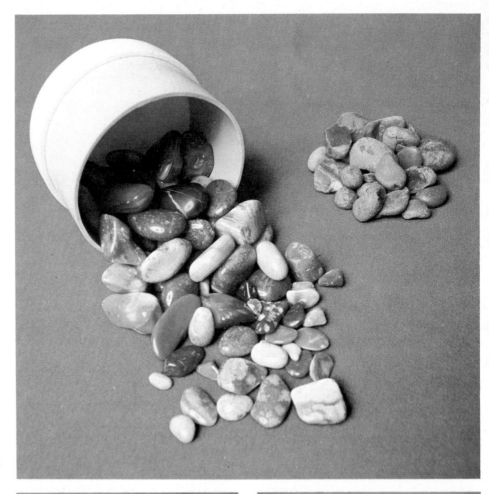

Top. *Here, the contrast is shown between the dull and uninspiring collection of unpolished pebbles on the right of the picture and the strikingly attractive pile of newly polished pebbles. The barrel of the tumbling machine should be filled with pebbles of varying sizes. —but equal hardness.*

Above left. *The machine shown here enables polished pebbles to be cut into slices.*

Above right. *A large pebble cut in two to reveal its intricate composition.*

pebbles can be cleaned off by wiping them over with a damp cloth.

The pebbled surface must now be protected. For this a piece of ⅜in. or 10mm plate or float glass —cut to size—should be used. The glass is fitted approximately ½in. (13mm) above the pebbled surface. To do this, lengths of deal batten must be cut to size to fit the four sides of the table. Use a rebate plane to cut grooves in each length of batten. These are for holding the glass in place. Now, fix the battens on to three sides of the table top, using tacks and pva wood adhesive. Having done this you should be able to slide the glass in place without too much difficulty. Make sure that the glass fits securely, and fix the batten to the fourth side of the table top. Once this has been done, simply paint the batten frame, and you will have made a strikingly original table top.

Only some of the decorative uses of polished pebbles have been mentioned in this chapter. Once you have mastered the basic techniques of pebble polishing, you will probably think of many more ideas for their use—ideas that can be used to their fullest advantage in beautifying your home.

Above. *The hard curves of this wrought iron plant holder make a pleasing contrast to the soft draping of flowers and greenery.*

Wrought iron screens

There are many possibilities for using decorative iron screens in the home. Doors and windows can be made more attractive, and large boxes or barrels can be decorated and used as planters or storage cases. Many people are, however, reluctant to construct such screens because they assume that the techniques needed require special training and equipment. But ordinary handyman's tools—a drill, hand saw, metal files and rivets—are all that's needed and the techniques can be easily learned in a matter of hours.

All designs for screens described in this chapter are simple to make but care must be taken if a professional-looking finish is to be obtained. If you choose to design your own screen, it will be necessary to work it out to the correct scale on some graph or squared paper.

Material required

Mild steel flats (strips) :

Outer frame—½in. or ¾in. x ¼in. thick (13mm or 19mm x 6mm)

Inner Design — ½in. or ¾in. x ⅛in. thick (13mm x 19mm x 3mm)

(The lengths and widths chosen are entirely optional and depend on your design.)

Rivets : ³⁄₁₆in. (5mm) diameter steel, flat-headed, counter-sunk, or snap-headed (see description below). The length will vary according to the design.

A setting-out board: made of ¼in. (6mm) hardwood or plywood which is two or three inches larger than your finished piece of work will be. A metal clad work surface on a bench will be ideal to use.

A large, adjustable spanner to use as a twisting tool or you can make a special tool from two lengths of 1in. x ⅜in. (25mm x 10mm) steel angle iron, two 1in. x ¼in. (25mm x 6mm) B.S.W. bolts, and ¼in. (6mm) washers to make up the spacers.

1in. (25mm) thick plywood or hardwood to make up bending formers for circles and other shapes. The quantity will depend upon the size of the design.

6 fire bricks, or thick asbestos, for fire protection when using the blow lamp.

Setting out the design

First, work out your design on a sheet of graph paper. Then, using chalk or a felt pen, draw a full size outline of the frame on to the setting-out board and divide the internal area up

Fig.1. Cut the metal to the required length with the scribed line just proud of the vice.

Fig.2. Measure the diameter of the rivets with a pair of calipers and drill the holes in the metal exactly to this size.

Fig.3. Lubricate the drill bit before drilling to prevent it binding in the metal.

Fig.4. Countersink the holes drilled in the metal if you use flat-head rivets.

Fig.5. With the ball of the hammer lightly tap the head of the rivet to push it into the countersunk hole.

Fig.6. Use the face of the hammer to beat the rivet head flush with the metal.

Fig.7. Support the head of snap- or round-head rivets in a bolster held in a vice. With a rivet snap, force the pieces of metal together.

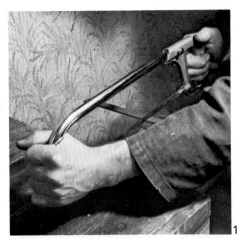

proportionately into the same number of squares as is on your design graph. Once this is done, you can transfer your design, enlarged to the actual size, on to the setting-out board with your felt pen or chalk.

If you are using one of the designs reproduced in this chapter you may find it necessary to elongate or condense the squares to suit your final shape exactly. Providing this will not alter the design significantly, it is perfectly all right to do so.

Having laid out the design, mark on to it the positions of the rivets using a different coloured chalk or pen. These marks should be made at right angles to the metal strips.

Cutting the metal strips

The metal strips must now be cut to length. The principles involved in marking and cutting metal are basically the same as those for timber. Marking is done with a hard-tipped metal scriber and cutting is done with a hacksaw. A metal working vice should be used to hold the strips since its jaws are designed to keep metal from slipping and will allow sufficient clearance of the working surface for the saw movement. A woodworking vice may be used but the wooden faces of the jaws may become damaged from holding the metal.

The outer frame

The perimeter of the outer frame should be carefully measured and the position of the joints decided upon—the joints should not be at a corner, but at a point where two rivets can be

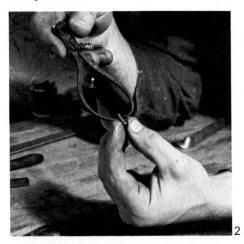

used to tie it in to the internal design. The overall length, including bends and twists, should now be marked out on a length of ¼in. (6mm) thick mild steel flat.

Then place the metal in the vice with the waste side hanging free and the scribed cutting mark about ¼in. or 6mm proud of the vice (see Fig.1). Holding the hacksaw as shown, cut to the waste side of the line. After sawing, smooth off the cut end with a flat metal file, pushing the file in a forward direction only.

Now transfer the positions of the rivets from the full size drawing to the metal strip. Mark them first with a felt pen or crayon and then indent the metal with a centre punch (or any hardened piece of pointed steel). This is used both to mark the centre of the hole and to prevent the drill bit from slipping when you begin drilling.

The holes must be drilled exactly to the size of the shank of the rivet (see Fig.2). Before beginning lubricate the tip of the drill with a drop of oil to stop the bit from binding in the metal and snapping in half (see Fig.3).

Flat-headed rivets must be countersunk to fit properly. Do this with a normal countersinking bit, the same size as the diameter of the rivet head (see Fig.4). When you are buying the rivets, be sure that the depth of the head does not exceed the thickness of the metal; if the rivets are a bit overlarge, grinding or filing down will be necessary. When the holes for the rivets have been drilled, clean off any jagged bits with a fine file held flat across the hole.

Bending right angles

Bending should be done with a blow lamp which has been set at the highest heat. (If you are using very thin metal, heat will not be necessary.) When using the lamp, always be sure that you enclose the area in which you are working with fire bricks or asbestos blocks. Mark the position for bending the metal strip and hold this corner mark in the tip of the central blue core—the hottest part of the flame. Heat the metal until it becomes red hot and then quickly place it in the vice. Gently tap the metal with a hammer and bend it into a right-angle. When you are satisfied with the shape, plunge the heated area into a bowl of water to cool and harden it.

Repeat this process for each corner, placing each bend on the setting-out board to ensure accuracy of work.

When the frame is laid flat it might be found that it is slightly out of winding; this may be easily straightened out by placing one side in the vice and twisting the frame straight from the opposite side.

Positioning the screen

Once the outer frame is finished, hold it in position against the door or window to which it will be finally fixed. Mark out the positions for drilling holes for the screws which will hold the screen in place. Be careful that you do not mark out places which will conflict with joints from the inner area of the screen. Now carefully drill holes in the metal frame to fit No. 8 black Japanned, round-headed screws. The number of screws you will need and the size will vary according to the weight and size of your screen,

Above. The first design incorporates three basic shapes which are easily reproduced using wood formers. The semi-circles on the edges link with the rocker-shaped cross bars with the 'S' shape in the middle forming a focal point. The lower design is very simple, consisting of large and small S shapes.

but 1in. to 2in. (25mm to 50mm) long screws should be adequate.

After drilling the holes, fit the frame back into its eventual position and use a nail to mark the corresponding positions through the screw holes on to the door or window frame.

The inner area

Measuring the lengths of strips for the decorative portion of the screen may be somewhat of a problem. When measuring curves it

will be useful to note that the formula for the distance round the circumference of a circle is $2\pi r$ or πd ($\pi = 3.14$ [$\frac{22}{7}$], (r = radius, d = diameter). Perhaps the easiest way of measuring, is to use a piece of string and match it carefully to the design. Stretch the string out straight afterwards and measure it.

Bending curves

Curves are best bent around a former which can be made from 1in. (25mm) thick plywood or hardwood. Cut out the shape of the curve wanted using a bow saw or electric jig saw; keep this former slightly smaller than the curve as drawn on the setting-out board, to allow for the 'spring' in the metal. After the former is cut screw it on to a slightly larger piece of timber. Now, at the starting point of the curve screw in a number of No. 10 or 12 screws at a distance away from the edge of the wood which equals the thickness of the metal strip precisely. Remove the screw heads with a hacksaw. (These screws will hold the metal strip in position while you are bending it). When you are satisfied that the wooden former is an accurate reproduction of the shape of your design, place the metal strip between the screws and the block and bend the strips around the curve. If the curves are particularly tight, you may find that you will need to heat the strips in the blow torch first and hammer them gently into shape around your former. Always check the bent shapes against the design on the setting-out board for accuracy.

Twists

Many of the designs shown incorporate twists. These are quite easy to do with mild steel strips. Use a twisting bar which can be made up with two pieces of 1in. x ⅜in. (25mm x 10mm) bar or hardwood and adjusted with ¼in. (6mm) B.S.W. bolts and washers.

To make slow twists in a flat strip, first mark out the area for each twist on the strip with chalk. Place the metal vertically in the vice, keeping the first chalk mark level with the top of the vice. Place the twisting bar over the strip and adjust it, if necessary, to hold the piece securely. Turn the bar with both hands.

Riveting

After all the shapes have been cut, bent, twisted, and drilled, the various pieces should be riveted together. Rivets are used to fix metal pieces together permanently; they are sold by weight and those used should be made of the same material as the metal pieces to prevent corrosion from occuring. The names of rivets are derived from the shape of the head. The designs given in this article can use either *flat-headed*, *countersunk*, or *snap-headed* (also called round head or cup head) rivets.

A few special tools are needed to do riveting properly. Those required are, primarily, the *rivet bolster* (or dolly) and the *rivet set*. The set is held over the shank of the rivet and is used for drawing the plates together before riveting. The bolster is normally held in a vice and supports the snap head of a rivet while a head is being formed at the other end. The snap is used to finish the formation of a snap head.

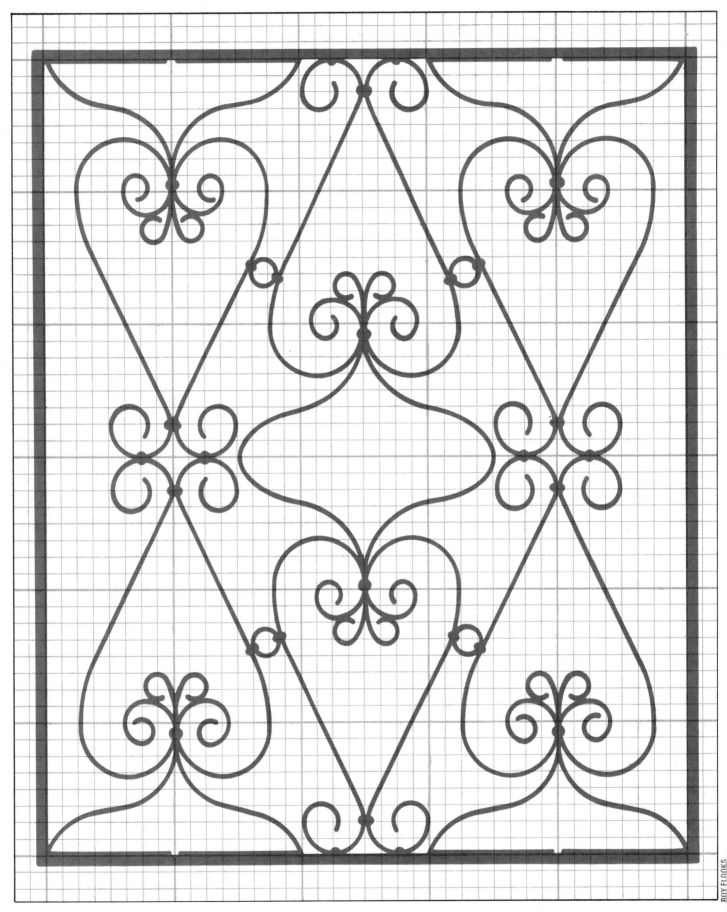

Countersinking rivets

All holes for countersinking rivets should be drilled beforehand, making sure that the outer edge of the countersink is the same diameter as the rivet head. Any burrs on the holes and metal cuttings between the two pieces being joined must be removed or the plates will not come together properly and the rivet may swell between them. A file held flat on the metal and drawn lightly over the holes will remove any burrs. The holes *must* be properly aligned to prevent the rivets from bending.

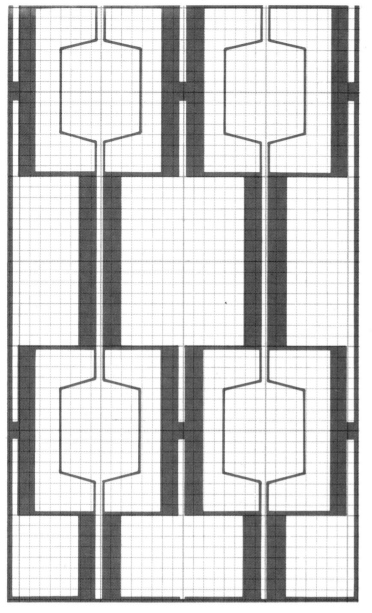

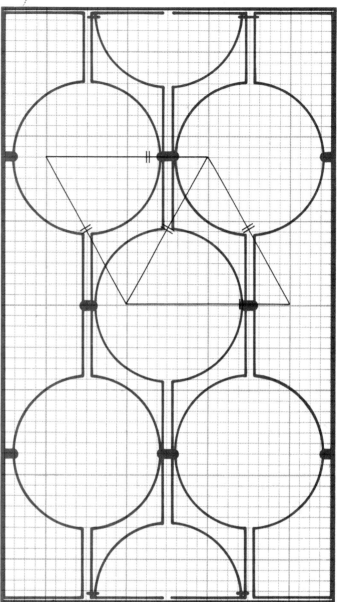

ROY FLOOKS

Left. Hearts and tightly curved flourishes form the basic shapes in the design of this screen, which possesses a pleasing symmetry.

Above left. An intriguing, eye catching geometric pattern with its sharp angles and wide horizontal strips make up this screen.

Above right. An eggtimer effect is achieved by this design which groups circles, open at the tops and bottoms, in a tight pattern.

Check to see that the size of your rivet snap or bolster is the same size as the rivet head you are using or, again, the joint will not be secure. For countersunk riveting, a length of rivet which equals the diameter of the shank should be left projecting from the metal pieces. It is important that the length of the rivet is correct or otherwise the heads may not fill the countersinking or may be misshapen. If you need to shorten a rivet, the waste, not the head, should be gripped in a vice during sawing. A hacksaw may be used for the cutting, and ends should be filed flat.

When beginning to fix countersunk rivets, place the two pieces of metal together with the holes aligned and the countersunk portions kept outermost. Insert the rivet and support the head on a flat surface. Using the ball end of a ball pein hammer, tap the projecting end of the rivet. This will cause it to expand and fill the countersunk hole (see Figs.5-6). Then use the flat face of the hammer to beat the surface flat. Finally, file the rivet flush to the surface.

Beware of making too shallow a countersink or the joint will be very weak.

To remove a countersunk rivet, drill it carefully to the depth of the countersink and punch the rivet out with a tapered punch.

Snap-head riveting

Snap- (or round-) headed rivets should have their heads supported by a bolster which is held in a vice (see Fig.7). The bolster has a hollow ground out of the top so that the rivet head can just fit into it. To form a snap-head at the projecting shank end (the amount of shank projecting should be $1\frac{1}{2}$ times the diameter of the rivet) begin by placing the rivet set over the shank and hammering with the flat end of a ball pein hammer to draw the two metal strips securely together. After a few taps, remove the set and, using the ball end of the hammer, strike the rivet shank until the head is roughly formed. Finish by holding the rivet snap over the end, giving the rivet a few sharp hammer blows. To

remove a snap-headed rivet, file off the head and then punch out the shank as for a countersunk head.

Finishing

Once the assembly of your decorative screen is completed, clean up all surfaces with a stiff wire brush and wipe down with turpentine. Cover the entire metal screen with a good quality metal primer. This will help to keep the metal from rusting and will also provide a good key for the top coat of paint to be applied. Black is the most common colour used on this type of screen, but another colour may be used if wanted. Enamel paint of a good quality gloss paint, suitable for exteriors should be used.

When the paint has dried, set the screen into position, aligning the screw holes drilled into the outer frame with these drilled into the window or door frame. Screw the frame into position, using No. 8, round-headed, black Japanned screws or a suitable equivalent.

Welding: new dimensions in DIY

Welding adds a new dimension to the home workshop and, when done on a small scale with the basic equipment described here, can open up a whole new field for the DIY enthusiast. In conjunction with the art of scrollwork and decorative iron work, electric welding not only speeds up the work but it can also be neater, cheaper and more satisfying to do.

Welding offers the neatest means of joining ferrous metals like iron and steel, although special electrodes are available for joining a number of dissimilar metals. The two pieces of metal are united by partially melting the substance of one piece into that of the other. A welded joint requires no large area of overlap under normal circumstances and can be much smaller in area than a rivetted one.

There are two basic types of fusion welding. One is gas welding, where a mixture of oxygen and acetylene is used to provide an intensely hot point of flame to melt the workpiece. This liquefies the metal at the joint, and by the addition of a filler material, in the form of a length of special wire called filler rod, produces a very strong, neat joint.

The other form of welding is electrical welding, also known as arc welding. Here the joint is again heated to the molten state and extra metal added from a rod. But in this case the rod is an electrode — a pencil-like object with a metallic core and a flux coating. At one

Fig. 1

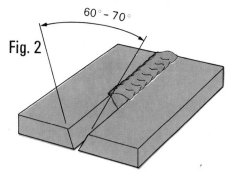

Fig. 2

60° - 70°

Fig. 3

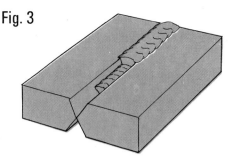

Fig. 4

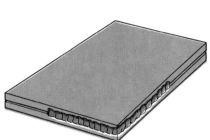

Fig.1. A simple square butt joint suitable for 16-gauge metal. *Fig.2.* For thicker material, the edges are chamfered to provide a V-shaped channel of about 60° to 70°. *Fig.3.* Very thick metal must be chamfered on each side in order to get sufficient weld penetration. Each side is welded several times in what is called the 'multi-run' technique. Each weld is cleaned up

before the next is made (see Figs.16-17) *Fig.4.* Simple lap-weld where one piece of metal is welded on to another. No chamfering is needed. *Fig.5.* Edge welding is used to close the edges of thin material. Again, no chamfering is needed. *Fig.6.* A fillet weld in thin plate such as 14- or 16-gauge. *Fig.7.* Thicker metal requires the multi-run technique (see Fig.3).

Fig. 5

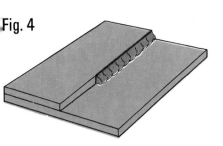

Fig. 6

Fig. 7

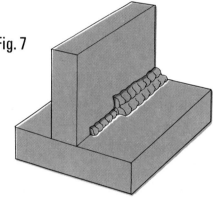

TRI-ART

nd, as with a pencil, a 'dot' of metal in the middle of the rod is exposed. At the other, a short length of the rod is left bare of flux so that it will make an electrical connection with the electrode holder. When a low voltage, high amperage current is passed through the electrode it jumps a fraction of an inch to the article being welded. This creates the welding arc—in effect, a continuous spark—which produces a heat of about 6,500°F (3,600°C), liquifying both the tip of the electrode and the edge of the workpiece.

From the amateur's point of view, gas welding needs expensive equipment, a great deal of practice to achieve the correct type of flame, and cumbersome gas cylinders. In unskilled hands, gas welding can be highly dangerous.

Electrical welding, on the other hand, calls for much simpler apparatus which can easily be bought or hired. Above all, relatively little practice is needed to produce a first-class job. Because of the low current consumption, there is no danger of electrocution, and with proper elementary safety precautions, the equipment is perfectly safe to use.

Home welding sets can be bought relatively cheaply, but for the casual DIY welder it is far cheaper to hire the apparatus for as long as he needs it. The cost of running the equipment is very low and the only expense is the electrode rods which can be bought in a variety of thicknesses in packs for less than £1.

The DIY welder's workshop should include a good solid work bench and a supply of clamps

and scrap timber for holding the job securely during work. Above all, there should be sufficient elbow room to allow free movement of the hand-held part of the equipment.

The equipment comprises a transformer which runs off the normal household power supply, the holder into which the electrode fits, a protective head shield containing a dark vision glass, a stiff wire brush and a cross-pane hammer, preferably with one pointed end.

In Britain, the transformer is connected by its three-core mains cable to a normal earthed 13-amp socket using a fused plug. It changes the working current to a safe voltage. Should you accidentally complete the circuit by touching both electrode and workpiece, a comparatively small current will flow giving you nothing more serious than a slight tingling sensation. At no time can this output rise to a dangerous level.

Leading from the transformer are two heavy-duty cables—they are thick to allow for the high amperage which has to be carried and they must not be replaced or extended with ordinary domestic cable. One of these cables normally terminates in a clip or clamp. This is fixed to the article being welded. The other cable is joined to the electrode holder into which is clamped the electrode rod. Some types of holder have a series of grooves in them which allows the rod to be secured at different angles to suit the convenience of the job. Alternatively the rod itself can be bent, although sharp bends should be avoided since this may cause the hardened

flux coating to flake off and its insulating property to be lost.

Safety precautions

Before attempting to use the equipment there are some safety points which you must observe. Welding constitutes a fire hazard and, because sparks and particles of molten metal may fly some distance, you should ensure that there are no inflammable materials anywhere near where you want to work. Oil-soaked rags, petrol, paraffin, white spirits, open cans of paint, wood shavings, curtains and plastics should be kept well out of the way. Keep a small fire extinguisher on hand or, at the very least, a bucket of water.

The welding screen is for the protection of your eyes and your face. It not only reduces the dangerous ultra-violet rays released during welding, which can blind you, but it allows you to watch exactly what you are doing. Dark goggles of the type used in gas welding are not suitable because they offer no protection for the rest of the face and with electrical welding extremely hot sparks fly. Because of this, never weld in shirt sleeves or with light clothing on. Ideally you should wear a leather apron but failing that wear an old jacket buttoned up or a full overall, and wear leather or asbestos gloves. Warn other members of your family not to watch unless wearing welding screens, and not to stand near you. Do not weld on a vertical surface and *NEVER* weld above your head. Try to keep the work-piece horizontal.

Welding produces heat; the end of the electrode and the weld line both become molten. Therefore do not handle either without first letting them cool, unless you wear heavy industrial gloves. Do not lay the electrode on the bench where you may inadvertently touch the hot end. A pair of pliers or tongs are ideal for handling the hot workpiece.

Although the welding current is low, do not stand on a damp floor and do not weld out of doors unless it is a dry day. Even then, you should stand on a thick rubber mat.

There is no hard and fast rule by which a particular gauge of electrode is selected. This is determined by the type of weld in relation to the thickness of the workpiece. A butt weld in 16 gauge steel sheet can be made by using either a 14 gauge or 16 gauge electrode, the only real difference being that the thicker 14 gauge electrode will do the job more quickly.

The degree to which the surface of the workpiece will be melted and re-cast by the intensity of the electrical arc is termed *penetration* and the greatest penetration results from the use of the larger gauge size electrodes. However, over-penetration may result if too thick a gauge is used and this means that the puddle of liquid metal will extend through to the other side and then drop out. This is called *blow-through*.

As a general guide, a 16 gauge electrode should be used for welding 18 to 16 gauge material; 14 gauge electrode for 16 to 12 gauge, and 12 gauge electrode for 10 gauge up to $\frac{1}{4}$in. thick plate. For material thicker than this, the 10 gauge electrode can be used, using what is called the *multiple-run* technique (see Fig.3)

to build up a large weld deposit. You cannot effectively arc weld material thinner than 18 gauge.

All that remains to be done is to decide on the amperage output of the transformer, using the selector switch provided. Each different sized electrode has a recommended current setting and generally four settings are available: 60amps, 75amps, 90amps and 100amps which are suitable for 16, 14, 12 and 10 gauge electrodes respectively. The selection of the current setting is largely a question of experience and, as with all things, there is a right way of welding and a wrong way. The correct current, the proper electrode and the right speed of the weld will produce a clean joint without spatter as shown in Fig.18. If the speed at which the electrode is moved is too slow, there will be a broad build-up of metal and lack of fusion at the edge due to the inclusion of the slag which forms on the molten metal. Too slow a speed on thin metal will result in over-penetration with a risk of burning through. If the current is too low again the build-up is high. With too high a current, the weld is very shallow with excessive spatter—this means that particles of molten metal are thrown out and stick to the surface on either side of the joint. With correct current and proper electrode gap, too fast a speed of weld will be characterized by a very narrow and hence weak weld line.

It is worth spending half an hour with some offcuts of scrap metal and deliberately varying current, electrode gap and speed so as to gain experience. A good weld should be clean, uniform in appearance and should (in the case

of a butt joint) protrude slightly above the surface of the metal.

Types of joint

There are basically only two types of joint encountered in welding; end-to-end joining and an overlapped join. Three different welding techniques are used depending on the particular job. These are the *fillet*, the *butt*, and the *edge* weld, illustrated in Figs.1-6.

The fillet is used where two pieces meet at a right angle and consists of a deposit of weld material along the join. No chamfering of the metal is needed under most conditions.

With a butt weld, where two pieces of metal are joined in the same plane, some preparation is necessary in order to offer the best conditions for fusion. If, for example, the pieces were welded in the 'as cut' state (just as hacksawed), it would be very difficult to achieve any penetration and the major portion of the weld would be on the surface. This would mean a weak and unsightly joint. The proper treatment is to chamfer the two edges with a file so as to produce a V-shaped trough. This not only makes it easier to contain a neat weld but it actually increases the surface area of the joint.

Edge welding is encountered where, as an example, two pieces of bar cross each other. In some instances, this will take the form of a fillet weld, but in other cases, as when two ends come together in the same plane (see Fig.4, where one piece is welded on top of another), it calls for the fusing together of a double edge. With metal up to, say, 12 gauge in thickness, no preparation is needed and the weld is just made along the joint. With thicker pieces, though, the edge weld is replaced by the butt weld technique, calling for the chamfering of both pieces. Because a weld may start wherever the electrode touches the workpiece, it is very difficult to weld into a corner, particularly if it forms an angle of less than about 60°. In welding scrollwork of the type the DIY man will most probably be involved with, tight corners such as where two scrolls meet can be avoided and a neat job made by edge-welding the sides of the scrolls where they touch.

Learning to weld

Firmly secure the pieces to be welded on the bench using clamps. Soft iron wire (an old coathanger for instance) can be used to hold pieces tightly together. Connect the earth lead to part of it using the clamp provided. **NEVER** let anybody hold the workpiece during welding.

The initial arc is 'struck' by bringing the electrode into contact with the metal, using a light tapping action. Any initial difficulty in striking the arc will be due either to dirt on the workpiece or to the flux shield of the electrode preventing metal-to-metal contact. Once the arc is started, withdraw the electrode slightly, or tilt it, to create a slight gap—it is this gap which creates the extreme heat of the arc, melting the electrode core wire and protective flux and the areas of base metal directly underneath the electric arc.

To maintain the arc, the electrode is moved steadily in one direction, either maintaining the gap by visual control or by tilting the electrode

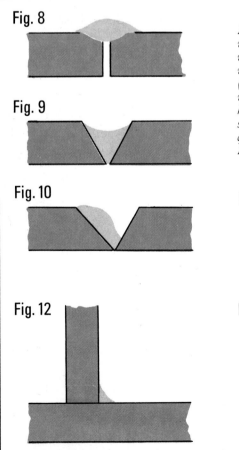

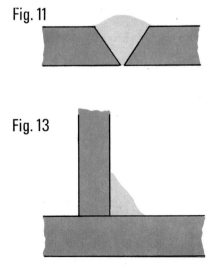

Fig.8. *A section through an unchamfered welded joint showing an obvious weakness.* **Fig.9.** *Section of a shallow weld made with too low an amperage (see Fig.18).* **Fig.10.** *An off-centre weld due to incorrect position of the hand electrode.* **Fig.11.** *A perfect weld showing good penetration.* **Fig.12.** *Poor quality fillet weld at a butt joint.* **Fig.13.** *A well-made fillet weld.*

TRI-ART

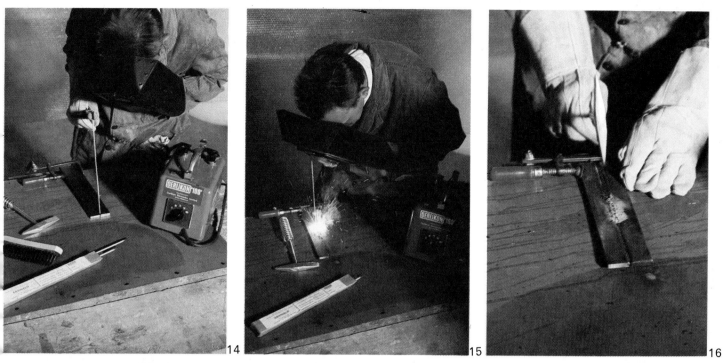

14   15   16

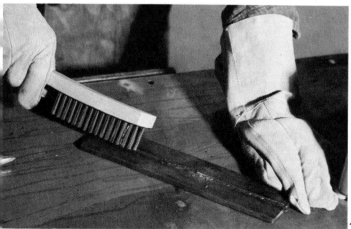

Fig.14. *The equipment which is used for amateur welding. The welder is about to strike the arc.* **Fig.15.** *The arc is struck and the weld is being made.* **Fig.16.** *After welding, the hard slag which forms over the weld line must be chipped off with a hammer. Special pointed-end welding hammers such as that being used here make the job easier but you can use an ordinary hammer.* **Fig.17.** *After removing the slag, the weld is scoured with a wire brush.* **Fig.18.** *These two bars have been butt-welded in four different ways to demonstrate good and bad welds. Top to bottom: a poor weld due to too large an electrode and too low an amperage; a spattered weld caused by the correct electrode and amperage but too great a spark gap between job and electrode; a perfect weld showing proper penetration and correct setting; a multi-run weld where two passes have been made.*
Fig.19. *Blow-through on thin sheet.* **Fig.20.** *Welded ironwork in the home, and a straight radiator cut and welded to fit neatly into a corner.*

17

18   19   20

so that it rests lightly on the workpiece. If you hold the electrode too close to the work, the arc will break and the electrode will stick. A quick twist of the wrist usually frees it. Otherwise you will have to switch off and chisel off the rod.

To stop welding, all you have to do is withdraw the electrode to break the arc.

One drawback of gas welding is that so much heat is put into the job that distortion may easily occur during cooling, and this often means cracking. With electrical welding, the amount of heat is extremely localized, so the problem does not arise. However, if you are attempting a long butt weld of, say, more than 4in. or 100mm, it is advisable to weld each end first to prevent creep or loss of alignment.

Unlike gas welding, electrical welding produces a deposit of slag over the molten metal and when cooled this forms a very hard crust. Before you can truly assess the quality of your welding this must be chipped off with a hammer and scrubbed with a wire brush. All the slag must be removed before painting your finished handiwork or rust may set in.

A word of warning here. When removing slag from welds, it is advisable to wear a pair of clear glass safety goggles or a clear plastic face shield.

Making a garden incinerator

You can gain experience in handling the electric welding equipment by making a garden incinerator. You will be producing something useful for a medium-sized garden and if your first welds are not perfect, then it is of little consequence since appearance is not vital.

The materials you will need for making the incinerator shown in Fig.21 are:
1) 26ft x 2in. x $\frac{1}{8}$in. (7.92m x 50mm x 3mm) of 10 gauge steel
2) 21ft x 1$\frac{1}{2}$in. x $\frac{1}{4}$in. (6.4m x 38mm x 6mm) steel bar
3) two or three packs of Easiweld 12 gauge rods (electrodes)

Start by forming the grid hoop for the bottom of the incinerator. A useful technique for bending a true circle in fairly thick bar is to start with a length of material several times longer than is needed. One end is then clamped in the vice and the other is bent in a hoop as shown in Fig.21. The advantage of this method is that, if you have a big enough vice and a sturdy bench, you can bend thick stock cold and furthermore the old problem which occurs when trying to bend a circle out of a piece the exact length (namely sustaining the bend at both ends as well as in the centre) is entirely avoided. The hoop produced is made to the right diameter by varying the bend. It is then hammered true if necessary and then a cut made through both ends. The hoop ends are then chamfered on both faces and twisted into alignment. Tack weld on the top and bottom edges to hold the hoop together.

You can save welding here by arranging the first grating bar so that the fillet weld also closes the hoop gap (Fig.21 top right).

It is only necessary to weld the grate bars on one side at each end. You will be able to save labour in shaping the ends of the grate bars if you just cut them square. The slight gap produced between the square end of the bar and the curve of the hoop will not prevent you from making a good welded joint.

When the grid is completed, shape the four legs and weld these to the grid sides. These are ordinary fillet welds. Make the top hoop in the same manner as the grid hoop. This fits outside the legs which are fillet-welded to the inside of the hoop. Again make the hoop joint coincide with one of these welds. If there is any tendency for the hoop to spring open, bind it tightly with wire during welding.

Then weld into place the 2in. (50mm) strips which form the basket, again using fillet welds. For a neat job, you should now edge-weld the tops of the legs and the basket strips to close the gaps between them and the top hoop. Finally chip off all the slag.

The incinerator is now completed and you will have gained enough experience to be able to tackle more attractive projects such as decorative iron work which can be put to good use in the making of garden furniture to enchance your patio or lawn.

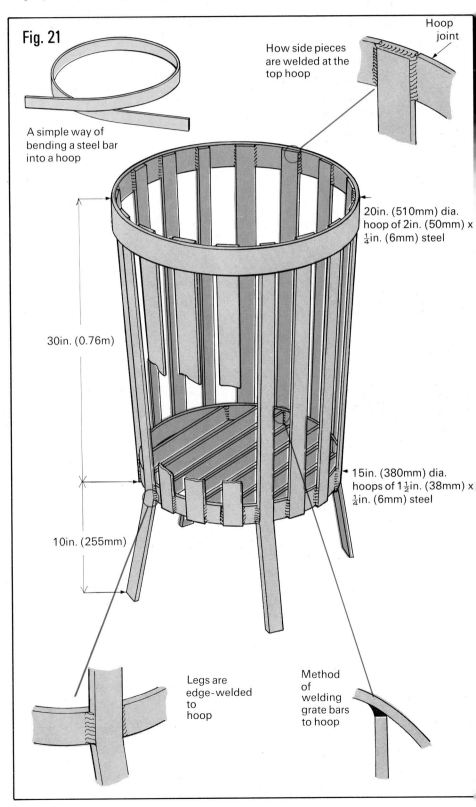

Fig. 21

A simple way of bending a steel bar into a hoop

How side pieces are welded at the top hoop

Hoop joint

20in. (510mm) dia. hoop of 2in. (50mm) x $\frac{1}{4}$in. (6mm) steel

30in. (0.76m)

15in. (380mm) dia. hoops of 1$\frac{1}{2}$in. (38mm) x $\frac{1}{4}$in. (6mm) steel

10in. (255mm)

Legs are edge-welded to hoop

Method of welding grate bars to hoop

Fig.1. This handsome copper bowl is an example of simple three-dimensional shaping which can easily be made by the novice.

Metalworking skills: a copper bowl

Working in metal is very simple and does not require expensive special tools or equipment. Any amateur handyman can use sheet metalwork techniques to improve his skills around the home and garden.

Types of thing that the sheet metalworker may wish to make include decorative copper jugs and bowls, fireplace canopies and utility items such as letter racks, tool racks, casings for hi-fi equipment, and so on. In the garage, sheet metalwork capability will extend the range of repair work you can undertake; for the garden, you can make items such as mower grass-boxes and wheelbarrows. This introduction to metalwork includes instructions on making a copper bowl.

Metalworking tools and equipment

For the workshop, you should have a stout bench or table. Your first need will be a metal-working vice. Buy the largest you can afford but don't get one with jaws smaller than 4in. (100mm) wide. Bolt this securely on to the bench projecting slightly beyond the front edge, so that when you have a length of metal clamped vertically between the jaws, it will hang clear of the forward edge of the bench.

The normal jaws as fitted to a vice are provided with serrated faces for a secure grip. For sheet metalwork this is not always an advantage since the ridges will cut into and disfigure thin metal, particularly aluminium and copper. Some vices have reversible jaws, the other sides being smooth. Special linings called *vice clams* are sold for padding serrated jaws. They are made of light alloy, steel or plastic. By far the best way, though, is to replace the jaws of the vice with a pair of smooth ones made of plain steel bar. Vice jaws take a great deal of hard use, so when you have made them and drilled them for their

43

attachment screws, take them if possible to your local engineering works and have them case-hardened.

If your bench is small, then it is a good idea to anchor it to the floor with steel brackets and screws to reduce 'hammer bounce' (a real problem in metalwork) and so cut down the amount of energy needed when working metals.

For marking out metal, an ordinary pencil cannot be used because it seldom leaves a legible mark and is not very precise. The proper tool, called a *scriber,* is like a steel pencil with a fine, sharp point. Again, an ordinary carpenters' wooden rule is inadequate for metalwork. Buy a good-quality 12-inch or 250mm steel rule, and also an engineers' flat try-square. A pair of steel dividers—special types are sold for metalwork—is also needed for transferring accurately dimensions from the rule to the metal, and drawing arcs and circles.

To mark the position of holes, or the centres of arcs, use a *centre punch* to make a small dot on the metal. There are two sorts: one is a small pointed rod which you strike with a hammer, and the other is a spring-loaded automatic punch which you push down on to the metal until the internal spring releases a hammer-blow on to the point. The second type is only really successful on alloys and other soft metals. The small pop mark produced will guide the point of a drill for subsequent hole-boring, or will locate one point of a pair of dividers for describing an arc.

The normal handyman's claw hammer is likely to be unsuitable for metalwork because most types have sharp edges which can bruise rather than bend metal. You should buy at least one, and preferably two *ball pein* hammers. The most necessary size is around 1lb (0.45kg) and you will find that a second one about half this weight will be useful. If you intend to do any fancy metalwork involving dishing or flanging (see the section on 'techniques' below), you will also have to buy a *cross-pein* hammer (around the 1lb size) and a *planishing* hammer. The ball-pein hammer has the usual more or less flat face on one side of the head, but the other side is in the shape of a ball. The cross-pein has one flat face and one in the form of a wedge, its chisel edge lying across the line of the handle. In Britain this is sometimes known as a Warrington hammer. The planishing hammer is used for forming flat metal into three-dimensional shapes; it has two highly-polished, domed faces of different sizes. A planishing hammer must never be used for anything else other than 'dressing' and shaping metal, since other uses might damage its faces.

There are several types of cutting tool. Hand shears known as *tin-snips* are used for metal up to about 18 gauge (1.22mm). Thicker gauges of soft metals can also be cut with tin-snips, but above this thickness the hacksaw is the usual tool. Tin-snips are available in two basic sorts—straight and cranked. The big advantage of cranked snips is that they enable you to keep your hand above the line you are cutting, thus making the job easier and avoiding skinning your knuckles on the sharp edges. Cranked snips are made in left- and right-handed versions; the left-handed ones usually have to be ordered specially.

Another cutting tool made especially for thin materials is the type of *double-shear* snips sold in Britain under such names as 'Goscut'. These remove a narrow strip of material from the cut line. The big advantage of this type of shear is that it does not distort the metal on either side of the cut, so that the sheet remains perfectly flat. You can also cut curves very easily. The disadvantage is that the cutters are only suitable for very thin sheet steel, or non-ferrous metals such as copper or aluminium up to about 18 gauge (1.22mm) and it is a slow tool to use since the blade cuts only about $\frac{1}{4}$in. (6mm) of the material at a time.

Hacksaws come in a variety of types and sizes. Choose one with a rigid (preferably tubular) frame which can be adjusted to take both the 10in. and the 12in. standard size of hacksaw blade. A useful feature found in a number of better makes is the provision for turning the blade through 90° for sawing through long, thin sections of metal. A totally-enclosed hand grip, such as you find on a good make of carpenters' saw, will prevent damage to your hands if the blade should break during use.

Hacksaw blades come in two main types—low tungsten steel for general work and high-speed steel for quality precision work. The main difference is that the high-speed steel blade is harder and lasts longer, and the teeth are less likely to break off in normal use. It is also more expensive. Blades are also graded by the number of teeth per inch, the standard numbers being 14, 18, 24 and 32. The greater the number of teeth, the slower the blade will cut, but the important thing is to choose the right blade for the job. If the teeth are wider apart than the thickness of the metal you are cutting, they will 'straddle' the metal, catch on it and chip off.

Another means of cutting steel which can produce very accurate cuts if used carefully is the *cold chisel.* The method of cutting with it is shown in Fig.2. The cold chisel is usually the best tool for removing a thin strip of metal from a bar or narrow plate thick enough to be held in the vice. To work properly, the edge of the chisel must be kept sharpened at the proper angle of 65° (see Fig.2)—the steel from which a modern cold chisel is made is not very hard and so you can easily sharpen it with an ordinary file.

Choosing and using files

Files for metalwork come in a wide variety of shapes and sizes, which can be very confusing. However, there are three main shapes and three usual degrees of coarseness. The shapes are flat, half round and round. Flat files are either *bellied* (this means that the edges have a slight convex curve) or *parallel.* Parallel files are made with one smooth edge, called a *safe edge,* so that you can file against a stop without cutting into it. These are called *hand* files.

The three grades of toughness are *smooth, second-cut (*sometimes called *medium),* and *bastard.* Files are also specified by length so that you can buy, for example, a 10in. half-round bastard, or a 12in. flat second-cut.

The choice of the right grade of file for the job can save a lot of hard work. Use a coarse or bastard file for heavy and rough work (there is a type of file called a Millenicut which has widely-spaced teeth; this is very good for heavy work), a second-cut for filing to size, and a smooth file

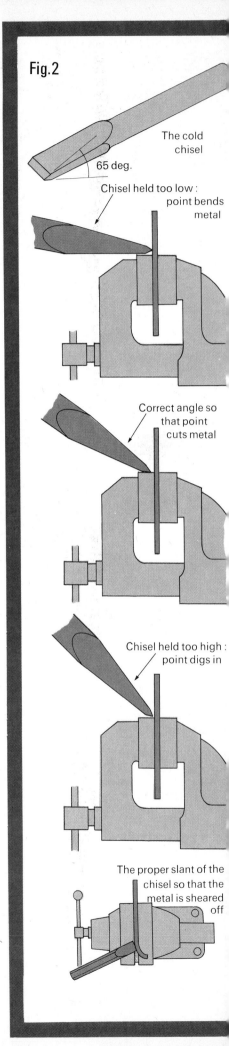

Fig.2

The cold chisel

65 deg.

Chisel held too low: point bends metal

Correct angle so that point cuts metal

Chisel held too high: point digs in

The proper slant of the chisel so that the metal is sheared off

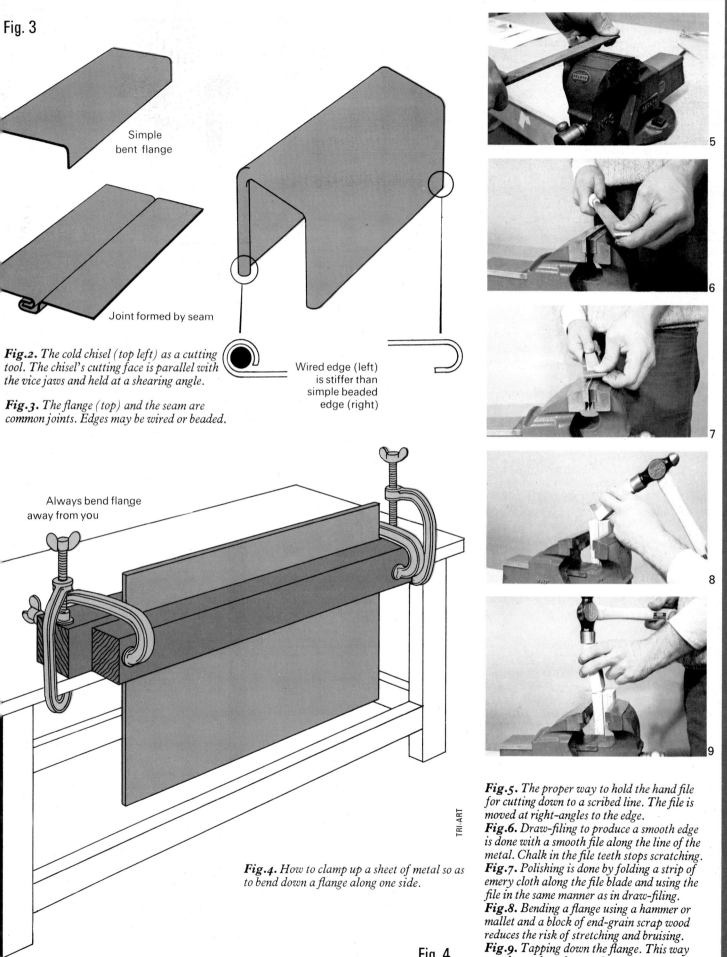

Fig. 3

Simple
bent flange

Joint formed by seam

Fig.2. *The cold chisel (top left) as a cutting tool. The chisel's cutting face is parallel with the vice jaws and held at a shearing angle.*

Fig.3. *The flange (top) and the seam are common joints. Edges may be wired or beaded.*

Wired edge (left)
is stiffer than
simple beaded
edge (right)

Always bend flange
away from you

TRI-ART

Fig.4. *How to clamp up a sheet of metal so as to bend down a flange along one side.*

Fig. 4

5

6

7

8

9

Fig.5. *The proper way to hold the hand file for cutting down to a scribed line. The file is moved at right-angles to the edge.*
Fig.6. *Draw-filing to produce a smooth edge is done with a smooth file along the line of the metal. Chalk in the file teeth stops scratching.*
Fig.7. *Polishing is done by folding a strip of emery cloth along the file blade and using the file in the same manner as in draw-filing.*
Fig.8. *Bending a flange using a hammer or mallet and a block of end-grain scrap wood reduces the risk of stretching and bruising.*
Fig.9. *Tapping down the flange. This way you do not dent the metal.*

for finishing. Finishing files include very small flat files called *warding* files, and small round, pointed files known as *rat-tail* files. There are also *three square* (triangular) files in small sizes for saw sharpening, and extremely small and smooth jewellers' files are available for delicate work.

In the handyman's workshop, there are many tools which are misused, mainly through ignorance but quite often through laziness. The file is seen by many as a sort of universal tool, and it is, for example, quite easy to knock in a nail with a file rather than reach across for a hammer. Treatment of this kind can ruin a file quite quickly.

Few people bother to learn how to use a file the right way, but correct use improves the neatness of results and makes the file last longer. Like the teeth on a saw, file teeth only cut one way—the file is pushed forward across the metal to do the work, and the return stroke does not cut. Many amateurs can be seen exerting equal pressure on the file on both the forward and return strokes, but the correct method is to put your weight behind the file on the forward stroke only, and draw it back lightly. Support the workpiece firmly in the vice and press hard enough to prevent the file from juddering. The file cuts best when its teeth can be felt to be cutting the metal—you will be able to feel this with a little practice. Don't file in short stabs, but use the whole length of the file and maintain an even pressure and speed of cut. The illustration Fig.5 shows the right way to hold the file.

Finish-filing or polishing is properly known as draw-filing and consists of filing along the edge of the metal rather than at right angles to it. The file is held as near parallel to the edge as possible, without catching your fingers on it, and is moved to and fro along the edge. Because the teeth of a file are cut in angled rows, draw-filing will often be more effective in one direction than in another, i.e. left to right will not finish so well as right to left (see Fig.6).

You can polish an edge by using finer and finer grades of file, finally rubbing chalk into the teeth of the file for a really high-grade finish. Alternatively, you can wrap a long strip of fine emery along the length of the file for polishing (see Fig.7).

When a file gets clogged with particles of metal, wood, glue or plastic, clean it by vigorous brushing with a file *scratch-card*, which is like a small wire brush with a flexible back. Obstinate clogging can often be removed by soaking the file in boiling water first. Light alloys nearly always clog file teeth, but this can often be prevented by rubbing a stick of chalk along the file before starting work.

A grindstone is a faster tool for removing metal than a file in certain situations. But use it carefully. It is a potentially lethal tool, whether a proper bench-mounted unit or just a small stone for use in an electric drill. The bursting forces built up through centrifugal force are very great, so if you are buying a replacement stone, make quite sure you get one made for the size and speed for your grinder to guard against the danger of the stone flying apart. A grindstone will only grind ferrous metals and is ruined very quickly by attempts to grind aluminium, copper or other alloys that are too soft. There are special types of grinding wheel used in engineering for grinding alloys, but these are not DIY tools.

For drilling holes, an electric drill is far easier and quicker to use than a hand drill. Choose one with a $\frac{5}{16}$'' chuck rather than the usual $\frac{1}{4}$''—the bigger drill has a reserve of power which gives a longer life.

Techniques

The most common operations in shaping sheet metal, apart from simple cutting, consist of *flanging, three-dimensional shaping, wiring,* and *joining*. Flanging means bending up an edge of the metal in such a way as to provide a means of attachment to something else such as another component, or to stiffen the metal sheet against bending. Three-dimensional shaping is used to produce a dished or bowl shape; wiring is a process in which the edge of a sheet-metal object is reinforced by a closed flange with a wire inside, and joining refers to any of several processes for fixing one piece of metal to another (see Fig.3).

A sheet of metal that is to be flanged or cut along a line should first be marked with a scriber and steel rule. Press hard enough to make a definite mark but avoid scoring the surface deeply. The scriber will mark soft metal quite clearly, and on polished steel it leaves a discernible trace. However, if you want to make the scribed lines show up more clearly, then you can paint a substance called Engineers' Blue on the metal first. This liquid dries very rapidly and leaves a coating that is removed by the scriber point. It can readily be washed off afterwards with turpentine substitute, or rubbed off with fine wire wool.

To flange a sheet of thin metal, clamp the sheet between two stout lengths of planed hardwood so that the amount of metal to be flanged protrudes (see Fig.4). Clamp the whole assembly in the vice. Note that the hardwood pieces are arranged to support the body of the sheet metal and that you bend the flange over, rather than the other way round. Never try to hold the flange part and bend the sheet of metal as this will usually result in producing a bowed (bent) flange, particularly if the flange is narrow.

Hammering metal stretches it, and the hammered-down flange will be thinned in places so that it is distorted. This can be avoided by laying a block of scrap wood against the metal to be bent and hitting the block with a mallet, so that the mallet blows are spread over a fairly large area of metal. This is shown in Fig.8. If the flange is more than, say, 6in. (150mm) long, then move the block along its length from one end to the other, bending a little at a time. If you hammer the flange right down at one spot at a time, then you will stretch the metal with the results already mentioned. But using a block and bending the metal gradually ensures an even, smooth bend.

Making a simple bowl

To shape something such as a bowl, the metal has to be stretched in such a way as to produce a three-dimensional curve. The ideal material for this sort of item is copper or soft aluminium. Generally speaking, copper is better, since it takes a fine polish and blends with almost any home decor scheme.

Shaping a bowl calls for the use of either the ball-pein hammer or, preferably, the planishing hammer. To support the metal during working and to allow for its changing shape, a small sandbag should be used. If you want to do a lot of this sort of work, then it is worth while making up a proper 'tin-basher's bag' which is like a circular cushion about 12in. (300mm) in diameter and 3in. (75mm) thick. It is made of two or three layers of calico with a top surface of fully-strained leather (ask for this at a saddler or leather shop) with the nap, or rough side, outermost. Alternatively you can work on a hardwood block or a large log of wood such as that shown in Fig.10.

Supposing that your bowl is to be 10in. (250mm) in diameter, then you should cut out of the flat metal sheet a disc which is larger, but only slightly larger than the finished diameter. The reason for this is that 'tin-bashing' depends for its success on the stretching of the metal in the middle of the piece, and this surplus has to be relieved (or taken up) at the edges. The more unwanted edge there is, the harder this job will be. As a rough guide, for a shallow dish like a soup-plate, add about five per cent to the finished diameter to arrive at the proper diameter of the disc of raw material. For deeply recessed bowls add up to ten per cent to the finished size. Don't forget that in this diameter you must allow for any turned or beaded edges (these terms are explained in Fig.3).

Place the sandbag on a rigid support such as the corner of your bench and press your hand into it to make an indentation. Hold your disc of flat metal in your left hand (unless you are left-handed, in which case these instructions must be reversed) so that its flat surface is inclined slightly towards you. Start hammering with the ball-pein or planishing hammer about half an inch from the near edge and, slowly rotating the disc of metal while keeping it at the same angle, make a series of closely-spaced, light and regular blows all around the edge. No matter how deep the finished bowl is to be, do not start in the middle. Always begin at the edge and gradually work inwards in a spiral rather like the groove on a gramophone record (see Figs. 10 and 11).

Wrinkles and kinks that form in the metal are easily removed by working them up the inside of the bowl to the edge. The hammer blows should be even in strength; you can save much time and effort in the way that you hold and use the hammer. Keep your wrist supple and let the hammer bounce back from one blow to relieve some of the effort of lifting it for the next. The left hand should meanwhile be engaged in slowly rotating the metal, always keeping it at such an angle that the hammer blow is making contact through the workpiece with the middle of the sandbag beneath. Hard blows are not necessary, but regularity is of great importance or the metal will stretch unevenly and your bowl will assume an unnatural shape.

The bowl is made deeper each time you complete a spiral from the edge to the centre and this process is repeated over and over again until the desired depth is reached. If the metal

Fig.10. First stage of shaping by hammering in concentric circles on an end-grain block. *Fig.11.* The process is repeated several times to increase the depth of the bowl. *Fig.12.* As the metal 'work-hardens' it should be annealed with heat either using a blow-lamp or a gas-jet, followed by quenching.

Fig.13 shows the flange being tapped down to avoid excessive cockling. *Fig.14.* The worker in these pictures is shaping the bowl inwards from the flanged edge and now transfers from the wood block in the bench vice to a large solid log into which a number of depressions of varying sizes have been carved. *Fig.15.* A shaped metal stake or end-grain woodblock is now used to hammer smooth the underside of the bowl with the planishing hammer.

Fig.16. The flange is hammered level on an old flat-iron. *Fig.17.* Defining the inner edge. *Fig.18.* Final smoothing of contours.

Fig.19. The bowl shown here was made in a few hours by an amateur craftsman. The material is 14 gauge copper.

Fig 20 Shaping the flat bottom of the bowl on a circular wooden stake. The completed copper bowl is featured in Fig. 1 on page 43.

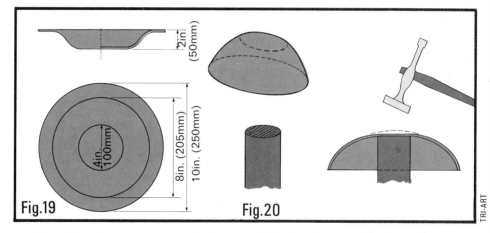

Fig.19   Fig.20

shows signs of becoming hard (this process is known as work-hardening and occurs in almost all metals, particularly aluminium and brass), the malleability, or 'stretchiness' of the metal can be restored by heating the entire surface with a blowlamp and cooling quickly in water. It need not be heated much; copper should be heated evenly until it shows a change in surface colour.

As the final shape is approached, the hammer blows should become lighter and closer-spaced. At this point make sure that the metal is clean and the hammer faces polished otherwise any imperfections in either will be transferred to the surface of the metal in the form of a blemish.

Select a suitable length of hardwood about 2in. by 2in. (50mm x 50mm) clamp this vertically in the vice and thoroughly radius its upper end (i.e. make it into a dome shape) using a 'Surform' or similar tool. Rest the bowl

over this *stake* and now hammer gently all over the outside with the flat face of the planishing hammer. You can use a domed steel stake, if you wish, but in this case you should use a wooden or hide-faced mallet. If you have a wooden stake, use a metal hammer. This is because metal (hammer) to metal (stake) contact will spread the bowl metal rapidly and, though this can be good for final shaping, where the hammer blows are extremely light, too much of this will make the metal wafer-thin and cause distortion.

The actual bottom of the bowl should be flat, otherwise it will not sit on your table. Take a cylindrical block of wood the exact diameter of the bottom and with the end grain at its circular end (see Fig.20), clamp this in the vice in place of the stake, invert the bowl over it and gently tap the bowl metal down on to the block, so creating a flat, circular base.

Now you must find the true edge of the bowl;

this is done by supporting the scriber horizontally at the right height above the workbench. You can do this by making a simple wooden scribing block. Press the bowl firmly on the table with one hand and either rotate the bowl against the scribing block or move the scribing block round the bowl so as to mark the proper height, and then above this mark the width of the rim or flange. Now tap the flange down flat; using a wooden or hide-faced mallet on a steel block held in the vice. This is shown in Fig.16. Again, rotate the job slowly and use steady, even hammer blows. An alternative method, in which the flange is formed in the actual shaping stage, is shown in the pictures here.

The flange can now be trimmed to the right diameter along the scribed line, and the whole bowl polished using fine grade wire wool followed by metal polish applied with muttoncloth. Wipe off all fingerprints before lacquering the metal.

A copper chimney hood to make

A copper chimney hood can be an eye-catching addition to a fireplace and chimney breast, and suits the mood of today's living rooms perfectly. If you are building your fireplace from scratch, it is easy to incorporate into the design; or it can be added to an existing free-standing flue pipe of the type found in many modern houses.

There are two types of chimney hood you can make (see Fig. 1). The simple, straight-folded hood is very easy to make, but its rather over-powering proportions and stark outline may obtrude on the decor of a room rather than enhance it. The flared chimney hood can be built with slender lines which will be both pleasing to the eye and a focal point of the room. It is, however, harder to make and calls for the use of the advanced technique of flanging a curved surface, and very accurate drilling and riveting.

The best materials to use are brass or copper. Aluminium, although easy to work, does not look good in most living rooms and will discolour to an unpleasant hue unless constantly polished. Some settings may benefit from the use of a 'black iron' (actually sheet steel) hood—this requires rather more effort to form, but the instructions given here still apply.

Design considerations

Before you start to plan your hood, study the following points. You cannot simply remove a fireplace and fit a chimney hood instead. If you have a free-standing flue-pipe then the process is relatively simple and you can add the hood directly to it. For most other types the entire fireplace and chimney structure will have to be removed from floor to roof and replaced from scratch. This is a far more complex and time-consuming task although still perfectly possible.

Begin by deciding on the size and proportions of your intended hood. A typical shape and size is shown in Fig.1. Remember that both copper and brass sheet are expensive, so try to keep within the dimensions of standard sheet sizes. Ask your sheet metal stockist what sizes he has. The thickness of the material for the hood shown here should be about 20 gauge, or roughly 1 mm. Anything much thicker than this will be unnecessarily hard to work with and add to the cost of the job, whilst anything much thinner will not lie flat and will dent easily. The bigger the hood, the thicker the metal needed to give it strength.

On a small hood, you can use very thin metal and stiffen the edges by the processes of bending or wiring (see Fig. 3, page 45) or by swaging. This technique consists of forming a shallow ridge across a piece of metal, either the whole way from one side to the other (a full swage) or part of the way across (a blind end swage). Swages in thin, soft metal are formed by squeezing a metal sheet between two shaped hardwood blocks. The pressure may be applied by means of a vice (for swages up to 8in. or 200mm long) or a row of G cramps (for longer swages). The technique is shown in Fig.3. Swages in thicker metal are formed by hammering using shaped wooden blocks.

The parts of the hood should be riveted together. Pop rivets are the easiest type to insert, but do not look very good in copper. A better idea is to use copper snaphead rivets, which are fairly soft and easy to use. The diameter should be $\frac{1}{8}$in. or 2mm, whichever is easier to get.

Flanging the curved sides

Unless the hood is very small and made without any curvature, you will need to make it from three pieces of metal—two sides and a front. Generally speaking you will find it easier and neatest to make the right-angled flanges for the riveted joints on the side pieces, leaving the front as a plain sheet bent in one direction only—from top to bottom. Flanging the sides, then, means flanging a curved edge and for this the technique shown in Fig. 4 of the previous chapter can be adapted. The easiest way of making a curved flange is to make shaped formers for it; these should be two pieces of thick plywood, block-board or solid hardwood board cut to the shape of the curve. The wood should be about $\frac{3}{4}$in. (20mm) thick.

Now cut out the metal for the side pieces, not forgetting to add extra length to allow for the curve. Also you must allow $\frac{3}{4}$in. (20mm) for the riveting flange, and also for the flange which will form the attachment of the hood to the wall. Do not forget that the two flanges will be bent in opposite directions, and in the opposite way on each side.

Clamp one of the pieces in between the two shaped boards and dress down the flange on the curved side, using a boxwood or hide-faced mallet. When this is completed, clamp in the second piece and form a similar flange in the opposite direction.

The flanges you have just made are the ones to which the front portion of the hood will be attached. Now bend up the straight flanges which will form the attachment of the finished hood to the wall. These bend in the opposite direction to the long curved flanges at the front and can be formed simply by using the method described in the earlier chapter. Do not drill any attachment holes yet, as they will be shifted by the distortion of the metal that is inevitable when it is bent.

Shaping the sides

The two side pieces now have to be curved along their length. Since the curve is gentle and shallow, the best way to make it is by hand,

48

bending the pieces carefully over something soft like a sandbag. If you hammer the edge of the front curved flange, this will spread the metal and help to distort the flange into a curve. Use a steel hammer on a steel block to achieve the maximum spread. The straight rear flange has to be shortened. You will find it easier to do this if you first distort the flange with a few mallet blows spaced at, say, 6in. (150mm) intervals. Once the side is bent, these irregularities can be tapped flat using a wooden mallet and a wooden block, which will compress the surplus metal. The thinner the metal you are using, the easier this will be to do.

Any springiness or over-flexibility in the sides will be held firmly in place by the front of the hood when it is riveted in place, and further stiffening will take place after the hood is fixed to the wall. The precise shape of the sides will also be determined by the shape of the edge of the hood front, so do not worry too much about shaping these sides exactly right.

Cutting and fixing the front

Now cut out the piece for the front of the hood. This should be cut very accurately to a line drawn on the copper with wax crayon, which will make an easily visible marking. Avoid scratching the copper surface.

Take the two sides and lay them on a clear floor in their proper relationship. If you clamp the bottom flanges to a batten of wood, they will stand up firmly enough for you to work on. Mark the rivet holes in the front piece. To avoid disfiguring the outer surface of the front piece by scoring it with a scriber, either mark out the position of the holes on the inside face (and subsequently drill pilot holes through from that side before drilling the main holes from the front) or mark the outer face with a wax crayon.

Drill all the rivet holes on the front piece. Then, starting at the top of the side pieces, transfer the position of the first hole very accurately onto the metal, using a pair of dividers. Drill this hole in each of the two side pieces. Bend the front piece approximately to shape and put it temporarily in place, attaching it through the holes you have just drilled with nuts and bolts. To keep the head of the bolt from scratching the outer face of the copper, use a fibre washer or a small piece of cardboard with a hole in it.

Now align the edge of the front with the edge of the flange and drill through another hole into the flange at, say, an interval of three or four holes from the first. Again put a small nut and bolt through this hole. Proceed in this way down both flanges, making sure that there are no

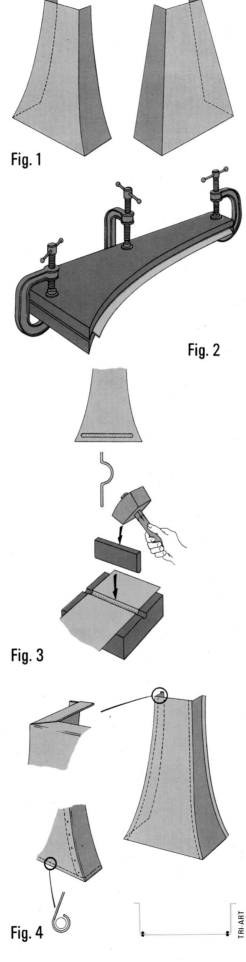

Fig. 1

Fig. 2

Fig. 3

Fig. 4

TRI-ART

Fig.1. *Two basic shapes of chimney hood. The proportions can be varied to suit the fireplace as in the picture on the opposite page.*
Fig.2. *How to flange a curved edge of metal. The piece is sandwiched between two shaped lengths of thick plywood and the edge tapped down with a boxwood or hide-faced mallet.*
Fig.3. *One method of stiffening thin metal is to form a swage in it. Here the principles of hand-swaging are shown. This will make your hood more rigid and you can form swages either across it or from top to bottom. The highlights created enhance appearance.*
Fig.4. *Details of suggested hood construction.*

hollows left between the flange and the hood front. These gaps would cause rivets inserted through some holes to drag the other holes out of alignment.

Riveting together

When all the rivet holes are drilled, undo all the locating bolts and take off the top piece. Clear out the drill swarf and remove any burrs around the undersides of the holes using a file. The rivets can be obtained from any ordinary hardware shop.

Re-assemble the pieces, again using nuts and bolts at regular spacings, and begin riveting. When all the clear holes have been riveted, remove the nuts and bolts and rivet these as well.

If you have used fairly thin metal, you should now turn the bottom edges to stiffen them. This is best done by cutting away the bottom ¼in. or 5mm of each flange, turning the hood over so that you can work from the inside, and tapping the edge upwards over a wood straight-edge, first along the front, then along the sides. For extra rigidity, bend the flange up to form a U and shape a length of 14 SWG (2mm) steel wire to fit the inside of the turned-over edge. Then close the copper right over the wire to produce a wired edge as illustrated in Fig. 3 of the previous chapter.

Finish and fixing

This completes the construction of the hood, except for attaching it to the wall, which can be done simply with plugs and screws. Before you install the hood, polish it with a proprietary metal polishing compound or (if you prefer a matt finish) very fine steel wool or, better still, brass wire wool. A spray lacquer will preserve the original brightness of the metal, but if the hood is likely to get very hot in use, you may find that the lacquer discolours and comes off.

An alternative finish that can be very decorative is a *beaten copper* finish; this can be done by hammering all over the surface of the hood with a polished ballpein hammer (an unpolished one might scar the surface unattractively). Hammer against a steel block held underneath the hood. The ideal way of producing a true hammered appearance, however, is to hammer the sheets *before* they are flanged and assembled. To do this, all you need to do is to clamp a heavy steel block (such as an old flat-iron) in your vice, hold the sheet on top of it with one hand and hammer through the sheet on to the block. You will find it easy to keep the sheet moving while hammering in the same position on the iron.

The finished hood should be attached to the chimney breast with round-head brass wood-screws set into fibre wall plugs in the brickwork. There is one point to watch though: the heat of the fire will cause warmed air to rise inside the hood and be expelled through any cracks. between the hood flange and the wall. If your wall is light-coloured, the places where this hot air comes through will eventually show up as dirty streaks on the wall. This can be simply prevented by sandwiching a strip of ordinary plastic foam draught excluder between the hood flange and the wall when you are fixing it up.

Fibreglass: a simple tray

Glass reinforced plastic, or fibreglass, has an enormous potential that has been virtually ignored by the handyman. Making this tray will introduce you to many more ambitious projects.

Fibreglass is, for most purposes, an economical material that can easily be moulded to many shapes. Examples include boat hulls, car bodies, furniture, trays and lampshades. It has immense strength, does not rust, and has great powers of adhesion, which also makes it a useful and popular material for repairs to metal car bodies and water tanks.

The basics of fibreglass

Making a fibreglass shell or shape is relatively simple, but some of the materials used will be unfamiliar to the home handyman. So it will be useful to run through the normal procedure for making a fibreglass shell, and follow this with a more detailed description of techniques and materials.

To make something simple such as a tray with an embossed pattern, you would require a 2in. or 50mm paint brush; a small roller, something like the type used for home decorating; a mould (another tray would do); a release agent, to prevent the plastic sticking to the mould; some glass fibre mat; liquid plastic or resin; colouring pigment; hardener, to make the resin set; and a bowl for mixing the resin and hardener.

You will also need sufficient space for the project. An ordinary kitchen table, covered with newspaper to soak up the inevitable drops of resin and hardener, will do. A cheap pair of rubber or plastic gloves will also come in handy.

Having laid out your materials, first coat the mould or tray with a release agent. It is only necessary to coat the area that will come in contact with the resin.

Next pour the resin into the mixing bowl, followed by the required quantity of hardener and pigment, and mix thoroughly.

With the paint brush, thickly coat the top of the tray with resin, making sure the surface is

Opposite page. Glass fibre is woven into many different types of fabric, some of which are shown here. The broad stranded material that looks like basket-weave is woven roving; the fibres are plaited into a cord, then woven as shown. It has enormous strength and is used for large projects such as boats. At the other end of the range, the fine weave of surfacing tissue makes it ideal for intricate mouldings. In between is glass scrim, which is more like cloth; and the loose-layered glass mat.

covered all over. This is called the 'gel' coat. Allow the gel coat to set.

Lay sufficient glass fibre mat over the mould to cover the area that has been coated with resin and press the mat into the resin with the roller.

Using the paint brush again, thickly coat the mat with resin, stippling the brush to work out bubbles. Then work the roller all over the surface to ensure that the mat is thoroughly impregnated with resin from both sides and to squeeze out any bubbles that have been trapped in the mat.

The above procedure—a layer of mat followed by a well-worked in coat of resin—is repeated as often as is required to build up the thickness of the shell.

When the resin has started to set, trim the edges of the shell where it overlaps the mould edges. At this stage you can do this with a pair of scissors.

If the shell is not too thick, say with only two layers of mat, then the shell will be ready to remove from the mould in about one day.

When you have removed the shell from the mould, you will have a tray; but the side that would normally be used as the top will have a surface like petrified coconut matting—the smooth side, with the pattern, will be underneath! This is because a mould always produces an 'opposite' shell. This is explained in greater detail in Fig.19.

To produce your tray, you have to repeat the whole process described above, using as a mould the fibreglass shell you have just made. In fact you can produce hundreds of trays from this mould if you wish. The only difference with this second mould is that you will lay the fibreglass over the 'bottom' or smooth side so that the final product is right way round.

That, basically, is all there is to it. But of course you will need to know more about glass reinforced plastic (GRP) if you are to become proficient in its techniques and wish to get involved in more ambitious projects.

Materials for glass fibre work

The mould can be one of two types, as shown in Fig.19. The negative or female mould (Fig.19B) is recessed and is used for articles that need to be finished or smooth on the convex surface. The positive or male mould is domed (Fig.19A) and the finished side is on the concave surface of the shell.

A mould can be made from a wide variety of materials—clay, wood, glass, metal, hardboard, plaster of paris (usually reinforced with wire net), rubber, or anything else that can produce a reasonably smooth surface.

If the mould is made from a porous material such as hardboard, wood, or plaster, then several coats of sealer such as a varnish should be applied. Each coat must be buffed down when thoroughly dry. Glass fibre moulding will produce articles which, without further finishing, have a glassy, smooth surface—but to achieve this, your mould too must be absolutely smooth.

Release agents are used to line the mould so that the shell or article can be easily removed. This is essential, because the resin used in fibreglass work will bond to most surfaces. Two different products are used: it depends on the

surface of the mould.

If the mould is made from a porous material that has been varnished, the surface must be treated with liquid cellulose acetate and, when this is dry, waxed and polished. The wax must be a hard variety such as carnauba. Ordinary domestic waxes are not suitable.

If the mould is made from non-porous material such as glass, steel, or fibreglass, the surface must be waxed first and then coated with a polyvinyl alcohol solution.

Whenever a release agent is being applied, make sure that it covers every single part of the mould. Even the tiniest spot left uncovered will make the shell extremely difficult to remove.

Polyester resin (usually just called resin) is a liquid unsaturated synthetic resin with the consistency of thick syrup. It is a binder which permeates and holds together the glass fibre strands.

Resin is naturally clear, with a slight yellow or blue tinge, but it can be tinted to any required colour by adding pigments.

There are many different resin formulas. Some are made specially for use on boat hulls; some are fire resistant and are used for car bonnets and boat bulkheads; and a clear resin is made for embedding specimens. There is a resin for virtually every conceivable job. Most manufacturers provide something like a dozen different resins, and each one calls a specific resin by a different name or code number. When you purchase your resin, tell your supplier exactly what you are using it for and he will sell you the correct type.

Hardener is usually an organic peroxide and is sold in liquid, powder or paste form. It is a catalyst, and when added to certain liquid substances such as resin, it will cause that substance to set.

However, it is not completely efficient on its own, and for this reason an accelerator is usually added both to speed up setting and to provide a final hard set.

Accelerator is a blue-coloured cobalt napthenate solution which is usually already added to the resin when you buy it. It accelerates the hardening process.

It is possible to buy hardener separately, but a word of warning: while it is relatively harmless when already added to resin, neat accelerator should **never** be added to hardener, as this could cause an explosion. If you ever find yourself with a job where extra accelerator is needed, always add it to the resin.

Pigments are usually sold in the form of paste which is added to the resin in the approximate proportion of 1 :14 by volume. They are specially selected to combine well with resin. Almost every conceivable colour is available—one pigment manufacturer has a chart of 80 resin pigments on his list.

Some pigments, notably black and blue, retard the setting time slightly, but not enough to cause any real inconvenience.

Most pigments are available in both opaque and translucent colours.

Other resin additives include anything that is added to the resin for a specific effect other than just colour. For instance, fine metal powders can be added to produce a metallic surface. Metal powders are usually added to the gel (the first,

51

Fig.1. *The first moulding has set on the metal tray which has been used as a first mould. Ease the edges off with a wooden spatula—a metal one could mark the resin.*

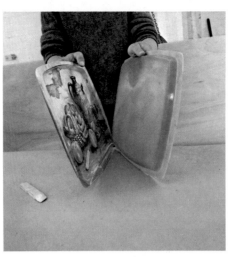

Fig.2. *Carefully ease the mould and moulding apart. The moulding will now become the male mould from which the final article is cast.*

Fig.3. *First apply the wax release agent. This must be polished in between each application, otherwise the moulding will reproduce the inevitable wax smears.*

Fig.4. *After waxing, the surface is coated with the final release agent, a polyvinyl alcohol solution which is applied with a soft cloth or a sponge.*

Fig.5. *Pour a quantity of resin into a container, then add the colouring paste in the proportions recommended by the manufacturer of the pigment.*

Fig.6. *Adding the hardener. This makes the resin set. Add strictly in accordance with the maker's instructions, otherwise the resin may craze or fail to set properly.*

Fig.7. *Applying the gel coat. This must be allowed to set before the fibre is laid, otherwise the strands of glass fibre will be visible on the surface.*

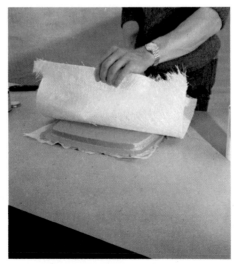

Fig.8. *Placing one of the layers of glass mat. To mould the mat round awkward corners, cut out any creases with a pair of scissors and 'tease' the cut edges together.*

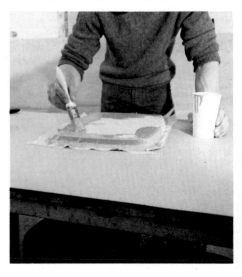

Fig.9. *Applying resin to a layer of glass mat. Stipple the brush vigorously into the material to ensure that it is thoroughly impregnated with resin.*

Fig.10. *After the resin has been worked into the mat with a brush, a small roller is pressed vigorously over the surface to force out any bubbles.*

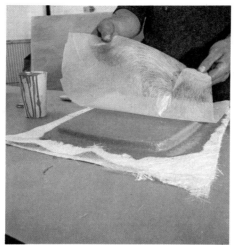

Fig.11. *Surfacing tissue is the last layer of glass fibre. It makes for a smoother surface, but is only used where a good finish on both sides is required.*

Fig.12. *Cutting away the superfluous material. This is done before the resin has properly set. A pair of sharp scissors can be used instead of the knife.*

Fig.13. *Use a very sharp handyman's knife for the final trim. This should be carried out immediately after the rough trim and before the resin has set.*

Fig.14. *When the resin has set, gently prise the two surfaces apart with a wood or plastic spatula. Metal or anything similar could mark the resin.*

Fig.15. *Separate the tray from the mould. If there are any irregularities or marks in the mould, the moulding will have reproduced the imperfections faithfully.*

Fig.16. *Using a flat file first, then a coarse glasspaper followed by a grade O glasspaper, pare down the rough edges of the tray to a smooth finish.*

Fig.17. *The surface of the tray will have a slight blue haze caused by the release agent. This is easily removed with clean cold water.*

Fig.18. *The finished tray. When you have completed this, you will have learnt some basic fibreglass techniques that can be used for many projects.*

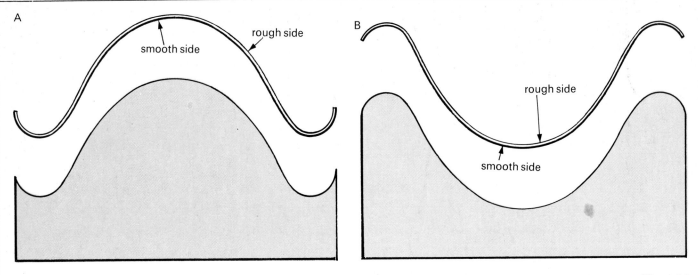

A male mould produces a moulding with a shiny concave surface.

A female mould produces a moulding with the polished surface on the convex.

visible coat or coats). The resin must be heavily saturated with the metal powder to produce a really metallic effect. Each manufacturer will give the right proportions.

Another attractive additive is bright, coloured, metal flakes. These are also sprinkled on the gel or visible coat. Used in conjunction with translucent pigment, a surface with real sparkle can be obtained.

Kinds of glass fibre

Glass fibre is actually a fabric composed of short strands of glass filament held together by a chemical which causes friction or 'binding', so that it will stay woven and handle easily. It is made, like other fabrics, in various weights and weaves.

Surfacing tissue is a very fine glass fabric. It can be used to cover the rather rough surface of glass matting when the reverse, or inside, of the finished article needs to be extra smooth.

Glass scrim is more like a cloth, and is used instead of glass mat when the mould has a deep or intricate curvature. As it will lay more easily into deep curves, there is less chance of trapped air remaining in the fibreglass to weaken the shell.

Glass mat is the material most often used for reinforcing the resin. The fibres are in random directions, and it is easy to 'tease' out some of the mat for joining it to another cut section of mat. It is sold in weights from 1 to 2oz (28 to 56g). The heavier mat, though obviously stronger, is much more difficult to impregnate with resin properly unless you have had some experience.

Woven rovings are filaments or strands of glass that are first plaited into a cord, and then woven into special cloths. This cloth has enormous strength and is used for large articles such as boat hulls.

Setting time

The time that resin takes to go completely hard, or set, depends on several factors. Resin in a single layer of mat should set in one day at the most. But if it takes longer than this, you have done something wrong, like adding insufficient hardener.

Temperature and humidity also play an important part in the setting time of resin. For quick setting, a warm, dry atmosphere is ideal. The worst possible conditions are cold and damp.

Tools and equipment

Unlike most home construction materials, fibreglass requires few tools, all inexpensive, and most of them are probably already being used in your home. The main ones are:—

Paint brush. To apply the first resin coat, and to stipple the second coat into the glass fibre. It is also used to apply the liquid release agent. Have two brushes ready, a 2in. or 50mm and a 1in. or 25mm.

Roller. When the resin is being applied to the glass fibre, it is impossible to work out all the bubbles by the stippling action of the brush. So the roller is used to work the area over and remove all bubbles. For most uses an ordinary size lambswool paint roller is adequate although some jobs will require a much smaller roller.

There are, however, special rollers made for fibreglass work. As this may be the only 'special' tool you will buy, it is hardly a great expense. These rollers have ridges round the working surface which ensure that the fibre is impregnated thoroughly and also aid in removing bubbles. They also sometimes have a splash guard which can prove valuable, because resin splashed on the furniture is a nuisance—and splashed in your eyes it could be serious.

Scissors. These are used to trim the edges of the shell before the resin has set properly. If you delay until it has set, forget the scissors—you will need a hacksaw and file !

Mixing bowl. For mixing the resin/hardener and possibly pigment or other additive. It can be made of any hard plastic (except polystyrene or, of course, glass fibre) or metal. Although it might seem tempting to use a bucket, remember that after adding the hardener you only have half an hour or so before the resin starts to gel. So a bucket would be necessary only if you are building something large like a boat.

Although the items listed below are not absolutely essential, they should be considered as part of the necessary equipment for this sort of work.

Acetone. For cleaning, brushes, rollers, and mixing bowls. Nothing else is quite so effective ; but do be careful of the fumes, which are highly inflammable, and clean only in a well-ventilated place.

Gloves. Rubber or plastic. Glass fibre, resin, and hardener can all cause nasty rashes and skin complaints, so always wear a pair of gloves.

Overalls, or a good apron. A very effective apron can be made from a sheet of polythene.

Barrier hand cream. For the same reason as the gloves.

The end product

You now have enough information to start on a simple project that will gain you some experience. A tray is a good object if you have one suitable that you can use as a mould—that is, provided you would like a duplicate.

Enough material will be needed to make two 'trays'. The first will be the reverse or positive mould, taken direct from the original tray as described at the beginning of this chapter; the second will be the actual tray for use.

Two layers of 1oz mat will be needed in each case, so purchase sufficient mat to cover the tray four times, with about ½in. or 12mm over all round for trimming. Using a general purpose resin, about 1½lb of resin is required for every square yard of 1oz mat. It is doubtful that you would want to make a clear fibreglass tray, so you will also require some pigment. The proportions for adding this are about 1 part pigment to 14 parts resin, but the exact proportions will come with the pigment instructions. Hardener is sold in 2oz bottles in the smallest size, and this is probably enough unless you are making several trays ; use the hardener in the quantities recommended on the bottle or box.

You can now start on your project, following the step-by-step instructions outlined above.

Next, you can try something more ambitious.

Plastic embedding

If you have ever picked a wild flower, then sadly watched it wilt and fade, here is a technique that should interest you. Anything—flowers, insects, coins, even photographs—can be set in a sparkling block of transparent plastic. You can use the same method to make other decorative items such as door finger plates and candle holders.

Embedding in plastic is an easy and inexpensive process. The only skills required are that you must follow instructions carefully and be prepared to experiment a little to create unusual and beautiful effects. The basic method is that some polyester resin is mixed with hardener and poured into a suitable mould to form a thin layer of liquid. The resin takes between 30 minutes and 3 hours to become gelatinous and sticky to the touch. Another layer is poured and the procedure repeated until the mould is full. The object to be encased is placed on top of a layer when the resin has become gelatinous and just before the next layer is poured. Variations include colouring each layer of resin differently from the rest.

Some distortion may be noticeable when the cast is viewed from the side and along the layers of resin. Therefore, always design the casting so that you will usually look at it at right angles to the layers of resin.

Materials

Polyester resin, hardener, and various pigments are obtainable from most art shops and a number of toy shops. The resin, a clear liquid, is available in tins ranging in size from 340g to 5 kilos (12oz-11lb). The liquid hardener is bought in small polythene bottles with a measure marked on the outside. Various pigments, both transparent and opaque, are available for colouring the resin.

Moulds can be bought from many art shops. They range from cube and cylindrical shapes to intricately-shaped ones for making jewellery. But it is not always necessary to purchase moulds, as you can often improvise with cups, bowls, dishes, or small trays. A mould should ideally be made of soft, pliable plastic such as that used for refrigerator containers. It is easier to remove the hardened resin from soft plastic moulds because the plastic 'gives', allowing the block to be squeezed out. On no account use any containers made of rigid, brittle plastic or polystyrene foam, for there is a strong likelihood of the resin reacting with the plastic. Most other materials, such as wood, glass or metal are suitable, provided you can get the block out of them afterwards.

Wax polish (not a silicone type) is used as a 'release agent' to coat the inside of the mould and prevent the resin from sticking to it. Paper cups or yoghurt cartons are ideal for mixing the resin and hardener in, as they can be thrown away afterwards. Cheap, disposable spatulas or ice-cream spoons are ideal for stirring the mixture. A bottle of dry-cleaning fluid or acetone is needed to remove spots of resin from table tops or clothes.

Other tools needed are a soft plastic jug with a scale marked on it, a pair of tweezers if you are encasing delicate objects, wet and dry papers ranging from coarse to very fine, some metal polish or special polishing paste, and a small sheet of glass.

Articles to be embedded

The range of objects that can be embedded or encased in resin is limitless, and it is this that makes the technique attractive to so many people. Dried grasses, flowers, or twigs can produce attractive effects; semi-precious stones and shells are equally effective. For the collector who wants an attractive way of displaying his pieces, resin is the ideal method: natural objects such as plants or insects, or man-made ones such as coins and medals can all look attractive when displayed in this way. Even photographs can be embedded in a block of resin, giving a '3D' effect.

Before you embed flowers, they must first be dried. Even if you buy 'everlasting' flowers or dyed grasses from a florist's, they must be hung in a warm room for two or three weeks so that they are completely free of moisture. Flowers or grasses picked fresh must be pressed between blotting paper in a warm room for at least two months before being embedded in resin. Most flowers lose their colour when pressed. Red flowers are among the worst in this respect, but yellow flowers and grasses seldom fade at all. It is possible to dye flowers once they have been pressed, but to start with, a mixture of grasses and yellow flowers will be very effective.

When embedding flowers or grasses in resin it is possible that small air bubbles may be produced. So when pouring layers of resin round the flowers, pour the layer so that it comes only 2/3 of the way up the flower. Any bubbles can then escape upwards before the next pouring.

Safety first

Once set, polyester resin is non-toxic and non-inflammable. But when it is in a liquid form it is inflammable and gives off a vapour which is harmful if breathed in large quantities. Therefore, always take the following precautions, and in all cases follow the manufacturer's instructions.

Keep the room well ventilated and do not inhale the fumes given off by the liquid resin. Be especially careful when pouring it into the moulds. Keep the liquid resin away from any naked flame. And finally, keep the hardener away from the eyes and skin as it is corrosive and poisonous. You should use rubber gloves when handling the hardener. If you do spill any, wash it off with luke-warm water.

Making a transparent cast

First choose your working area. The reaction between the resin and hardener will take place at any temperature above 59°F (15°C), but 68°F (20°C) is more satisfactory.

Prepare the working area, making sure that there is adequate ventilation in the room. Check with a spirit level that the working surface is level; otherwise the liquid will not fill the moulds to an even depth all the way across. Cover the working surface with newspaper or cellophane.

Wash and dry the mould and then rub some wax (non-silicone) polish over the inside and then polish it. Enough of the wax film will be left on the inside of the mould to prevent the resin from sticking to it.

Place the mould on your level working surface. Then fill the mould with water up to the level the cast is to reach. Pour the water from the mould into the measuring jug and note the volume of water. Empty, then dry, the jug and mould. Fill the jug with resin to just above the level of the water reached, so that there is approximately 5%-10% more resin by volume in the jug than there was water. You need the extra volume of resin as some is certain to remain in the jug when you pour it again. If you are going to use different coloured layers of resin (see below), pour some extra resin into the jug. Then refer to the manufacturer's instructions and add the required amount of hardener to the liquid. This is normally 2%, but the right proportion is marked on the sides of the bottle containing the hardener. Mix thoroughly using the wooden spoon or spatula, and stir for at least a minute.

Pouring the resin

Now pour the first layer of resin into the mould, and then cover the top of the jug and place it in a bowl of cold water. This will prevent it from hardening before you use it again. The depth of this and following layers can vary within a considerable margin. The depth is regulated by the fact that the setting resin heats up. If the layer is too thick, too little heat will escape from the mould and there will be a build-up of heat that will crack the resin. This is particularly disastrous if you want a perfectly transparent cast. Alternatively, if the layers, and therefore the finished product, are too thin, it may crack. Keep the layers between $\frac{1}{8}$in. and $\frac{1}{2}$in. (3-13mm) thick.

Allow the resin to begin to set. The time needed depends on a number of variables. The thinner the layer of resin, the more hardener there is mixed with the resin, and the higher the room temperature, the quicker the resin will begin to gel and become thick and sticky to touch. The resin may remain tacky for only about 20 minutes, so it is important to check at

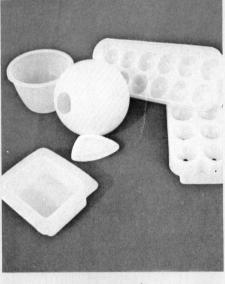

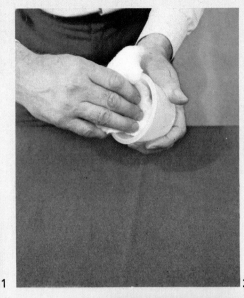

Fig.1. Soft plastic shapes suitable for moulds. Fill the chosen mould with water and then pour it into a jug and note the level.
Fig.2. Then polish the mould with wax (non-silicone) polish so that the resin cast will slip out easily when set.
Figs.3 and *4.* Pour resin into the jug to just above the level of water previously noted and add the appropriate amount of hardener.
Fig.5. Then mix thoroughly.
Fig.6. Pour layers of resin in the mould between $\frac{1}{8}$in. and $\frac{1}{2}$in. (3mm-13mm) thick.

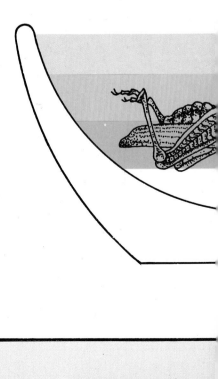

regular intervals how far the setting has progressed. Use a clean wooden spoon to check. Do not be afraid of leaving a mark if the resin has partially set; it has the convenient property of 'closing up' after the surface has been disturbed.

If you are embedding any objects or adding another layer of resin they should be added when the resin has become tacky, but not hard. Embedding objects in the cast is done simply by placing the object on top of one layer of resin. It will not sink in. As many layers as necessary are then poured until the object is completely covered.

Removing the mould and finishing

When the last layer of resin has been poured leave it to set for as long as possible; preferably overnight but for at least 8 hours in any case. Flexible plastic moulds are easy to remove as they 'give', allowing the casting to be eased out. If the casting does stick, carefully run a thin-bladed knife round the edges.

China, glass or metal moulds must first be put in very hot water for at least 10 minutes and then plunged directly into cold water and left there for 10 minutes. If available, ice cubes should be added to the water to keep it cool. Then remove the mould, hold it upside down and tap it gently

against a table top. The cast should slip out easily. If it does not slip out and the mould is still slightly warm, put it back in the cold water for a little longer.

If the last, or bottom layer, of resin has set rough it should be smoothed. Wrap a fairly coarse piece of wet-and-dry paper around a flat-sided block of wood. Wet the paper and smooth the base of the casting, moving the block in small circles. Use successively finer grades of paper until the base is smooth all over. This will produce a flat eggshell finish which can be an attractive base for a number of castings. If a clear sparkling finish is needed, metal polish or special polishing paste for resin should be applied, and then rubbed with a soft duster.

The surface of the cast is fairly robust, but as the resin continues to harden for a few weeks it is best to treat it carefully to begin with.

Further techniques

Coloured effects can easily be obtained by adding pigment to the mixture of resin and hardener. If you want different coloured layers, pour some of the mixture of resin and hardener into one of the paper cups and then add the pigment in the proportions recommended by the manufacturers. The resin is then poured in the

6

7

8

Figs.7 and *8.* When the resin has set put the object in position and pour further layers.
Fig.9. Leave the final layer to harden for at least 8 hours. Then squeeze the plastic mould around until the cast slips out.
Fig.10. The surface of the last layer of resin poured may be uneven. To obtain a smooth clear finish, lay sheets of various grades of wet and dry paper on a flat surface and rub the mould across it in a circular motion.
Fig.11. A cross-section of a mould. You can use more than one layer to embed an object.

9

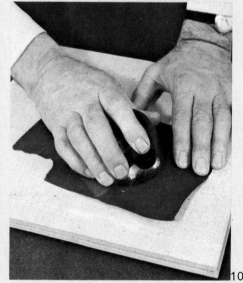

10

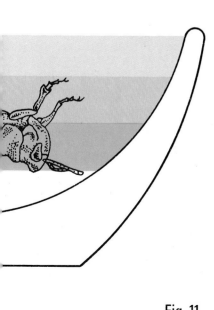

Fig. 11

normal way. The transparent pigments are ideal for colouring a whole cast ; the opaque pigments are for using in the final layer of resin as a background against which to set the objects.

An attractive effect can often be made by creating faults or fissures in the cast. To do this add more hardener than usual to the resin. About 3% will usually be sufficient. Then pour extra-thick layers of resin into the mould. 1in. or 2in. (25-50mm) layers are about right. More heat than usual will be created in the cast, resulting in the appearance of fissures. When the cast has set and been removed from the mould the fissures may come to the surface on all sides of the cast. Then take some resin with the usual amount of hardener added, perhaps with the addition of a colouring pigment, and pour it into any fissure that breaks the surface. Wipe any surplus from the surface of the cast. When dry, the surface should be smoothed as described previously.

Another interesting effect can be produced by adding a little water to the mixture of resin and hardener. Stir thoroughly just before pouring. This gives the appearance of bubbled glass.

In certain circumstances, a perfect finish to the bottom of a moulding can be achieved without using wet-and-dry paper. If the mould

is filled to the top with resin the following method can be used. Pour the last layer of resin so that it is very slightly above the lip of the mould. Then carefully slide a piece of pre-waxed glass across the surface of the resin before it sets. Then, with the glass still in place, leave the mould so that the resin hardens thoroughly. The cast should then have a smooth, clear surface all the way round.

If liquid resin is poured onto a casting that has already set, a firm connection will be made. Separate castings, once set, can be attached to each other or to most other materials with an epoxy resin adhesive such as Araldite, or a mixture of resin and hardener in which the percentage of hardener has been increased to 4%. The resin can also be cast directly onto most clean dry surfaces and will stick to them. But with metal, it is best to roughen the surface first to provide a good key. Wood should first be primed with a mixture of resin, hardener and acetone.

Polyester resin castings can be cut with a hacksaw and holes made in them with a twist drill. Any resultant rough edges should be smoothed using wet and dry paper. When making screw holes in finger plates, always finish the edges of the holes as neatly as possible, since they will probably be visible.

Moulding in resin and plaster: a chess set

Casting attractive ornamental objects in resin or plaster is more than just a fascinating hobby. Consider the advantages of designing and making your own chess set, for example. As well as the satisfaction you will feel at producing an original design, there is the added pleasure of knowing that your work will cost a fraction of a shop-bought chess set.

Polyester resin is a comparatively new synthetic material which has particularly wide applications in the production of cast objects. Unlike traditional casting materials, such as plaster, it is extremely durable, and it can be treated to produce a wide range of textures and colours. Also, when suitably reinforced, particularly with glass fibre, resin is extremely strong and can be used for car and boat shells and a host of other industrial uses.

Polyester resin can also be put to a multitude of these uses within the home, some of which have already been discussed in earlier chapters. This section concentrates on the ways in which resin can be moulded into beautiful objects for decoration and for more practical uses.

As an introduction to the techniques of casting resin, you are told how to make a complete chess set. In carrying out such a project, you learn not only how to handle and work the materials, but also something of the range of designs to which resin and plaster can be moulded. There is an additional attraction too. Shop-bought chess sets are usually very expensive and the more original the design, the more they cost. By making your own, you save money and, in fact, the demand for original

chess sets being large, you can easily sell your work, and thus combine a pleasant hobby with an attractive way of earning 'pocket money'.

Materials you will need

Resin: Polyester resin is a syrupy liquid which turns solid on the addition of a liquid hardener (catalyst). The addition of hardener by itself, entails a long curing time; to speed up the process, an accelerator must be added in accurately measured amounts. Suitable resins are now available from many handycraft outlets and usually contain the correct amount of accelerator, requiring only the addition of the catalyst to effect a cure.

Cleaners: The very properties which make resin such a durable material make it virtually resistant to ordinary household cleaners. Before starting work, therefore, equip yourself with a can of polyester resin solvent for cleaning equipment and surfaces, and a cleansing cream specifically designed for removing resin from the hands. Never clean your hands with solvents; they can cause dermatitis. In fact, you are advised to wear thin rubber gloves when handling resin.

Fillers: These improve the texture of the resin, increase its hardness and provide a suitable base for the addition of pigments. While any compatible powder may be used as a filler, striking effects are obtained by adding metal or stone filler (bronze, copper, granite, etc.) in the ratio, by weight, of 5-7:1 (of resin). Pigments can be obtained in a wide range of colours and form from 2%-10% of the mix. They can be used in combination to neutralize 'loud' colours.

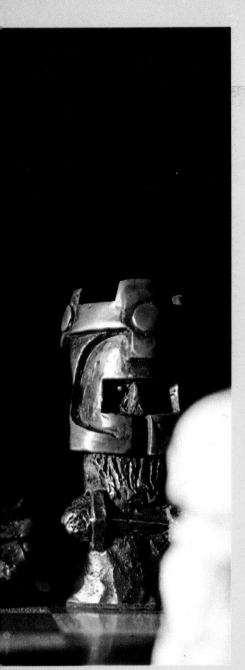

Left. Using the resin casting techniques described here, you can make yourself a set of individualistic and distinctive chessmen.

Measuring and mixing containers: It is important that the ingredients of the resin are accurately measured. Some manufacturers supply the hardener in calibrated bottles and also sell calibrated disposable cups for measuring the resin. When mixing and measuring out the filler and resin, use separate plastic bowls and sieve out any lumps in the filler.

Moulding materials: Plaster of Paris is only suitable for 'one off' moulds and is not recommended for making a chess set. A superior material is latex rubber, or better still, a rubber compound which can be applied, melted down and re-used again. Handycraft shops, DIY merchants and other outlets for home moulding materials will supply or procure these materials.

Other materials and tools: As well as the specific items listed above, you will require a modelling material such as clay or plasticine, mixing spoons, a sable paint brush for applying the latex, some fine plaster, and cardboard racks for holding the moulds.

The list of materials may seem large, but apart from the basic ingredients they can be used time and time again. False economy will only make the work longer and more complicated, and in the long run will affect the quality of the end product.

Some points to bear in mind

1. Although the materials are not dangerous when they are handled correctly, you should observe certain rules. Always work in a well ventilated room and avoid skin contact with the resin as much as possible.

2. Protect the work surface with newspaper.

3. Use only the recommended cleaners and solvents.

4. Keep all the materials away from naked flames. You can hasten the curing process by directing a fan heater at the work.

5. Once the resin has been catalysed it begins to harden, a process which is speeded up by the addition of an accelerator. As it cures the resin becomes jelly-like and cannot be moulded

again. For this reason make up no more resin than you can use before it gels.

6. Store all polyester resins and liquid hardeners in a cool, dark place, away from liquid accelerators.

Designing and modelling a chess set

It is possible to buy chessmen kits, which come complete with moulds, materials and instructions. You can also make moulds from an existing chess set. However, you will obtain far more satisfaction in producing chess pieces to an original design, and though you can learn the techniques with the aid of a kit, this should be your eventual aim.

Begin by drawing a series of thumbnail sketches of the various chessmen and try to keep to a uniform design. In recent years chessmen have been modelled on political and military figures, but though this gives ample scope for individual expression, the beginner is advised to stick to stylized figures.

Such a set is best represented by the Staunton chess pieces, first designed in 1835 by Nathaniel Cook. To minimize confusion between pieces, Cook used symbols rather than lifelike figures—thus a crown for a king, a coronet for the queen, a mitre for a bishop, a horse's head for the knight, and for the lowly pawn, a ball. Because each piece is readily distinguished the Staunton chessmen are now the most widely used.

If, however, you prefer something different, and can devise a theme on which the pieces can be modelled, there is plenty of scope for the imagination. Look through one of the many books which have been written on chessmen, or go along to see a museum collection.

Once you have worked out the rough designs, re-draw them accurately, full size. Obviously, the actual size of the pieces will depend on the size of board you intend to play on, but it is important to achieve a balanced visual effect—as much to prevent confusion as for appearance. Having added any detail, look at the designs objectively and work out whether they can easily be modelled. If not, modify the designs—removing any unnecessary detail.

The type of modelling material is dependent on the design and the mould material. Plasticine, which is inexpensive, is the ideal for simpler designs which do not incorporate many projections or undercuts. A more complicated design is best modelled in modeller's wax, which takes very fine detail. Modelling clay is best used for larger figures which are not too detailed. Another factor is the type of mould material used. Both plasticine and wax can be painted with latex, but hot-melt rubber should only be applied to clay or similar materials.

Having decided on the modelling material, build up an example of each piece, with the exception of the pawn, of which you should make at least two. When working the clay, concentrate on getting the basic form and size before adding any detail.

Making the moulds

If you are using liquid latex, making the moulds is simply achieved by painting the latex onto the model, using a sable hair brush. Be sure to cover the whole surface of the model, taking particular care over undercuts or ornamentation, and avoid trapping air bubbles in the mixture. Allow the first coat of latex to set, then apply more coats in the same way until the mould is a suitable thickness. Between applications, keep the head of the brush immersed in water to prevent it 'gumming up'. If this should occur, rinse the brush in paint stripper and, when the latex has been removed, wash it out in cold water.

To allow you to remove the mould easily, make a lip round the base of the mould. This projecting latex lip also allows the mould to be hung in a circular cut-out when waiting for the resin to cure.

If you are using hot-melt rubber, first melt it over a very low heat—preferably in a steamer. Once it is liquid, you can either apply coats to the model as described above, or use the dip method. This method, which is only recommended for moulding materials which do not distort or melt under heat, involves dipping the model into the melt enough times to produce a mould of the correct thickness. Add a lip to each mould, as shown in the step-by-step series.

Making the resin/filler mix

Having gauged the amount of resin required and the correct proportion of filler mix, mix them with a spoon in a plastic bowl, together with a measured amount of pigment. Filler powder,

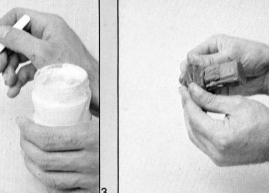
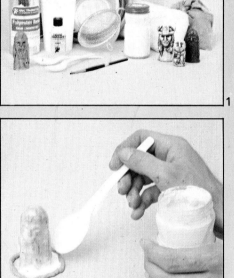

Step-by-step (1): Mixing basins, spoons, sieve, sable paint brush, measuring jug and calibrated beaker, and, of course, the various raw materials used—hardly a grand outlay for an end product of such aesthetic quality and physical durability.
(2): The object to be moulded off, which may either be a chess piece as such, or a model moulded from something like plasticine or wax, is carefully coated with the liquid latex.
(3): A rim of latex is included at the base of the mould (to allow it to be racked up as the resin sets), using a plasticine 'dam'.
(4): In the process of setting, the latex mould darkens in colour. It is simply peeled off the casting model.
(5): Filler and pigment are measured out.

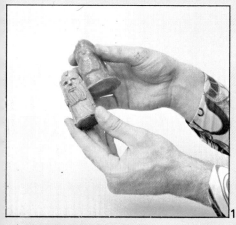

which gives texture and 'body' to the resin casting, is only available in black or white and must usually be dyed. The pigments used for this purpose are very strong colours which should be mixed to produce the correct shade. Don't feel that chessmen have to be either black or white. Provided each side is easily distinguishable you can produce any attractive colour combination. One helpful point to remember is that, because you can only have a vague idea of the eventual colour of the casting, black and white filler mixed to a grey powder can be dyed to the shade you desire more easily than black or white filler used by themselves. To prevent particles of filler 'lumping' in the mould, sieve it into the resin and stir well.

At this stage, before pouring the mix into the moulds, make a set of makeshift racks or holders from cardboard of a suitable thickness. Then check the mix for any air bubbles it may contain and leave it to settle for about fifteen minutes.

Next, add the appropriate quantity of catalyst (liquid hardener) to the mix, stirring it carefully to avoid forming air bubbles, but firmly enough to disperse the catalyst evenly throughout the mix. If you are using powdered hardener, take particular care to avoid getting any in your eyes. Should this occur, rinse them immediately in cold water and, if the pain persists, see a doctor.

Now take each mould in turn and pour in the catalysed mix until they are about three quarters full. Gently pinch the mould in order to eliminate air-pockets—paying particular attention to undercuts and ornamented surfaces. Then top up the moulds and place them in the previously prepared racks. After about five minutes the level of the mix may fall as it settles in the mould and more should be added.

Depending on the concentration of the catalyst, the casts should be cured in approximately thirty minutes. About ten minutes after the addition of the catalyst the chemical reaction begins to work and the mix begins to gel and becomes extremely hot. This heat production is quite normal in an exothermic reaction of this type.

When the cast has fully cured (i.e. no tackiness remains on the surface of the cast) and has cooled down sufficiently to be handled, wet the mould with water and peel it off. The casting is now ready for any finishing treatments and the

Step-by-step (6): The ratio, by weight, of filler to resin that you decide on determines the physical 'feel' of the casting. The more filler is used, the more predominant are the characteristics of the filler materials in the finished piece. A high proportion of, say, a granite filler will mean a very 'stonelike' end product, whereas more resin will result in a more purely 'resin' finish. The special measuring beaker, calibrated in 'resin-ounces', which thus enables you to measure directly in terms of weight rather than volume of liquid resin, is available from your resin supplier.
(7): The final step in preparing the mix.
(8): Filling the first mould.
(9): Tapping to dislodge any air bubbles.
(10): The fruit of your labours !

mould can be re-used in exactly the same way.

Finishing off

Once you have completed casting the whole set, check that no tacky surfaces occur on any of the pieces. If they are at all sticky, place them immediately in warm water and detergent and scrub them gently with a soft brush.

An electric drill, fitted with a fine sander, can be used to smooth the bases of the chessmen. To polish them, use ordinary boot polish of the correct shade. A textured and etched surface can be created on the white pieces by washing

Above. *Any full-size chessboard laid with pieces such as these assumes a vitality and an interest even before the first pawn or knight makes the opening move.*

them in a dilute solution of household cleaner or very weak hydrochloric acid.

Finally, you can paint the pieces if desired, and add felt to their bases to prevent damage to the pieces and the board. You are now ready to make the opening moves in a game of chess, using pieces you have designed and built yourself. While your game may never pose a threat to

Fischer, the satisfaction of handling intricate pieces made with your own skills will give lasting pleasure—and from the moulds you can make several sets in resin or plaster.

Of course the applications of resin and plaster casting are much wider. Now that you have mastered the techniques, a whole range of projects opens up. Garden ornaments, book ends—in fact any object small enough to cast—can be made quickly and cheaply. The praise with which your chess set will be greeted will, no doubt, encourage you to explore these and other satisfying projects.

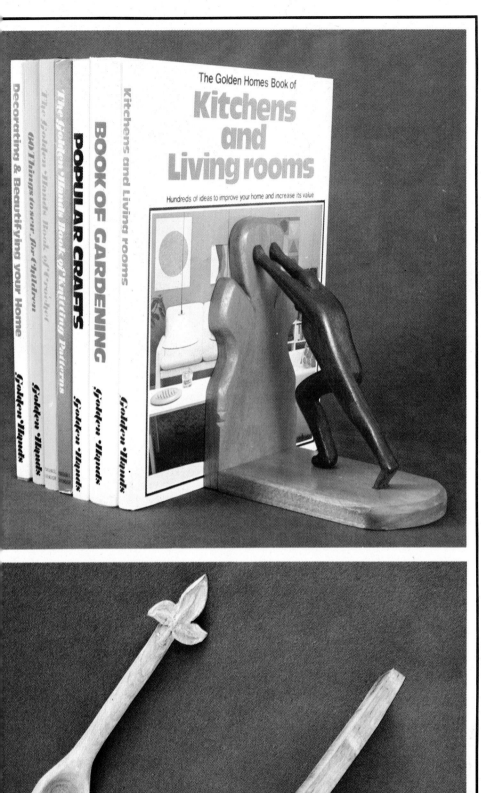

Decorative wood carving

The carpenter who learns the fascinating craft of wood carving adds a new dimension to his work. This chapter shows you how to carve an attractive book-end and spoon, and teaches you the basic carving techniques which can be applied to furniture decoration.

From earliest time, carpenters have decorated their work with wood carving. In the middle ages it was practised more as an art than as a craft, and perhaps the finest examples of wood carving skills are represented by the carved screens and figures found in many medieval churches.

Wood carving as a means of decorating furniture was most popular towards the end of the nineteenth century, but though much of this work shows considerable skill, a lot of it is too ornate for modern tastes. By the beginning of this century wood carving had fallen from favour, and since then furniture design has become increasingly simple to the point of starkness.

In recent years however, decorated furniture has become more popular and interest in wood carving has revived. This is partly because of the attractive and original results that can be obtained, but another factor is the sheer creative pleasure that wood carving gives.

There are two styles of carving practised nowadays—the traditional style and the modern. Modern carving differs in that the work is carved in smooth, shallow sweeps and the finished product may be sanded and polished. Because modern carving is less intricate, it does

Above left. *This unusual bookend provides a suitable introduction to the craft of wood carving. In making it, the beginner will learn many of the basic carving techniques and learn how to handle the unfamiliar carving tools.*
Left. *The Welsh love spoon presents a more advanced wood carving project. Traditionally, sycamore was used for these items but oak is a suitable alternative. The leaf pattern is often seen on decorative carved work.*

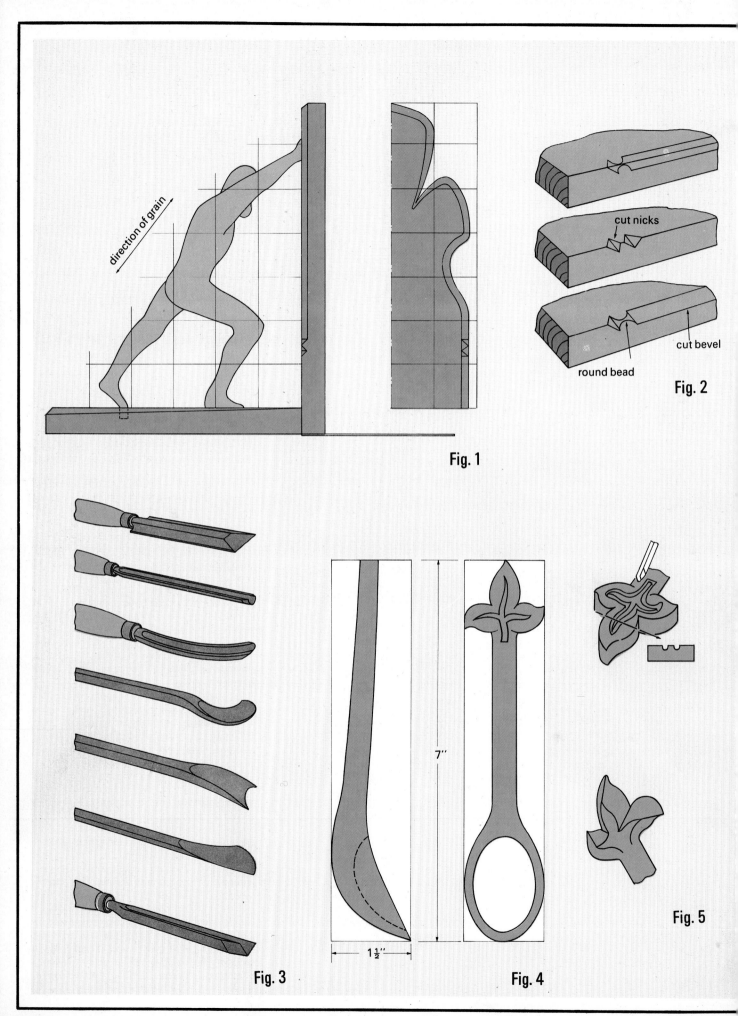

direction of grain

Fig. 1

cut nicks

round bead

cut bevel

Fig. 2

Fig. 3

7"

1½"

Fig. 4

Fig. 5

not require a large range of tools, and some that are essential will be already part of the handyman's tool-kit.

Wood carving tools

Some of the modern wood carving processes can be carried out using ordinary wood chisels of the bevel edged type (Fig.3). However, more complicated work requires the use of proper wood carving gouges, a comprehensive selection of which is shown in Figs. 3 and 7. Traditional wood carvers often owned over a hundred different gouges to handle all the intricacies of their work. But you can start with two or three gouges, and add to your kit as the need arises. Alternatively, you can buy one of the excellent boxed kits available which contain all the necessary tools.

A comprehensive selection of gouges will include not only straight gouges but also spoon bit, back bent and spade or fish tail gouges. At one time these tools were available in a large range of widths and with blade curvatures ranging from almost flat to a deep 'U'. Nowadays the range is much smaller, but still adequate for most work.

For detailed work, a very narrow gouge is essential. This type is called a 'fluter' or 'veiner' from its use in cutting out the veins on leaf work. V-shaped grooves are cut with a double-sided chisel called a V tool and the beginner is advised to use one with a 60° blade section. Preliminary roughing to shape is best done with a toothed file or rasp, such as a Surform. A coping saw is useful for removing surplus wood.

A lot of the carving processes are done with both hands on the tool—one pushing on the handle, while the other, on the blade, acts as a guide. Consequently, cramps, holdfasts and vices are needed to hold the work. An engineer's vice with padded jaws is more useful than a carpenter's vice, because it stands above the bench and allows the carver to work right round the job. With the work held in a vice, deeper cuts can be made by hitting the tool with a mallet. Traditionally the mallet is short-handled and round-headed, but an ordinary carpenter's mallet is adequate.

Tool maintenance

Good results depend on the sharpness of wood carving tools, and it is essential that the

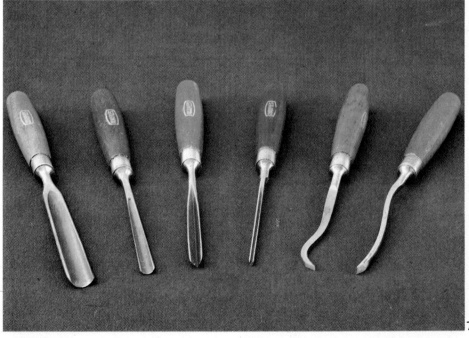

Fig.1. Side profile of the figure and a scaled outline of half the bookend. Too much detail on the figure is inappropriate, a stylized form is more striking.
Fig.2. Bevelling is one of the most recurrent features of the carvers' art and these simple bevels and beads on the bookend are a valuable introduction to this aspect of carved decorations.
Fig.3. A selection of the various chisels and gouges which the novice wood carver should have. More complicated work demands a wider selection of tools.
Fig.4. Side and top profiles of the love spoon. Preliminary cutting out is done with a coping saw.
Fig.5. Views of upper and lower surfaces of the leaf design on the spoon handle, showing details of the 'veining'.

beginner learns how to maintain his tools. Chisels and the outer surfaces of gouges can be sharpened by rubbing them on an oilstone, but for the inside edges of gouges, slip stones are needed. These are small oilstones which have different curves on two edges. The curves need not necessarily correspond exactly to the curves of the gouges, but the wood carver who owns an extensive kit of gouges will need several slip stones of different blade curvatures.

Preliminary sharpening of tools can be done with a grinding wheel, but care should be taken

Fig.6. Apart from gouges and chisels, the wood carver should be equipped with a coping saw, mallet, rough files and a padded vice.
Fig.7. The person who takes up wood carving can buy a matched set of gouges for first projects. As he or she progresses, tools for advanced work can be added to the collection.

especially when using a high speed power grinder, that the carving tool is not overheated and so have its temper drawn. After grinding and sharpening the tool on a stone, a finer finish can

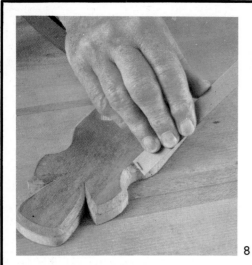

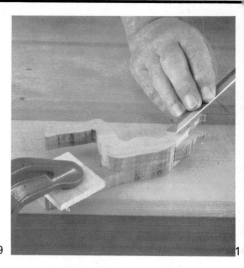

Fig.8. *When the bookend has been cut out, carve a bevel on the edge of one surface. This bevel extends $\frac{1}{16}$in. from both sides of the cut edge and narrows at the 'leaf' intersections.*

Fig.9. *Mark out and cut the outline of the figure with a coping saw, from wood with its grain running in the same direction as a medial line drawn through the figure.*

Fig.10. *Smooth off the surfaces of the figure and add a shallow groove under the arms. Here a bevel edged chisel is being used, but a V tool is more suitable for this job.*

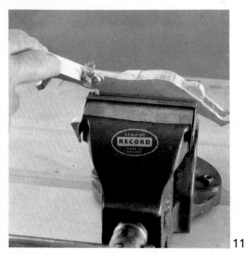
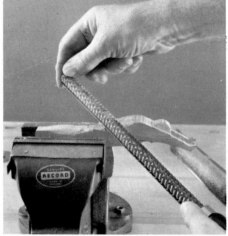

Fig.11. *With a chisel, slightly round off all the edges. For finer work, such as is required on the head, use an appropriately curved gouge.*

Fig.12. *Clamp the figure in a vice and round off all the surfaces with a rough file, such as a Surform. Final touches can then be added with gouges and the figure sanded.*

Fig.13. *To cut out and shape the spoon bowl, hold it in a vice and, working from the outside to the centre with a curved gouge, cut the hollow out to the required depth.*

Fig.14. *Shape the outside curve of the bowl with gouges and files. There is no need to make this outer curve match the inner. Refer to Fig.4 for the ideal shape.*

Fig.15. *Once the leaf has been cut out with its edges slightly undulating, carve the veins to the pattern shown in Fig.5 and then pare a slope from the edges to the veins.*

Fig.16. *The handle is rounded to run into the leaf. Extend the centre vein a little onto the handle, and outline it by cutting back a little round the handle.*

be obtained by stropping it on a piece of leather treated with a fine abrasive, such as pumice powder, mixed in a vaseline base.

Once a tool has been properly sharpened, do not allow it to become so blunt that it has to be reground. Regular treatment with an oilstone and slipstone will reduce the need for regrinding except at very long intervals.

Making a carved bookend

The book end illustrated in Fig.1 is a suitable wood carving project for the beginner. Its construction introduces the correct carving techniques, as well as detailing the elements of figure work and bevelling. Bevelling is an important part of the wood carver's craft with many applications in furniture decoration. It can be used on chair and table legs to add interest to a straight edge, and as a pattern round the borders of trays and frames.

Suitable woods

Most woods can be carved, with varying results, but the ones most suitable are close-grained hardwoods such as sycamore, beech, mahogany and oak. Choose a piece that has a uniform, even grain and is free of knots or discoloration.

Begin by making a template of half of the book end as shown in Fig.1. Lay this on the wood, draw round it, mark the centre line, then reverse the template to complete the pattern. Cut the curved outline with a coping saw, leaving a very small margin round the pattern which is then sanded down exactly to the mark. Clean up and smooth all the cut edges, then pencil in the area to be bevelled as shown in Fig.1.

This bevel should extend $\frac{3}{16}$in. from both sides of the cut edge and appears on only one surface of the book end. Where the 'leaves' intersect, the bevel becomes progressively narrower. The bevelled edge stops in a double triangular notch and bead (Figs.1 and 2). This simple pattern, which breaks up the outline of the book end, is called 'wagon bevelling', so called because it was used extensively by wheelwrights to decorate the edges of farm wagons.

To cut the bevel, hold the wood in a vice and pare progressively down to the lines with a wide chisel. Always cut with the grain, but if the wood should start to tear up, reverse the direction of the cut. A useful hint is to imagine the lines of the grain as a bundle of straws to be cut in the direction that would stroke them down, rather than lift them up. When cutting straight or outside curves, hold the flat of the chisel against the wood. To cut the bevel on inside curves or hollows, use the chisel with its bevel edge downwards. The bead at the end of the bevel is made by cutting small nicks about $\frac{3}{8}$in. (10mm) apart and working the area between them into the bead shape. For a small article like the bookend, one bead is adequate, larger works, such as screens, can be decorated with many beads of different shapes.

Much of the charm of carved pieces is in their 'rough' appearance. For this reason it is not necessary to sand the bevelled edges, as any rounding of corners will spoil the characteristic clean-cut appearance which distinguishes it from inferior machine-made decorations.

The base

Cut out the base from a piece of wood measuring 6in. x 3$\frac{3}{4}$in. (150mm x 85mm), and round off one end. The upper edge of the rounded end is bevelled in the same way as the outline of the end. The upper long edges of the base are then taper bevelled from the rounded edge, so that the bevel becomes progressively narrower towards the book end. The base can then be fixed into the upright by dovetail joints or by screws, and a thin metal plate glued and screwed to the bottom of the upright.

The figure

Only a skilled wood carver working on a large scale can hope to make an exact reproduction of the human form. For this reason the figure is highly stylized while preserving an essentially life-like appearance. Anybody with some artistic ability can attempt a more life-like appearance, but too fine detail is inappropriate. As facial features are hard to carve, the head is hidden between the arms.

The figure may be carved in the same wood as used for the stand, or in a contrasting hardwood. Choose a piece which can be carved so that the lines of the figure correspond to the direction of the grain.

Copy the pattern given in Fig.1 to give a template of the side profile of the figure. Draw the outline on a suitable piece of wood measuring approximately 8$\frac{1}{2}$in. x 5in. x 1$\frac{1}{4}$in. (250mm x 125mm x 32mm) and cut out the figure with a coping saw. Reduce the width of each leg to about $\frac{1}{2}$in. (13mm) with a saw, similarly, cut out the arms by sawing out a piece $\frac{1}{2}$in. (13mm) wide as far back as the head.

At this stage round off all cut edges and surfaces. Then, starting at the head and working downwards, add any features by paring away with chisels and gouges. The top of the head is completely rounded, and a shallow groove cut under the arms with a V tool. A small tenon is cut on the extended foot, and a corresponding mortice cut into the base.

Carved pieces should not be varnished but oiled. Three parts of linseed oil to one part of turpentine may be applied in several coats, and the piece polished with a soft cloth to produce a dull gloss. The final step is to glue the figure into the base, the book end is then ready for use.

Carving a Welsh love spoon

This project introduces more advanced carving work and demonstrates how to make a leaf pattern—a recurrent design in traditional carved pieces. The spoon has interesting associations. It was a tradition in Wales that a young man carved a decorative spoon and presented it to the lady of his choice. If she kept it, she had accepted him and they were betrothed. Although these love spoons were never meant to be used, they were given ordinary spoon ends, but the handle was decorated in any way the maker chose.

Sycamore is the traditional wood to use, but oak, though difficult to work, is a suitable alternative. The spoon may be curved or, if it is to be hung on a wall, can be left flat. A piece of wood about 7in. (175mm) long and 1$\frac{1}{2}$in. (38mm) square is sufficient. Use only wood with a fine, even grain.

Commence by making a template of the spoon, using Fig.4 as a guide. Draw this out, but do not cut out the entire shape just yet.

Cut out the spoon end and work the hollow before cutting the rest to shape. Hold the piece in a vice and cut the hollow, working from the outside to the centre, with a curved gouge. If the cutting edge of the gouge is not allowed to go too far below the surface, you will reduce the chances of splitting the wood. When the bulk of the waste wood has been removed, use a flatter gouge to pare round the bowl until a pleasing shape is obtained.

Now saw the rest of the outline (as shown in Figs.4 and 5) taking special care over the leaf pattern. Using a gouge or file, cut each leaf so that its edges are slightly undulating—giving a more realistic appearance. Mark the outlines of the veins as shown in Fig.5, then cut out to shape with a V tool and veiner. With a small gouge of fairly flat section, pare the surface of the leaf to make a slope from the edges in to each vein.

Return to the bowl. With the handle held in a vice, remove surplus wood from the outside of the bowl by paring and filing. There is no need to make this outside curve match the curve of the bowl so long as the bowl has a 'light' appearance.

The handle is approximately square in section at this stage, and its centre should be left square to provide grip for the vice until both ends of the spoon are completed. At the bowl end, pare the handle to give a rounded section into which the shape of the bowl blends. Round the edge of the rim of the bowl by careful paring. This edge, and the outside of the bowl, may be sanded smooth, but the inside of the bowl looks better if the tool marks remain.

At the other end of the handle, round its section so that it blends into the edge of the leaf, but cut a clean edge to the sides of the leaf so that it is clearly defined. Extend the centre vein a little onto the handle, and outline it by cutting back a little round the handle.

The leaf would be weakened if it was thinned too much, but its appearance can be lightened by bevelling the underside (Fig.5). Pare carefully with the grain, changing direction as you follow the outline. Keep the cuts light and support the piece as you work. Sand the back of the leaf, if you wish, but leave the front as tooled.

Only the centre part of the handle remains. Pare this to match the curves at each end. The tool marks on the handle can either be left or sanded smooth. Usually, these spoons are not given any surface treatment, but an application of wax polish will not detract from its appearance. The finished spoon can now be hung on a ribbon as a wall decoration.

Further work

Both the projects described, while simple, use techniques applicable to more advanced work on furniture. Wood carving is a fascinating craft and once you have mastered the basic techniques you will be eager to progress to more complicated work. In an age of machine made furniture it is pleasant to apply a traditional craft which gives results as original as they are attractive.

Above. *A hand-carved house name board adds a distinctive touch to the exterior of your home, as well as showing your address clearly and attractively. Also, in making it, you will learn the techniques for carved lettering.*

Relief carving: a name plate for your home

Add an attractive and individual touch to your home with this carved house name board. Apart from being a very useful item, its construction teaches you the art of carved lettering—an extension to the very simple basic techniques of wood carving described in the preceding chapter.

Carving a house sign may seem, at first sight, a fairly simple task but, in fact, is one which can prove quite exacting. This is largely due to the nature of letter carving—an art which demands not only a basic sense of design, but also a fair degree of precise work. Unlike most wood carving, which is stylised and done in the round, letter carving requires the ability to carve unbroken lines, whether straight or curved. However, provided you realise that letter carving involves some preliminary draughtsmanship and the ability to work patiently and exactly, you can produce excellent results.

Lettering

Like most other aspects of wood carving, carved lettering has a long history. Go into almost any church and you will find examples of the craft, some of them dating back to the Middle Ages. The best work is that which conveys the written message quickly, clearly and beautifully, and these qualities do not necessarily depend on the style of carving.

There are four styles of letter carving commonly practised—incised, raised, rounded and sunk and squared and sunk. In theory any one style can be used for the name board, but some are easier to carve than others.

Incised lettering is carved to a sunken V-shaped section, which means working not only to the outlines, but also to a centre line through each part of each letter. Any errors with a cutting tool are difficult to erase and a uniform section is difficult to maintain when cutting rounded letters. For this reason it is best applied to the carving of Roman capitals with their emphasis on straight vertical strokes. Sunken and rounded or squared lettering combines the difficulties of both incised and raised or relief carving, and should not be attempted by the beginner. Plain relief carving is most suited to the novice, as errors in cutting can be effectively disguised without ruining the overall composition.

The other consideration is style of lettering. One style, Roman capitals, has already been mentioned as relatively simple to carve (and draw), emphasising as it does bold, straight lines. However, one of the main attractions of wood carving is the opportunity it gives for original, individual expression. For this reason you will find it much more satisfying to devise your own lettering style, remembering only not to make it so intricate that it is difficult to carve.

Materials

Every species of timber has a character of its own which affects the manner in which it can be carved. While most timber can be carved, softwoods are prone to splitting and warping and are unsuitable for the name board. Most hardwoods give good results, but the ideal timber is one which is close grained, uniform in texture and durable enough to withstand exposure outdoors. Oak, Teak and some of the tropical hardwoods such as Mahogony answer all these requirements well, but Teak is probably the best choice for the beginner.

A comprehensive list of carving tools for the beginner was given in the preceding chapter. For relief carving the requirements are almost the same. Straight and curved edge chisels of various widths and blade curvatures and different gouges are all necessary. Other essential equipment includes a short, round-headed mallet, a padded vice, sharpening equipment and rasps. Depending upon the complexity of your chosen letter design you may also need additional tools. If you do not possess any carving tools and have difficulty in choosing individual chisels and gouges, you are advised to buy one of the excellent boxed sets which contain a balanced selection of tools.

Drawing out

Having decided on a style of lettering, you must now draw out the name, full size on the board. This is not as easy as it sounds as it requires not only basic draughtsmanship, but also a sense of composition. The satisfactory spacing of letters is just as important as their design, and the only way to achieve this is by first practising drawing them out on paper.

Take a large sheet of paper and divide it into two halves. On one half draw in the full size

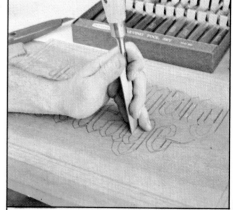

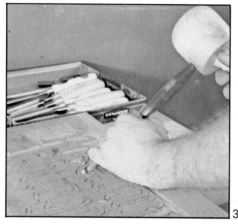

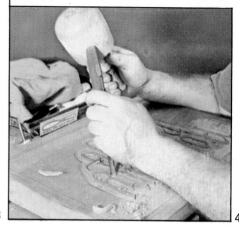

Fig.1. When you have devised a satisfactory composition, transfer it to the board with the aid of carbon paper.

Fig.2. Using a straight-edged chisel, cut the straight parts of the letter outlines to a depth equal to ⅓ the width of each stroke.

Fig.3. With a narrow, deep U-shaped gouge, cut along the edges of the letters to bring them into bold relief.

Fig.4. When carving the serifs on the letters, take extra care. A small slip with the gouge at this stage can mar the final composition. You can avoid this by cutting away from each letter.

Fig.5. Carve out the background with a wide gouge and smooth with a wood carver's router.

outline of the board. On the other half make several drawings of the board on a reduced scale. Now mark in the lettering on one of the smaller drawings and, when you have finished, examine it critically. The overall composition should be good, with the letters correctly scaled in proportion to the surrounding area and properly spaced. If the lettering is not completely clear, perhaps it is too intricate, and you must devise or copy a different style. In this you can be aided by books which illustrate the various lettering styles.

Having worked out any faults in your design, re-draw it in another small frame and keep on doing this till you are completely satisfied with the result. Transfer this arrangement to the full-size frame, drawing very carefully as this will be the final composition.

Marking out

It is possible to re-draw the composition on

the board freehand, but this is not recommended for the amateur. An alternative method is to divide up the board into areas representing individual letters, words and lines, with the aid of a T square, and then using each dividing line as a reference point for freehand lettering. By far the easiest method, though, is to trace out the words with the help of carbon paper.

Take a piece of carbon paper of the same size as the board and pin it onto the board. Lay the full-size drawing over this, making sure it is centred correctly, and secure it so that it cannot slip. With a soft, sharp pencil, carefully but firmly trace out the outlines of the letters. Remove the paper and, if necessary, emphasise the traced outlines. Never use anything but pencil on the board itself in case you have to clean up any unwanted marks.

Cutting out

Begin by cutting the outlines of all the letters.

Rather than complete each letter separately, cut the straight lines first and then the curved lines and serifs. Before making any cuts at all you must first calculate how deep they should be. As a general rule, relief lettering is shown to best advantage if the distance that it stands proud of the surface is about one third the width of each stroke. Skill in achieving this can only be gained by trial and error, and for this reason you are advised to carve a practice letter on a waste piece of timber.

When you are confident that you have the 'feel' of both the wood and the tools, cut out the straight parts of the letter outlines. Best results will be obtained by using a straight-edged chisel with a blade width ¼in. (6mm) shorter than the line to be cut. If you use a wider chisel you risk intruding into curved lines. If you use a narrower chisel, you will have to make more cuts per straight line and risk making an uneven line.

Place the chisel in position on the straight line at 60° to the surface. Strike the head of the chisel with a round-headed mallet, taking care not to let the chisel slip. If the wood you are carving is particularly hard, do not try and cut to the required depth with one stroke. Provided you hold the chisel in the correct position, you can work down to the right depth in stages. Complete all the straight parts of the outline before cutting any curved lines.

Depending on the style of lettering chosen, the rounded letters will all exhibit different curves which require different chisels to cut them out. One curve may require as many as four different chisels to complete. Before making any cuts, match the chisels to the curves and work out if there are any lines which present special problems. Having assessed which tools will be needed, cut out the curves in strict order and link them to the straight cuts. Particular care should be taken when cutting out finely tapering serifs and, in fact, the beginner should not make these too thin.

The background

Once you have cut all the outlines out, you must cut out the surrounding wood to the correct depth. The area immediately round the letters must be cut away with great care—a less delicate approach can be employed on the rest of the background.

At this stage, a few words about the carving tools and their handling may prove useful. Whereas the choice of chisels and gouges for cutting the outlines is straightforward and their use is fairly mechanical, the choice of tools for cutting round the letters, and their method of use, is less clear cut. Initially you will require a fairly wide gouge which has a blade curved in a fairly shallow U. This tool is used to cut up to the letters and for carving out most of the background. Narrower gouges with a highly curved blade are used to clean up the edges of the letters. How the gouges are handled will vary from person to person. The experienced wood carver or the gifted novice who has a 'feel' for wood, will tend to cut with bold, deep strokes, removing as much waste wood as possible at each cut. The less experienced carver will work more cautiously in shallow sweeps and will cut down to the required depth in stages. However,

both the expert and the novice should work in a strict order of procedure.

After making a few preliminary practice cuts in a piece of waste wood with a wide, shallow gouge, place the tool in position about ½in. (13mm) from the edge of a letter and at right angles to it. With one hand holding down the blade, push the gouge towards the letter. The ease with which the blade cuts through the wood depends on the timber species, the sharpness of the blade, and how much force is exerted. Working with a very hard timber like oak, even the sharpest blade cuts with difficulty. Use only as much force as is necessary and always keep control of the blade. If you try and cut too deep, you may either split the wood or scar the surface of the letter. Depending on the hardness of the wood and its grain, cut up to the outline in stages and, if you don't feel confident of cutting right up to the outline exactly, stop a little short.

Once you have cut right round all the letters so that they all stand proud of the surface, cut down the rest of the background. This will be a long and tiring job which involves constant sharpening of the tools. Cut in one direction only, preferably with the grain, till you have reached the required depth.

Now return to the lettering. With a narrow, deep U-shaped gouge, cut along the outlines to bring the letters into bold relief. A good method to employ is to rest the back (i.e. the non-cutting part) of the gouge against the side of the raised letter and gently push it along the outline in short sweeps. It is very likely that you will not have cut deep enough with the straight

chisels in the first stage, and it will be necessary to redefine the outlines and deepen the cuts. If you have to do this, remember that the sides of the letters should slope outwards, as shown in Fig.5, which means that when cutting outlines at this intermediate stage, the chisel should be set a little out from the top edges of the lettering.

With all the letters cut out evenly, finish the background. No matter how skilfully you handle the carving tools, the background will be uneven and show up the individual strokes. Although a lot of wood carving is left in the unfinished state, the lettering on a board is shown to best advantage if it is set against a smooth, plain background. A wood carver's router set to the required depth will smooth the background and help emphasize the lettering.

Finishing off

If desired, you can cut a simple stepped frame round the board which helps throw the lettering into bold relief. As the board will be exposed to the weather, it will need an application of wood preservative, and when this has soaked in well you can oil the board or varnish it.

For a really luxurious name board, you can have the original cast in bronze or some other material. But whether you make a casting or use the original board, you will have the satisfaction of having made a useful and beautiful item with the finest traditional skills and methods.

Right. *The finished carving can be left plain, gilded, or cast in another material.* **Below.** *When drawing out, you can use the lettering below or devise your own style.*

Lathework for beginners: 1

A lathe adds a whole new dimension to your carpentry skills. For the first time, you move beyond square, plain shapes, and you can make round objects of any contour and with as much (or as little) decoration as you like. Lathework is not difficult, and is as enjoyable to perform as the results are satisfactory.

Wood-turning lathes are available in a range of sizes, from small ones powered by electric drills to huge professional models that can make sections for newel posts that are several feet long. Drill-powered lathes can do good work provided you don't try to make anything too large. But if you can afford a purpose-built integral lathe (one with its own motor) you will find it much more versatile than a drill-powered one.

The lathe

All lathes, drill-powered or integral, are designed in much the same way. The main frame, to which all the other parts are attached, is called the *lathe bed*. The size of the lathe bed controls the maximum length of the piece of wood that can be fitted into the lathe. On the smallest drill-powered lathes, it is about 2 ft 6in. (0.75m) long ; integral lathes have much longer beds.

The *headstock* is a strong support mounted at the left-hand end of the lathe bed. In integral lathes it houses a revolving cylindrical *mandrel*. This is threaded on the outside and has a hole down the middle so that fitments to hold the workpiece can be attached to it in two ways as described below. In drill-powered lathes the headstock is simply a clamp for the drill and the mandrel is screwed directly to the shaft of the drill. In integral lathes the mandrel is driven by an electric motor underneath the headstock by means of a belt and pulley.

At the other end of the lathe bed is another support, the *tailstock*, which is used for the turning of long objects such as lamp stands. The tailstock can be slid up and down the lathe bed to suit the length of the work piece and can

Below. Spindle turning on a Myford ML8 lathe, using a standard gouge for the basic roughing out. The correct holding position is illustrated, with the tool at the right angle.

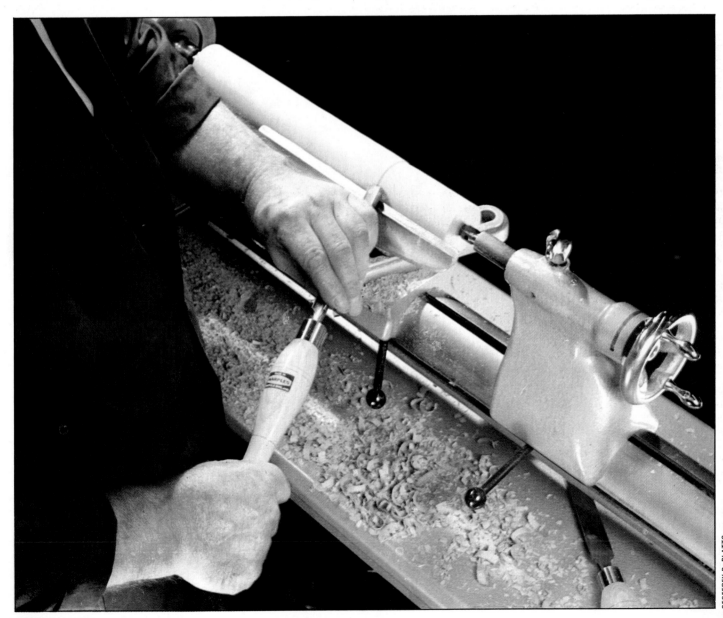

be fixed in any position. In *spindle work*, the workpiece is clamped between headstock and tailstock and spins on a *dead centre*, a flat plate with a blunt central spike, fixed to the tailstock. A *cup centre*, which is cup-shaped and has a removable spike, is found on some lathes.

In *face plate* work—the turning of wide, flat objects such as bowls—the tailstock is not used and the object is fastened to the headstock only. This is why the mandrel provides two methods of attachment. Spindle work is fixed on a *morse tapered driving fork* inserted into the hole in the mandrel. Face plate work is fixed firmly with large wood screws to a flat face plate, and the face plate is in turn screwed on to the threaded end of the mandrel.

On the near side of the lathe bed there is a *tool rest*, sometimes called a *tee rest* because of its shape. The tools used for shaping the wood are held against, and slid along, this rest, which can be adjusted in all directions to suit any type of work.

Some larger integral lathes have an outside face plate attachment that allows a face plate to be fastened to the outer end of the headstock. This allows you to work on very large items that would otherwise foul the lathe bed. This face plate must have a left-hand thread to prevent it from unscrewing while being used. Drill-powered lathes don't have this feature; they are anyway unsuitable for turning large pieces.

Lathe tools

Special tools are made for lathework. There are three main kinds: gouges, chisels and scrapers. At first sight, they may look like ordinary bench chisels, but there are important differences and bench tools should never be used for lathe work.

Lathe tools have very robust blades and extra-long handles which are usually made of beech or ash and have strong brass ferrules. Gouges and chisels are available in three sizes: long and strong, which are about 20 in. (500mm) long including the handle and are used for heavy work by professional craftsmen; standard, about 16in. (400mm) long and the normal type for professional and amateurs alike; and small, about 13in. (330mm) long and suitable for light work on drill-powered lathes.

All lathe tools are supplied ready ground to shape, but you have to sharpen them yourself. This must be done in a special way for each type, as described below.

Gouges are used for roughing, or cutting wood roughly to shape. A gouge blade is U-shaped at an angle of 40° around the outside of the U. It can be ground in two shapes: straight across, which makes the gouge suitable for cutting flat, open surfaces, and with the corners ground further back than the centre, which makes the gouge right for cutting inside curves such as the insides of bowls.

Gouges come in sizes from ¼in. (6mm) to 1in. (25mm) wide. The wider sizes are used for roughing straight lengths and the narrower ones for sharp inside curves. In addition, the ¼in. gouge can be used for boring, such as is done in the middle of a bowl to mark the depth to which it should be cut (see below).

Chisels are used for finishing work once it has been roughed out with a gouge. They have a straight cutting edge, which may be ground square across or on the skew. The range of widths is the same as for gouges, but unlike gouges (and ordinary bench chisels) they are ground on both sides at an angle of 15°, so they come to an edge at 30°. Skew-edged chisels are commoner, because they are easier to hold in the correct position. Both types, however, are used for the same purpose.

There is also a special type of chisel called a parting tool, which is made in one size only. The blade is like that of a chisel, but its end is ground in a V shape rather like a spear. It is used for cutting a finished piece away from the waste wood left at its end. It is also useful for marking out a block before you start cutting it to shape.

Scrapers are similar to chisels, but are used for fine finishing work. They are ground at the very shallow angle of 10°. One popular and useful type of scraper has a round 'nose', or sharp edge. Another commonly available type has a shallow V-shaped nose which most people re-grind to suit their particular needs.

All lathe tools are normally sold with their handles. If you do happen to buy some in 'blade only' form, make sure that the handles you buy for them are the special extra-large lathe tool handles and not ordinary chisel handles. These ordinary chisel handles are too small either to accept the tang of a lathe tool blade or to hold firmly when working.

Grinding and sharpening

When you buy lathe tools, they are generally ground to shape but not sharpened. The method of sharpening differs from that for ordinary bench gouges and chisels: the sharpening angle is the same as the grinding angle so that, when they are sharpened, an equal thickness of metal is removed from all over the ground edge, and its surface remains perfectly flat. Sharpening in this way takes longer, and needs more care, than the conventional method, but is absolutely **necessary if the tools are to be used in the right way** and, hence, to achieve the best possible results with the finished article.

You will need three abrasive blocks for sharpening your chisels, gouges and scrapers: two Indiastones both 5–8in. x 2in. x 1in. (130mm–200mm x 50mm x 25mm) and a shaped oilstone slip of a suitable size to fit the inside curve of your gouges. One Indiastone should be used for gouges, which wear stones unevenly, and the other kept exclusively for chisels and scrapers, which need a perfectly flat surface. Slips have an egg-shaped cross-section, so one slip will be suitable for all the curves on your various gouges if you choose it of the correct size.

Gouges should be sharpened at an angle of exactly 40°. To do this, hold the gouge with one hand at each end and apply the point bevel side down to the stone with its bevelled edge exactly parallel to the surface of the stone—you can feel the angle by raising and lowering the handle until the bevel lies flat on the stone.

Run the gouge backwards and forwards over the stone and rock it from side to side at the same time, so that all of the curved surface of the bevel touches the stone on each pass. Since you are sharpening the blade only on one side, a burr or wire edge will appear on the upper, visible side of the edge. If this burr appears all round the curve it will show that you are moving the blade in the right way.

As soon as the burr has appeared all round the edge stop sharpening and rest the blade, still bevel side down, on the tool rest of the lathe or some solid surface. Then lay the oilstone slip flat in the groove of the gouge and slide it carefully over the edge to remove the burr—this should happen quite quickly.

Chisels should be sharpened on both sides at 15°. Apply the chisel to your perfectly flat India-stone with its bevel resting flat on the stone as before. Then move it backwards and forwards (but not, of course, rocking it) until a burr appears as before. Turn the chisel over and sharpen the other side in the same way. Remove the burr very carefully on the flat surface of the stone.

Scrapers are sharpened in the same way, but on one side only and at 10° instead of 15°. Remove the burr by laying the unground side of the scraper flat on the stone.

To consolidate and smooth the edge of a scraper after sharpening, it is usually *ticketed* with a special *ticketer*. This can be bought in large hardware stores, but is very easy to make yourself. Take a 4in. (100mm) length of hardened silver steel rod, or grind the teeth off an old 4in. three square file and round the corners—it doesn't matter if a ticketer is round or triangular. Set this tool in a file handle.

Use your ticketer first of all to burnish the edge on the flat side of the scraper. Lay the scraper flat side up on the bench and rub the ticketer along the edge, keeping it absolutely flat and being careful not to tilt it.

Then turn the scraper over and apply the ticketer to the bevel edge, moving it up and down until you feel the bevel. Lower the handle of the ticketer very slightly—not by more than 2°—and draw it along the edge of the scraper, pressing quite hard to create a slight burr on the other side. This burr should not be removed.

Preparing the wood

Wood that is to be turned is normally square in cross-section. It is time-consuming and messy—and can be dangerous—to cut the corners off entirely on the lathe, so it has to be trimmed very roughly to a circular cross-section before you begin.

A piece of wood that is to be spindle turned should be about 2in. (50mm) longer than the finished article to allow for the waste at either end to be cut off when turning is finished.

Find the exact centre of the wood at each end by marking the diagonals from corner to corner. Then draw the largest circle on this centre that will fit on to the end of the wood and plane the corners off the wood all along its length to make it roughly octagonal in cross-section. Take care not to cut below the line of the circle at any point.

Use a tenon saw or a chisel to prepare one end of the timber to receive the driving fork, making sure that the slot is a tight fit and perfectly central. Prepare the other end for the dead centre of the tailstock by denting the centre mark with a center punch, and apply a little oil or grease to the mark to make the wood revolve freely.

GEOFFREY B. PLATTS

1

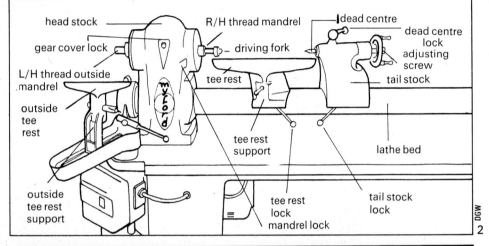

head stock — R/H thread mandrel — dead centre

gear cover lock — driving fork

dead centre lock adjusting screw

L/H thread outside mandrel

tee rest

tail stock

outside tee rest

tee rest support

lathe bed

outside tee rest support

tee rest lock

tail stock lock

mandrel lock

DGW

2

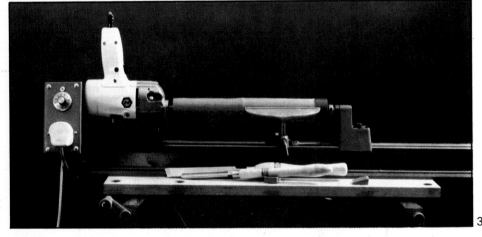

3

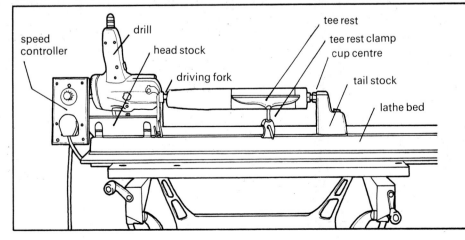

speed controller

drill

head stock

driving fork

tee rest

tee rest clamp

cup centre

tail stock

lathe bed

DGW

4

The wood is now ready for clamping between the headstock and tailstock. This is done simply by tapping the driving fork well home on to its slots, screwing it on to the headstock, sliding the tailstock firmly up to the other end and locking it in position. Adjust the tool rest as close as possible to the wood, and turn the wood around once by hand to make sure that it does not catch. The rest should be set just above the centre line of the lathe.

Wood for face plate turning should be just over 1in. (25mm) thicker than the finished work. Plane one face perfectly flat, draw the diagonals and the circle as before, and saw off the corners of the block nearly down to the line of the circle. Lay the face plate exactly over the centre of the block, mark and pre-drill screw holes in the block through the holes in the face plate, and fasten the plate firmly to the block with stout 1in. screws.

Screw the block and plate on to the mandrel and set the tool rest as close as possible to the face of the work, but just below the centre line.

Safety precautions

Never wear loose clothing when working on a lathe; anything that gets caught will be rapidly wound into the machinery, taking you with it. So remove all loose clothing such as a baggy jersey, a tie or an apron. If you have long hair, tie it well out of the way, preferably under a cap. Roll your sleeves well up. The ideal clothing is a buttoned-up overall, but it should not have any holes in it; these can be particularly dangerous.

Just in case something does happen, make sure that the 'off' switch of your lathe is placed so that you can reach it with one hand, in a hurry and without looking.

Don't allow anybody to stand near you when turning wood. They might be injured by flying chips, or simply tempted to meddle.

Before you start work, always make sure that the workpiece is firmly fixed to the lathe, the lathe is firmly clamped down and all its parts are secure. These last two points are particularly important in the case of a drill-driven lathe which you have to assemble every time you use it.

Lathe speeds

The ideal speed for a particular turning job depends both on the operation being performed and on the diameter of the workpiece. The wider a workpiece is, the faster is its speed (in inches per second) at the outside edge for a given lathe speed (in revolutions per minute). So for

Fig.1. This is a purpose-built commercial lathe. *Fig.2.* This is a key of the various parts of the lathe.
Figs.3-4. An electric drill driven lathe and its component parts.
Fig.5. A block of wood with the corners removed has been turned out for face plate turning. The face plate is mounted on the block with screws, and a piece of hardboard is placed between the work and the face plate to prevent damage to the chisels.
Fig.6. In this illustration the face plate with the work attached is being screwed to the mandrel of the headstock.

most ordinary operations (other than end boring, finishing and final parting off) the smaller the piece the faster it should turn. A list of ideal speeds is given in the list below.

diameter of work	nature of work	lathe speed (in rpm)
under $\frac{3}{4}$in. (19mm)	roughing and general turning	2600-2800
$\frac{3}{4}$in. (19mm)-7in. (180mm)	,,	1400
7in. (18mm)-12in. (300mm)	,,	900
all sizes	sanding, burnishing	2600-2800
all sizes	end boring, lathe drilling, parting off	280-300

If you are using a drill-driven lathe, you are most unlikely to be able to vary its speed to this extent. Most two-speed drills can be set to 900rpm and 2400rpm. These speeds are all right for some operations but no good at all for end boring, which you are quite likely to have to do at some time.

The solution to this problem is to buy a variable speed controller for your drill, but there is an important point to observe in choosing one. Some speed controllers reduce the drill speed simply by cutting the voltage and power, and these will prevent the drill from turning at all when heavy work is being done at a low speed. The type to buy is a thyristorized speed controller, which reduces speed but maintains almost full power under load.

Another point to watch is that the speed control must be of the correct wattage for your drill. For example, one common British thyristorized variable speed controller, the Fotherly Willis ETC 500, is rated at 500 watts. This is suitable for a medium-sized British drill such as the Black and Decker D 720 which is rated at 370 watts and well within the safety margin.

The controller is marked from 1 to 10, 1 giving roughly one-tenth of and 10 giving full speed. So to achieve a speed of roughly 300 rpm, set the drill to 900 rpm and the controller to the third notch. This will give you three-tenths of 900 rpm, or 270 rpm approximately.

The second part of this chapter deals from start to finish with making a table lamp describin in all the techniques that are necessary. It also shows the additional techniques you need to use for making a bowl.

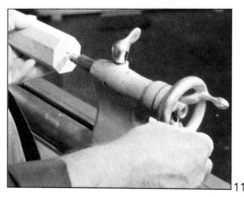

GEOFFREY B. PLATTS

Fig.7. A $\frac{1}{4}$in. standard gouge being used for boring the centre of the face plate work. This not only removes the centre of the work, but can be marked with a crayon so as to gauge the required depth of the bowl.

Fig.8. This is how lathe tools should be sharpened. The gouge is held comfortably against the inside forearm, with the bevel side flat on the stone. Here a gouge is being sharpened so that the angle between gouge and stone is 40°. The sharpening action is a back and forward motion, pivoting smoothly from the shoulder.

Fig.9. After the gouge has been honed on a
flat stone, it will be necessary to remove the burr from the edge. This is done with a slip stone, with the gouge resting firmly on a surface while a convenient radius of the slip stone is held flat upon the inside surface of the gouge.

Fig.10. A piece of prepared timber is being fixed to the driving fork on the headstock mandrel. The two parallel saw cuts fit over
the staggered chisel edges, which ensures accuracy when centring the work piece.

Fig.11. When the work piece is fixed, the tail stock is brought up close to the end and the cup centre wound up into a previously punched centre mark on the work.

Fig.12. This is a Black and Decker lathe unit, used in conjunction with a Fotherby Willis speed controller.

Lathework
for beginners: 2

The first part of this chapter dealt with various kinds of lathe, the different types of lathe tool and their maintenance, and setting up the lathe and the workpiece for spindle and end plate work. This part tells you how to make a table lamp base, which uses both techniques, and a bowl, which introduces inside end plate work.

If you carefully follow the techniques described below, you will soon be able to produce superb pieces of individually crafted furniture.

To achieve good results, it is important to use the lathe tools in exactly the right way. If they are not held at the correct angle for their type, they may 'dig in', catch on the wood and be wrenched from your grasp. This is not only extremely dangerous but makes a mess of the surface of the wood. Used correctly, on the other hand, well-sharpened tools can achieve such a high standard of finish that no sanding is necessary.

Turning techniques

When removing wood with a gouge or chisel, the tool is held point upwards on the tool rest with its bevel towards the workpiece and flat against it. The handle of the tool is then raised slightly to bring the cutting edge into contact with the work. This is why the edge has to be sharpened at the same angle at which it is ground. If there were a double slope the handle would have to be raised a long way to make the edge touch the work, and it would then be likely to catch and fly out of your hand.

The tool must never be pressed against the work or it may catch, or vibrate and chip the wood. But it has to be held firmly, or it will be thrown down by the force of the lathe. For this reason, it must be held with both hands, one as near the point as possible and the other taking a firm grip on the opposite end of the handle. The tool should be supported against the tool rest before it is slid up to come in contact with the wood.

The way that various tools are held is shown in Figs.1-9. Note that the full width of the cutting edge is never used but only the section of the edge that is nearest the tool rest. The tool should be applied to the workpiece at one end (or side for end plate turning) and moved

Opposite. This elegant lamp base has been turned in beech, and the bowl in a variety of woods that have been glued together before turning. These items can be made quite easily using basic lathework techniques.

smoothly across to the other side (or the centre) in a continuous movement. If you stop, it will create a ridge that will be difficult to remove.

Finding the correct angle and movement requires careful practice, so you should try the techniques out on worthless scrap timber until you get them right.

In spindle turning, the length of the finished object should first be marked on to the prepared timber with the parting-off chisel (the speed at which the lathe should be running is discussed below). This tool should be laid flat on the tool rest and brought into contact with the workpiece to mark it with a neat V-shaped groove.

After the timber has been marked, it should be roughly cut to shape with a 1in. (25mm) wide gouge; in some cases the parting chisel can be used. The gouge can be held flat on the rest and the centre of the cutting edge used to cut, or tilted at an angle and slid across the work point first, depending on the contour of the part you are cutting. Be very careful that the far, upper edge of the cutting surface does not catch on the wood through incorrect angling.

Once the work is roughly cut to shape it should be smoothed. The correct tool for this is a chisel. Whether you use a straight or skew-edged chisel is entirely a matter of preference; some manufacturers make a special deep-throated gouge with the sides of the 'U' shape parallel and this can be used on its side as a chisel.

When you switch from gouge to chisel, lower the tool rest to below the centre line of the workpiece and again move it as near to the wood as possible. You must stop the lathe to do this. Then restart the lathe and lay the chisel on the tool rest with the skew of its edge (if any) tilted towards the centre line of the workpiece, and the edge itself angled at about 45 to the centre line. Raise the handle until the end of the edge nearer the tool rest comes into contact with the wood, then sweep it across smoothly as before.

Final smoothing is done with the scraper, which is used in a different way from the other tools. The tool rest remains slightly below the centre line and the scraper is laid on it horizontal and bevel side down, so that it meets the work below the centre line at about 60°. It should be used with great care and the overhang between the tool rest and the workpiece should be kept to an absolute minimum to keep the tool from vibrating.

End plate turning is done in a slightly different way. The sides of gouges used should be ground well back to make them round-nosed, or they will catch. You will be cutting into a vertical surface instead of one that slopes away from

you, so the tools will be held much nearer the vertical. This means that the tool rest should be kept below the centre line all the time, and moved further below it for chisel and scraper work.

A tool should be applied to the wood with its bevel flat against it as before, but it should not be angled to start the cut. Instead, it should just be pushed gently towards the wood, which will start the cut less violently.

When you are working across the face of a block, you will find that when you get to the middle, the rotation of the block tends to twist the tool around. Even if you hold it firmly to resist this, it will still not cut properly. There is a special technique to overcome this difficulty; it also marks the depth of the centre of a bowl at the same time.

First use the parting tool to draw a circle $\frac{1}{8}$in. (3mm) from the centre of the block. Then mark the intended depth of the bowl on the blade of a $\frac{1}{4}$in. (6mm) round-nosed gouge by sticking on a piece of adhesive tape. Start a cut with the gouge about $\frac{1}{2}$in. (13mm) from the centre and cut towards the centre in the conventional way. When the trailing edge, which is doing the cutting, reaches the marked circle, swing the handle of the gouge around smoothly so that it is at 90 to the face of the wood. You can then use the gouge as a drill to cut a $\frac{1}{4}$in. hole into the wood until the tape is level with the surface.

The table lamp shaft

The vertical shaft of a table lamp base is an ideal starting-ground for spindle work. It introduces all the basic techniques of marking out, turning, finishing, end boring and making a round tenon to fit into a mortise in the base.

The lamp base can be made out of any wood, though a close-grained hardwood is easiest to work. The piece for the shaft should be prepared and set up between headstock and tailstock as described in the first part, and the tool rest brought as close to it as possible without fouling.

Set the lathe to the correct speed for the size of the workpiece, then use a deep 1in. (25mm) gouge to take the corners off the wood. The piece will be roughly octagonal in cross section to start with, and only the corners of the octagon will touch the gouge. Hold the tool firmly but lightly so that it just takes tiny chips off the wood, and sweep it from end to end along the whole length of the piece. Continue in this way, gradually cutting the corners off until the piece is a true cylinder. Reposition the rest as you do this to keep it as close as possible to the work, stopping the lathe each time you do so.

At this point, the position of 'throats'—hollowed-out areas—and of the ends of the spindle and the shoulder of its tenon should be marked on the wood with the parting-off tool.

Use a straight-across gouge to shape the throats, working from the outside (i.e. the high side) to the centre from each side of the throat alternately. Don't make the tenon yet; just cut the visible part of the shaft roughly to shape.

Once the piece is approximately the right shape, finish it off and put a smooth surface on it with a chisel, which should be used very lightly with a planing action, so that it produces

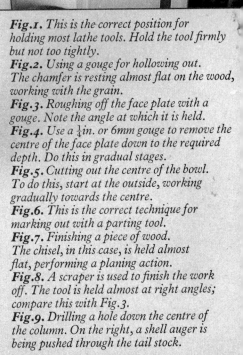

Fig.1. This is the correct position for holding most lathe tools. Hold the tool firmly but not too tightly.

Fig.2. Using a gouge for hollowing out. The chamfer is resting almost flat on the wood, working with the grain.

Fig.3. Roughing off the face plate with a gouge. Note the angle at which it is held.

Fig.4. Use a ¼in. or 6mm gouge to remove the centre of the face plate down to the required depth. Do this in gradual stages.

Fig.5. Cutting out the centre of the bowl. To do this, start at the outside, working gradually towards the centre.

Fig.6. This is the correct technique for marking out with a parting tool.

Fig.7. Finishing a piece of wood. The chisel, in this case, is held almost flat, performing a planing action.

Fig.8. A scraper is used to finish the work off. The tool is held almost at right angles; compare this with Fig.3.

Fig.9. Drilling a hole down the centre of the column. On the right, a shell auger is being pushed through the tail stock.

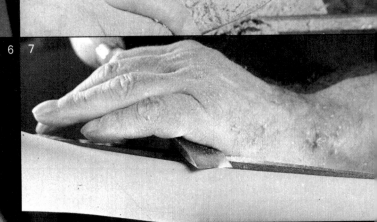

shavings and not chips. For the final smoothing, use a scraper—square-edged for outside curves, round-nosed for inside.

Now make the tenon on the bottom. First cut it considerably oversize with a gouge, then set a pair of outside calipers to the size of one of your larger lathe drill bits and use a chisel to reduce the wood to exactly that size. The tenon should be the same thickness all the way along and not tapered.

This completes the shaping work. Provided you are working on a good, close-grained wood, all you need to do now is burnish it with a handful of wood shavings while it revolves at full speed. If there are any blemishes on the wood, they can be sanded off with fine sandpaper; this must be moved constantly from side to side and never allowed to rest in one place, or it will score the wood.

For instructions on drilling the hole down the middle for the flex, see below. Don't part the lamp shaft off the scrap at the ends before you read this section.

The table lamp base

Prepare the wood and mount it on the end plate as described. On a wide item like a lamp base, you can save yourself a lot of tiresome parting-off work at the end by making the block only as thick as the finished base, without allowing any waste, and screwing it directly to the end plate. You can hide the screw holes later by covering the base with felt. But you must screw the block on top of a hardboard or ply spacer the same size as the block and at least $\frac{1}{8}$in. (3mm) thick. If you don't do this, the tools will collide with the metal end plate and have to be resharpened.

Fasten the end plate to the headstock and turn the wood down to a circle as before. Remove the centre as described above (this applies to a lamp base as well as a bowl) and run a gouge across the face several times to make it perfectly flat and smooth. Mark out any rings you wish to turn on it with the parting-off tool. Then cut the wood roughly to shape with a gouge.

Do the smoothing work with a chisel on the outside edge and outside curves, and a gouge on inside curves. Add the finishing touches with a scraper, and sandpaper if needed.

Lathe drilling

You will need to drill three holes in the table lamp base: one right down the middle of the shaft for the flex, one through the edge of the base, also for the flex, and a much larger hole for the mortise in the base to take the tenon of the shaft.

The large mortise hole is the easiest. Leave the workpiece on the end plate and mount a chuck on the tailstock to take a drill bit. Only integral lathes have this facility. Remove the centre point of the cup centre by undoing two screws with an Allen key and fit the chuck in instead, doing up the screws to hold it stationary and stop it from revolving. Then insert a bit the same size as the tenon, start the lathe and slide the tailstock up to the workpiece.

The bit must be marked with a piece of tape to indicate the maximum depth of the hole; this will stop you from drilling into the end plate.

Press the tailstock gently so that the bit enters the workpiece and continue pressing very lightly to drill the hole. If the bit is not a self-clearing one, i.e. it does not have a spiral shaft to remove wood chips, it must be removed from the hole after every few seconds' drilling to clear it, or it will clog and jam. Shell augers, which are often used for this type of work, are not self-clearing.

Drill-powered lathes have tailstocks that cannot be dismantled. If you have one of these, drill the hole in the base by hand with a brace and bit.

The long, thin holes for the flex, however, must be lathe drilled. The technique varies for integral and drill-powered lathes.

Integral lathes have a tailstock with a removable centre as described, and also a special drilling jig that fits in place of the tool rest. This jig fits along the centre line of the lathe and is designed to hold a shell auger steady and stationary, but at the same time allow it to be pushed forward. The auger should be of the type with its own handle.

Part the waste off the tailstock end of the lamp shaft, but leave it attached to the driving fork on the headstock as it was when it was being turned. Remove the centre from the tailstock, fit the jig to the tool rest stand and select a narrow shell auger of the required length. Mark the depth of the hole with tape.

Now poke the auger through the hole and up to the wood as if it were a tailstock centre, until it just touches. Start the lathe and very gently press the auger into the wood, holding it as steady as possible. Drill right up to the end in this way, using very light pressure. But every time the drill has advanced 1in. (25mm) remove and clear it, or it will jam.

On a drill-powered lathe, there is no drilling jig. Instead, improvise a horizontal drill stand by making a wooden jig that fits over the lathe bed to support the shaft at the centre line of the lathe. Tack a pair of battens to the jig so that the shaft can be slid up the lathe bed between them without any sideways movement. If the shaft is smaller at one end than the other, make a shaped block to support the narrow end firmly and tape it securely to the shaft.

Insert a long, thin twist drill bit (special extra-long ones can be bought) in the chuck of the drill and then slide the shaft carefully up the jig so that the bit drills it from end to end. The jig, the battens and your hands must be rock steady to do this successfully, and you must grip the shaft firmly to stop it from spinning.

The base is drilled from the edge, so it can't be done while on its end plate (and certainly not while spinning). It must be set horizontally on a jig as described (on both integral and drill-powered lathes) and slid towards a bit set in the headstock or chuck. If the tenon on the shaft is set into the mortise in the base while this is done, it will drill the small transverse hole to link up with the centre hole of the shaft in exactly the right place. You might have to enlarge this small hole in the shaft later to get the lamp flex round the corner—a tricky job.

This completes the actual woodwork on the base. It is now a simple matter to fix a lampholder on the top and fit the shade of your choice.

Built-up bowl

Built-up work is lathework done on several layers of contrasting wood stuck together and turned as one piece. A built-up bowl is shown in Fig.0. Whether you like the striped effect or not is a matter of taste, but the actual work is fun to do. The lathe techniques are exactly the same as for solid work.

Note that the layers can either run across the work as shown, or along it, which gives a much more dramatic effect. But the second type should never be attempted by a beginner, because an improperly glued joint or an accidental 'dig in' can cause the work to come apart with the force of an explosion. If you want to do this type of work, wait till you have the necessary experience.

The layers of wood should be glued together with ordinary pva adhesive cramped up extra firmly and left to dry for several times the recommended period to make absolutely sure they are properly joined.

You won't want screw holes in the bottom of the bowl, so glue on a scrap layer that can be parted off later. In the case of a solid bowl, make this block from which it will be turned 1in. (25mm) too thick and part off the excess. In either case, no spacer will be needed on the end plate.

Mark a circle on the block, cut it down to an octagon and mount it on the end plate, then screw the end plate to the headstock. Shape the outside of the bowl as before.

The inside will need more care. Smooth the face of the work and remove the centre as described. Move the tool rest as close to the smoothed face of the work as it will go and set it well below the centre line. Then gradually hollow out the inside of the bowl with a deep gouge with its corners cut well back. This must be done very lightly indeed, or the gouge will catch. Keep moving the tool rest inward. (Stop the lathe to do this.)

When the bowl is almost down to the required depth, smooth it with a shallow gouge. A chisel is the wrong shape for the inside, though it can be used on the outside as normal. Finish off with a round-nosed scraper for the inside and a square one for the outside. Sand if necessary and burnish before parting off. Built-up work with the layers running along the centre line of the lathe (i.e. the difficult type) should not be sanded, since it tends to impregnate the light layers with dark wood dust and spoil the appearance.

Polishes

Certain types of polish are better than others for specific woods, so check this with your local supplier before you start.

Although the wood should be burnished with the lathe running, it should be polished after it has been removed or the wax will be overheated by the friction. The correct procedure for wax polishing is to burnish the wood thoroughly with the lathe running at full speed, then remove it and rub off the dust of burnishing with a clean dry cloth. (This would be dangerous with the bowl revolving.) The polish should then be applied by hand and rubbed to a shine with circular motions of a fairly coarse (though not abrasive) cloth.

Basics of marquetry: a chess board

Marquetry, the art of inlaying different textured timbers, is undergoing something of a revival. With a range of over 100 different kinds of wood available in veneer form, cut to precision-made thickness, the scope for artistic expression via this medium has widened to an almost unlimited degree. A useful introduction to marquetry is provided by making up a simple geometric design such as a chessboard, the step by step construction of which, with the aid of a cutting board, is fully described and illustrated in this chapter.

Above. *A simple geometric design such as a chessboard makes an ideal introduction to marquetry. Modern veneers, of standard precision-made thickness, greatly simplify construction and assembly.*

The craft of marquetry dates back to the days of ancient Egypt; perhaps the first examples to be found were the rather crude wood mosaics found in the tomb of Tutankhamen. In England, marquetry first appeared during the 16th century, and by the end of the following century the craft had reached a high degree of sophistication.

But the finest examples were produced on the Continent by such mastercraftsmen as Roentgen, Boulle, Oeben and Riesner. Some magnificent examples of their work can be seen today in museums—and occasionally in an auction room.

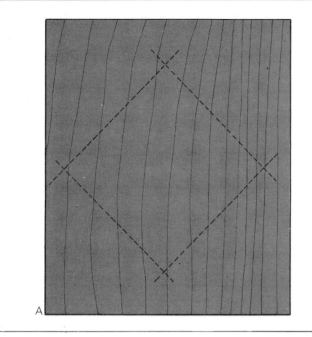

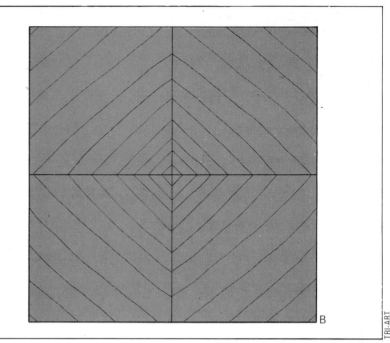

TRI-ART

Preparations

For a chessboard with a 12in. (305mm) square playing area, the following materials will be required:

(a) a baseboard of ½in. (13mm) thick plywood or chipboard, about 14in. (356mm) square to allow for a border;

(b) two pieces of contrasting veneer; these pieces should be at least 12in. x 8in. (305mm x 203mm) and preferably larger to permit trimming.

(c) a third veneer in sufficient quantity to cover the back of the chessboard, viz. 14in. x 14in. (356mm x 356mm), and the border and edges—about 14in. x 6in. (356mm x 152mm), again allowing excess for trimming.

Also required will be adhesive tape, glue such as Evostik Resin-W (if suitable press is available) or a contact adhesive such as Dunlop Thixofix. If you haven't a press, fine grades of glasspaper or garnet-paper, and a suitable polish such as Furniglas Home French Polish or Hardset. The only tools required are a sharp trimming knife, a 2ft (600mm) steel rule, a set-square and a cutting board.

Buying veneer

DIY and veneer shops sell veneer in a good range of woods. The trouble is that they will almost certainly want to sell you whole sheets. As a rule, these measure 3ft x 1ft 6in. (914mm x 457mm). A sheet of this size is quite expensive, particularly in a rare wood. Before you commit yourself to paying for a whole sheet, try the antique shops in your locality. Many of them repair their own furniture, and some may have an offcut of the veneer you want.

It is worth trying, anyway.

Nearly all veneer is of the same thickness: about $\frac{1}{16}$in. (1.6mm). You will probably not be able to get the veneers you have in mind, but the main thing is to select two contrasting veneers, such as mahogany and sycamore, walnut and avodire, or, for a really top-class result, burr walnut and satinwood. Any two contrasting veneers will do.

Fig.1. This shows the procedure for making the backing veneer:
(A) How the diamond is cut from a piece of veneer to give a diagonal pattern;
(B) The diamonds are matched from four pieces which are cut from consecutive—i.e., almost identical, leaves of veneer.

Cutting board

A cutting board may not be regarded as essential, but it will more than repay the small amount of time spent in making it. A suitable design for a cutting board is illustrated in Fig.2. It is made from ½in. (13mm) thick plywood or chipboard and some pieces of hardwood strip. Note the adjustable stops which, for our chessboard, should be set to give a uniform distance of 1½in. (38mm) between the steel rule placed firmly against the stops and the hardwood strip along the back edge of the cutting board.

Construction

Begin the chessboard by cutting the light and dark veneers into 1½in. (38mm) strips, each at least 12in. (305mm) long, and if possible slightly longer, to be trimmed at a later stage.

The cutting board enables this task to be carried out quickly and accurately by simply positioning the veneer against the hardwood strip, placing the steel rule on the veneer and firmly against the stops, and then cutting cleanly against the rule.

Do not try to cut right through the veneer in one stroke; use several lighter cuts to avoid splintering or tearing the veneer. Naturally, the knife must be kept very sharp. Cut four strips of dark veneer, then five strips of the light.

It is worth emphasising at this stage that throughout this project great accuracy in cutting and assembling the veneers is essential.

Using strips of adhesive tape, fit the nine strips of veneer together in alternate sequence as shown in Fig.3.

Note that the strips should be assembled in the same order in which they were cut, and with the grain running in the same direction; in other

words, no strip should be reversed in relation to its fellows. Check that all strips fit tightly against one another with no gaps along their whole length.

The next step is to trim the assembly along one end at right angles to the direction of the veneer strips; use the steel rule and the set-square for this.

The assembly is then positioned on the cutting board with the trimmed edge firmly against the hardwood strip, so that the veneer strips are at right angles to the steel rule held against the stops.

Now carefully cut through the assembly so that a new 1½in. (38mm) wide strip is obtained, comprising nine squares of alternately light and dark veneer. Handle these pieces with care, as the squares of veneer are joined together only by the adhesive tape. In the same manner cut seven more 1½in. (38mm) wide strips of nine squares each.

Keeping these strips in the same order, lay them out on the cutting board and stagger them alternately to form a chequer pattern.

With adhesive tape, fix the strips together, again making certain that the joints are tight between adjacent pieces of veneer, and checking that the squares meet exactly at the corners. It will be found that there are eight squares of light veneer projecting from the assembly. Cut these off and discard.

Final trimming of the chequer pattern can now take place. If the procedure has been followed with care, the result will be the familiar chessboard pattern in a perfect square, with each of the small squares meeting its neighbours exactly at the corners. If all has gone well, the border can now be fitted and the complete pattern mounted on the base board.

Border

The type of border chosen for the basic chessboard is largely a matter of personal taste. It can be simply made from four pieces of veneer of a shade chosen to contrast with those used in the chequer board; or it could be a more elaborate frame, in which various inlay bandings, or even marquetry scrolls, are used.

In general, a relatively simple border of 1in. (25mm) width would prove quite satisfactory; usually a dark border is more pleasing in appearance than a light one. The effect can be further enhanced by the use of a light coloured 'stringer'—a thin strip of veneer of contrasting colour running around the whole perimeter.

The border on the chessboard illustrated was made from four 14in. (356mm) long composite pieces consisting of a $\frac{1}{4}$in. (6mm) strip of dark veneer, a $\frac{1}{4}$in. (6mm) strip of light veneer and a $\frac{1}{2}$in. (13mm) strip of dark veneer. These strips must be taped together, once again ensuring that all the joints are tight.

To improve the corners, $2\frac{1}{2}$in. (63mm) lengths of the light veneer at the ends of each border piece can be replaced by a contrasting dark veneer, as shown in Fig.4. The border pieces are then taped along the edges of the squared veneer assembly, overlapping each other at the corners. To form the mitres, the two borders at each corner are carefully cut together along the diagonal.

The offcuts of veneer are removed and the corners carefully joined and secured with tape.

The top of the chessboard is now complete. However, before it can be glued to the base board it is necessary to ensure that one side is entirely free from adhesive tape. Select the surface which is to be polished eventually and remove all the tape from the other side, taking care not to pull the pieces apart or to tear up the grain of the wood. If gummed paper tape has been used, it will be necessary to moisten it slightly before it can be removed; but check first that there is sufficient tape on the front side to prevent the assembly from coming apart.

The work is now ready for laying, and it can be put aside while the base board is prepared.

The base board

Either plywood or chipboard. $\frac{1}{2}$in. (13mm) thick and perfectly square, would be suitable for the base board. For the sake of appearance, and also to counteract any tendency to warp, the back of the board and all the edges should be veneered.

A single sheet of veneer, cut slightly oversize, would be perfectly satisfactory for the back, although for a more professional job matching quartered veneers might be preferred. Either way, the back should be veneered first, then the edges, and finally the front (top) surface.

To make a quarter or diamond-matched pattern it is necessary to obtain four pieces of veneer, sliced consecutively from the same log, and at least 10in. (254mm) square. Identical pieces, each slightly larger than 7in. (178mm) square are cut from these with the grain running diagonally; these pieces are then taped to-

Fig.2. The cutting board; adjustable stops are set to give a uniform distance of $1\frac{1}{2}$in. (38mm) between the steel rule and the hardwood strip along the back edge.
Fig.3. The strips are assembled in the same order in which they were cut, with the grain running in the same direction.
Fig.4. How the border-pieces are assembled and fitted and the corners mitred.

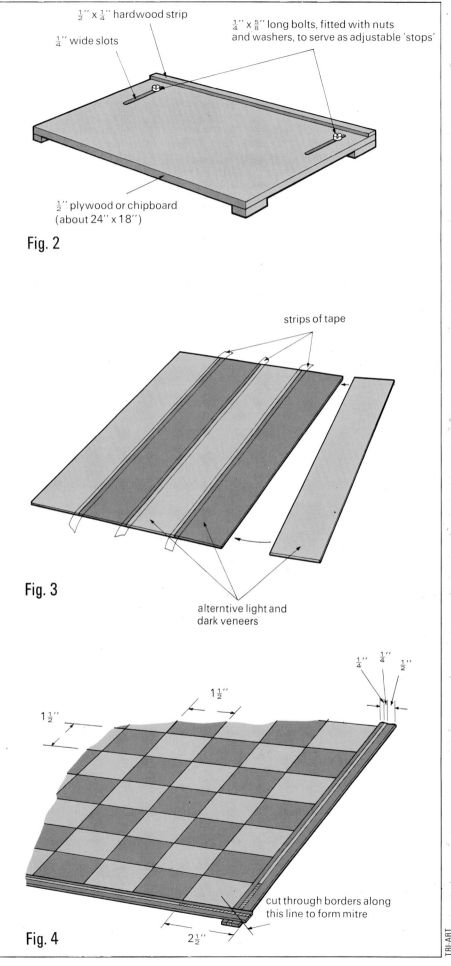

$\frac{1}{2}$" x $\frac{1}{4}$" hardwood strip
$\frac{1}{4}$" wide slots
$\frac{1}{4}$" x $\frac{5}{8}$" long bolts, fitted with nuts and washers, to serve as adjustable 'stops'
$\frac{1}{2}$" plywood or chipboard (about 24" x 18")

Fig. 2

strips of tape
Fig. 3
alterntive light and dark veneers

$1\frac{1}{2}$"
$1\frac{1}{2}$"
$\frac{1}{4}$" $\frac{1}{4}$" $\frac{1}{2}$"
cut through borders along this line to form mitre
$2\frac{1}{2}$"
Fig. 4

TRI-ART

85

gether, their grains being matched to yield the diamond formation.

Fixing

To anyone not familiar with the techniques of veneering, the use of a contact adhesive such as Dunlop Thixofix is probably the easiest for fixing the veneers. The adhesive is spread on the base board first, and then onto the backing veneer. After about 15 minutes drying, the veneer is very carefully placed in position and pressed down evenly, ensuring that no air is trapped underneath. The overhanging lip is then smoothed off with a sanding block.

Four strips of veneer are now cut—slightly over-size for the edges of the board. An opposite pair of these is glued into position and the projecting edges trimmed off; the second pair is then treated in the same way.

Finally, the chequer assembly is glued to the top surface. Make sure that it is exactly square to the board. The greatest care must be taken with this operation since, when using contact adhesive, it is almost impossible to move the veneer once it has been wrongly positioned.

At this stage, all the remaining adhesive tape can be removed from the chessboard. It is now ready for sanding and polishing.

Finishing

Using the finest grade of glasspaper on a cork sanding block, the surfaces of the veneers are gradually rubbed down. Take care neither to round off the corners nor to rub through the thin veneer at any point. This process continues with increasingly fine grades of glass or garnet-paper until the whole surface of the chessboard is absolutely smooth. The better the surface

preparation at this stage, the easier it will be to obtain a good polish subsequently.

The chessboard can be polished using any one of the various brands of synthetic French polish which are available. Naturally, a clear or 'white' polish should be used to avoid discolouring the light veneers. Alternatively, the traditional French polishing technique can be adopted and will give an excellent result, again provided that white polish, available from most hardware shops, and not the usual button polish is used.

Alternative use

This chapter describes a basic chessboard, but the chequer pattern could serve equally well as a centre piece for a coffee table.

In this case, the assembled chequer pattern would be let into the solid wood table-top, or it

would be cut into a single piece of veneer of suitable size.

An even better result would be obtained by using consecutive leaves of veneer in a two-piece or four-piece matching pattern and setting the taped veneer assembly into this.

After glueing the veneer to the table-top, sand and lightly polish, then cover with a sheet of plate glass held in place by hardwood lipping.

Fig.5. Here are the materials and equipment you will need to make the chessboard: sheets of veneer, cutting board, knife, steel rule, tape and adhesive.

Fig.6. Begin the chessboard by cutting the light and dark veneers into $1\frac{1}{2}$in. (38mm) strips, each at least 12in. (305mm) long. The cutting board enables this task to be carried out quickly and accurately. With the

veneer placed against the hardwood strip and the steel rule held firmly against the stops, the strips are cut.

Fig.7. Taking care to keep the veneers in the order in which they were cut, the strips are taped together with colours alternated.

Fig.8. Again using the cutting board, strips consisting of nine $1\frac{1}{2}$in. (38mm) squares are cut.

Fig.9. The strips are kept in the same order, but with alternate ones offset to form the chequer pattern.

Fig.10. Composite strips form the borders, and these are taped to the trimmed.

Fig.11. The taped assembly is accurately positioned on the baseboard and is fixed with contact adhesive.

Fig.12. The chessboard is finished, and is ready for sanding and polishing.

The result is a most attractive and functional piece of furniture.

Cutting list

Material	Imperial	Metric
Plywood or chipboard		
1 piece	$14 \times 14 \times \frac{1}{2}$	$356 \times 356 \times 13$
veneer		
2 pieces	$12 \times 8 \times \frac{1}{16}$	$305 \times 203 \times 1.6$
1 piece	$14 \times 14 \times \frac{1}{16}$	$356 \times 356 \times 1.6$
1 piece	$14 \times 6 \times \frac{1}{16}$	$356 \times 152 \times 1.6$
4 edging strips	$14 \times \frac{5}{8} \times \frac{1}{16}$	$356 \times 16 \times 1.6$

You will also need:
adhesive tape, glue or contact adhesive, glass-paper or garnetpaper, polish; a sharp trimming knife, a 2ft. (600mm) steel rule, set-square, cutting board.

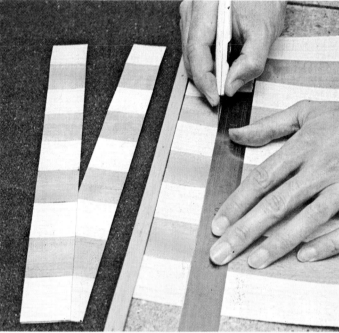

7

11

12

Marquetry: a screen

Once you have mastered the basic techniques of marquetry—the art of inlaying different textured wood veneers—you can go on to more ambitious projects that will give a delightful originality and appeal to any wooden surface. This chapter tells you how to make a marquetry picture that will be an eye catching centre point of your decor wherever you choose to use it.

The chessboard described in the preceding chapter involved the use of the relatively simple marquetry technique of making straight-line cut-outs. In order to make pictorial designs you need rather more advanced skills—in particular, the technique of fitting what are often complex irregular shapes together accurately.

The traditional method of cutting out complex shapes, and one still used by the few professional marquetry craftsmen, involves cutting the veneers with a very fine saw-blade mounted in a machine (rather like a mechanical fretsaw) called a 'donkey'. With the production of thinner modern veneers, however, knife cutting became popular, and this is the method used by non-professional marquetry carftsmen.

Pictorial marquetry

The applications of pictorial marquetry are many, ranging from conventional pictures to miniatures the size of a playing card and smaller, and from large items of furniture to tiny trinket boxes.

The design 'Irises' described in this chapter can be put to a variety of decorative uses. It can be used to decorate the door of a small cupboard, a tea-tray or a coffee-table. Here it is used as a centre-piece for a free-standing firescreen, as shown in the photograph opposite. Use the design full size if possible, but if you require a slightly smaller format the grid can be redrawn to the reduced scale and the design carefully copied.

It must be stressed at the outset that marquetry is not a craft for the impatient, and the 'Irises' design is rather more than a beginners' picture. With care and patience though, anyone with an average ability should be able to make up the panel.

Tools required

The only tools needed to make up the panel are a knife, a stylus for tracing the design (an

Left. Pictorial marquetry can be put to superb decorative use in the home. This panel can be used on its own as a beautiful picture.

old ball-point pen will do) and a cutting board. Use a knife that is light and comfortable to hold and has a fine pointed blade—in contrast to the relatively heavy trimming knife used for projects such as •the chessboard, which involves geometrical marquetry. A surgical scalpel fitted with a pointed blade is ideal, though perhaps a little awkward for the beginner to handle. Some practice at cutting veneers with a slightly heavier craft knife would be useful. For the cutting board, any piece of plywood or blockboard (or even hardboard) with a good clean surface will suffice.

Materials

The materials required include an assortment of veneers, gummed paper tape, a pva adhesive, fine grades of glasspaper and garnet paper and a suitable polish such as Furniglas 'Home French Polish' or 'Hardset'.

The firescreen shown here consists of a 2ft x 2ft (610mm x 610mm) piece of $\frac{5}{8}$in. (16mm) to $\frac{3}{4}$in. (19mm) plywood or chipboard. You will also need some hardwood edging strip and hardwood blocks for the feet and handle. To mount the marquetry panel onto the baseboard of the firescreen, or other location, use a contact adhesive if you do not have a press.

Designing your panel

The first step in making a marquetry panel is obviously the selection of a design. For convenience, the design 'Irises' is reproduced on page 90 (Fig. 1), but you may prefer to draw up your own pattern.

Almost any subject is suitable—landscape, animal or bird, and floral or abstract designs can all be used as the basis of the marquetry panel. It is essential though to keep in mind the nature of the material with which you are working. The natural tones of the woods, though beautiful and varied, are nevertheless subdued. It is useless to attempt a picture that relies for its impact on bright colours, as this impact cannot be achieved in marquetry without the use of dyed veneers. (Dyed veneers are available in a range of colours, but they tend to look out of place in a marquetry picture amongst the more delicate hues of natural wood.) It is also better to choose a design comprised of large area of similar tone, than one with a lot of minute detail. The essence of marquetry as an art lies in the skilful use of natural tone, texture and figure of the wood to achieve the effect desired.

Making the panel

When you have chosen the subject, a line drawing is made on tracing paper by carefully tracing round the areas of different tone whch

will be represented by the different wood veneers. This line drawing is the 'pattern' for the marquetry panel and care at this stage will be repaid in the final result. Whatever the subject, the basic procedure for making up the design in veneer is the same. The following description relates to the design 'Irises' but the steps can easily be adapted to any other pattern.

First, transfer the main feature of the design to a suitable background. For the Irises a pale pink veneer such as guara, gaboon or a light mahogany would set off the white and red-brown blooms as well. With black carbon paper between the line drawing and the veneer, trace the outline of the six leaves with the stylus. Then, taking care to hold the knife upright, cut round the shape of the first leaf and remove it from the background. Do not try to cut right through the veneer with one stroke unless it is very soft—several lighter strokes will give a cleaner result and reduce the chances of the veneer splitting. Use a pricking action when cutting sharp curves.

The hole or 'window' in the background veneer forms the template to which a contrasting veneer can be cut. An ideal veneer for the leaves is a greenish-brown magnolia. Place this veneer behind the 'window' in the background and position it for the best effect (Fig.2). Hold the veneers firmly together on the cutting board (with tape if necessary) and, again making sure that the knife is perfectly upright, cut the dark veneer around the inside edge of the 'window'. If you do this job accurately the leaf shape will fit exactly into the hole in the background veneer. Hold it in place in the background veneer with either adhesive spread around the edge of the leaf or with gummed paper tape across the back of the veneers. Now cut and fit the remaining leaves in the same way.

The next step is to transfer the outlines of the flowers, buds and stems onto the panel. Do this by carefully aligning the line drawing over the leaves, now cut into the background, then sliding the carbon paper into position and tracing over the outline with the stylus. Each shape can now be cut in turn from the background veneer and replaced with a veneer of suitable grain and shade.

When making up the flowers, careful selection of veneer is vital if you are to achieve the best effect. Fig.1 gives suggestion for the type of veneer and direction of the grain that can be used but you do not have to follow this rigorously. The best approach is to use the 'window' method described previously—this allows you to see the effect of one veneer against another.

A dark figured mahogany is suitable for the reddish-brown falls (the petals which hang down—5 in Fig.1) with a lighter shade veneer for the underside. For the standards (the petals which stand up—7, 8, 9 and 10 in Fig.1) a much lighter blend of veneers can be used—willow, avodire, maple, aspen and canarium are suitable.

Trace, cut and assemble the flower buds and stems in the manner described above to complete the panel. Now stand back from the work and study the general effect of the design and the selection of veneers. It is a simple matter at this stage to replace something that isn't quite right aesthetically. Examine the panel for faulty cutting which, at this stage, can easily be

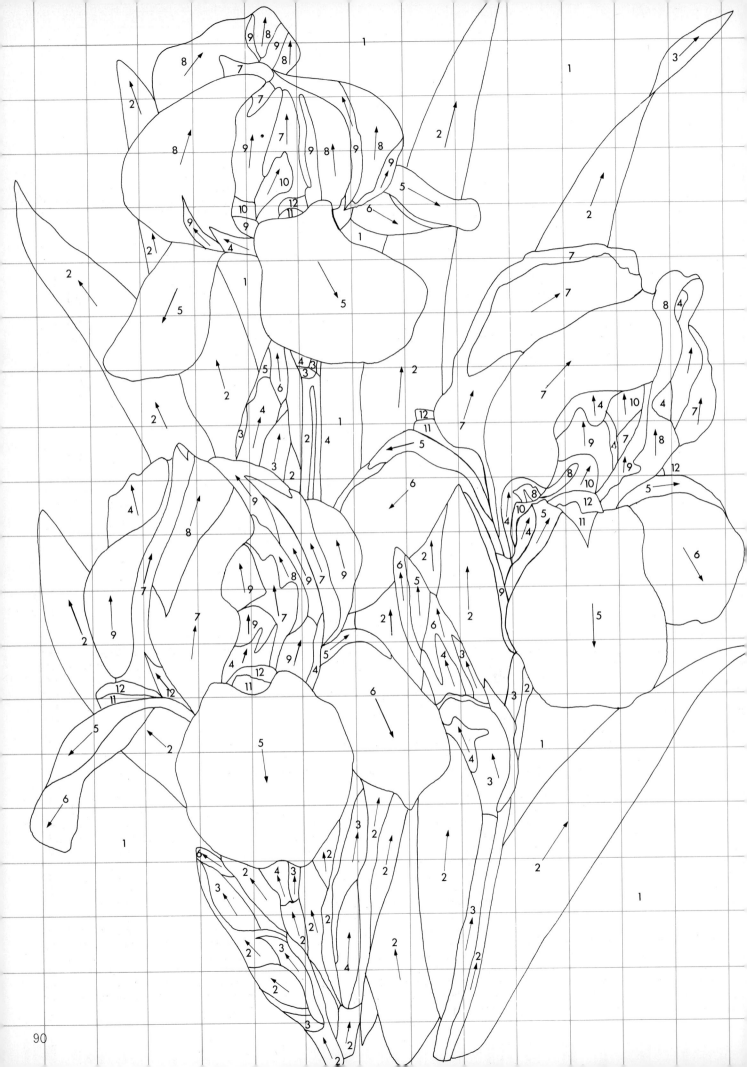

90

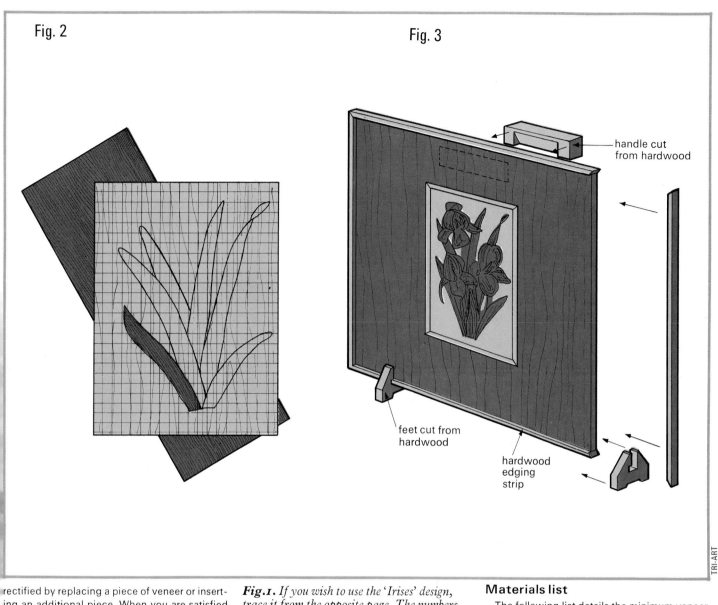

Fig. 2

Fig. 3

handle cut
from hardwood

feet cut from
hardwood

hardwood
edging
strip

TRI-ART

rectified by replacing a piece of veneer or inserting an additional piece. When you are satisfied with the panel put it to one side. You can now prepare the groundwork on which the panel will be mounted.

Assembling the firescreen

If you intend to feature the marquetry panel on a firescreen as described here, the size of the groundwork panel will obviously be determined by the size of your fireplace. Plywood or chipboard is ideal and it should be ⅝in. (16mm) or ¾in. (19mm) thick. Since the marquetry panel measures 12in. x 9in. (305mm x 229mm) it will be necessary to have a surround of suitable veneer around it when mounted—a firescreen will usually have to be bigger than this. The veneer surround can either match or contrast with the panel and its appearance will be considerably improved if you include a plain stringer or inlay banding around the panel.

Now prepare the veneers and the marquetry panel for glueing to the front of the firescreen. First trim the panel so that opposite edges are parallel and then tape thin stringers or inlay bandings along these edges. Then tape the surround veneer to the marquetry panel and cover the whole face of the panel with tape. This keeps the assembly together while you remove

Fig.1. If you wish to use the 'Irises' design, trace it from the opposite page. The numbers refer to the different veneers, as given below.
Fig.2. To cut the veneers properly, cut through the graph paper into a sheet of veneer. By doing this an accurate shape is achieved.
Fig.3. The components of the firescreen.

the surplus glue and tape from the back of the panel. Make sure you remove every scrap of glue or tape before you apply the panel to the firescreen.

Apply glue to the panel and take great care to position it correctly on the firescreen. When the glue has dried, clean up the edges of the firescreen with fine glasspaper. Remove the tape carefully from the front of the panel and sand the front of the panel with progressively finer grades of glasspaper and garnet paper, then polish the surface carefully.

The hardwood edging strip can now be applied to the exposed edges of the firescreen, and the hardwood feet and handle screwed in place as shown in Fig.3. The final step is to polish the hardwood fittings to the same finish as the other surfaces.

Your marquetry project is now complete and ready to form the focal point of any room in your home.

Materials list

The following list details the minimum veneer requirement for the marquetry panel 'Irises'. Naturally a larger assortment of veneers would be preferable, as this would give a greater freedom of choice when selecting the most suitable tone and texture of veneer to achieve a desired effect.

Background	1	guatea or light mahogany	12" x 9"
Leaves and stems	2	magnolia	10" x 6"
	3	imbuia	4" x 2"
	4	light mansonia	2" x 2"
Blooms, etc.	5	dark figured mahogany	5" x 3"
	6	bubinga	4" x 3"
	7	avodire	5" x 3"
	8	willow	3" x 3"
	9	canarium	3" x 3"
	10	quilted maple	2" x 2"
	11	light harewood	1" x 1"
	12	movingui	1" x 1"

For the firescreen the following additional materials are required; the quantity depending on the size of the screen :—
Plywood or chipboard for groundwork (⅜" or ¾" thickness), veneer for front and back, hardwood lipping, ¾" x ½". hardwood blocks for feet and handle.

Fig.4. The outline of the leaves is traced from the pattern onto the background veneer.

Fig.5. Once the design has been traced, the shape of the first leaf can be cut.

Fig.6. Using the 'window' in the background veneer as a template, cut the leaf from the sheet of veneer placed underneath.

Fig.7. Once they have been cut, fit three leaves into the background veneer and secure them with tape. Care should be taken not to snap any of the thin veneer sheets.

Fig.8. Now, fit all the other leaves in place onto the background veneer, and trace on the rest of the pattern.

Fig.9. After all the leaves have been fitted into place, the same procedure is followed to fit one of the blooms. Once this has been done, the other blooms can be fixed in the same way without too much difficulty.

Fig.10. The finished panel. A beautifully decorative piece like this does not have to become a firescreen. The same kind of design could easily become an attractive picture, or the centre-piece of any item of furniture.

Pyrography and pokerwork

You may not be very familiar with the word 'pyrography', but if the term 'pokerwork' is mentioned, you'll probably grasp the basic idea behind the technique. Ever since the introduction of a small electric machine, the popularity of pyrography has increased by leaps and bounds. With the aid of this ingenious piece of equipment you'll be able to master the necessary pyrography skills after only a little practice—and produce some striking ornaments to decorate your home.

Machine pyrography is only an advanced form of pokerwork. The art of pokerwork is either used on its own, or in conjunction with the wood engraving technique. Pokerwork has been used for many years in the making of wooden nameplates and the like.

Origins of pokerwork

Primitive pokerwork was—as the name implies—the use of a hot poker, or rod of iron, to burn patterns into the surface of a piece of timber. This art dates back centuries, and, although the equipment has become much

Above. The picture on this attractive plaque was burnt into the wood, using the pyrography machine. Pyrography is a remarkably simple art to master.

more sophisticated, the basic technique is still the same today. It seems to have originated as a peasant art, which was most widely practised in Northern European countries. Many antique examples of this early pokerwork are still to be seen.

Modern pyrography

As mentioned earlier, the basic techniques of pyrography are much the same as those of early pokerwork—only the tools have changed. Where a poker, or rod of iron, used to be employed, a wire pointed 'pencil' is now used. The points are made from lengths of nickel chromium alloy wire, and can be easily formed to provide any shape. Because of this, the possible variation in styles available to you is considerable. The modern pyrography machine has made the art much more simple for the beginner to master. Before going on to discuss the pyrography technique itself, it will be

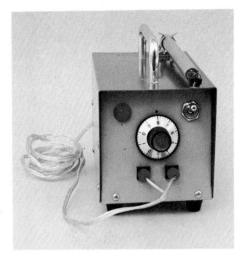

Above. *The pyrography machine itself. It is very easy to operate and comprises a control unit and a 'pencil'. This is connected to the control unit by low voltage cable.*

useful for you to know exactly what the electric pyrography machine consists of.

The pyrography machine

The electric pyrography machine was first introduced some years ago, and has since been perfected to meet the requirements of more sophisticated pokerwork and the special needs of the pyrography artist. The most important advantage of using this machine is that it enables an amateur with little experience to produce some strikingly attractive pieces of pyrographic work. Two main parts make up the machine—the 'pencil' and the control unit.

The *'pencil'* is handled in exactly the same way as an ordinary lead pencil. To ensure cool running, the handle is designed to prevent the points overheating. These points are easily replaceable, and can be formed to almost any shape you may require. Spare points and extra wire are provided with the machine and you can also buy them separately. Pencils can easily be interchanged. Because it plugs directly into the control unit, you'll find it a simple matter to switch to a spare pencil with a different point. This ease of operation greatly increases the versatility of the machine, as you'll be able to switch from one style of burn to another with very little delay.

The heart of the modern pyrography machine is the *control unit*. It is A.C. mains operated. Because of this, very little power is used up. The on/off switch is of the standard toggle design—although type of switch is not important. A useful feature of the control unit is that it is fitted with a pilot light. This enables you to see at a glance whether the machine is switched on or not. To control precisely, and to vary the heat of the point, a knob—calibrated from 1 to 9—is provided. The figures are very clearly marked to reduce the possibility of mistakes. For extra durability the case of the control unit is made of stove enamelled steel. The whole thing rests on soft rubber feet. To minimize the risk of damaging the pencil when it is not in use there is a storage clip fixed to the case of the control unit. One of the best features of the machine is that it is almost completely

Above. To burn a pattern into a piece of timber without causing ugly blobs, the pencil should be moved across the wood firmly—and at an even speed.
Left. A superb example of intricate pyrography work. This portrait of a fox displays great attention to detail. To complete the work, a coat of clear varnish is applied.

safe. Also, there is not enough heat reserve in the point to give a serious burn if touched accidentally.

Replacing the points on the pencil is quite a straightforward job. All you need to do is to loosen the two terminal screws nearest the point. Be careful not to touch the other two screws you'll see there. Remove the old point by gently pulling it out, and replace with a new point. Now, tighten the screws. This should be done carefully so as not to bend the terminal posts.

Basic pokerwork technique

As mentioned above, pokerwork is the scorching of patterns using a pointed tool such as a poker. There is a pokerwork machine available which uses a pointed loop of special wire. This is electrically heated to red heat.

With the aid of this modern method of poker-work, ornamentation and lettering can be placed upon useful wooden objects like spice racks, house nameplates, clock faces and wooden jewellery. Wooden toys can also be decorated and detailed by using the pokerwork technique. Also, it can be employed in the signing of wooden works of art—especially marquetry pictures. Just about any wood can be used, but a light coloured fine grained timber is best of all.

As a beginner you would be well advised to trace your design onto the wood to provide a guide to work from. Alternatively, you could draw the design onto the timber in pencil. This supposes that your piece of wood is smooth enough for this. Birch plywood—sanded very smooth—gives a very good surface to practice on. Try to make the burn as black as possible. If you do this it will lessen the possibility of the pattern fading under strong light. You can work the wire loop to virtually any shape by using pointed pliers to provide a 'brand' for simple repeat decoration. It is for this reason that extra wire is supplied with the machine. When you

95

have completed your piece of pokerwork it is important to seal it against dirt, using a good quality clear varnish.

If you wish you can tint with dye, stain or paint the finished pokerwork. The pokerwork lines will prevent the colours from running uncontrollably. Pokerwork relies on quite deep burns for its effect.

The pyrography technique

The skills involved in pyrography are somewhat more advanced than the comparatively crude pokerwork. A good piece of pyrography work relies for its effect on burning the surface of a panel of timber to various shades of brown to produce a picture. It can also be employed to burn patterns on leather. Many of the designs seen on belts were achieved in this way. The effect is remarkably similar to that of a pen and ink drawing or an engraving. It is capable, however, of more subtle and striking qualities. A great many beautiful works of art have been produced in the pyrography medium. The

early nineteenth century produced a number of interesting examples—notably some of the Pinto collection which are now to be seen in Britain in the Birmingham Museum. These early artists did not possess the benefit of the pyrography machine. They had to make do with the application of a variety of steel tools heated over a charcoal fire. This method was sometimes supplemented by the use of acid or hot silver. You can see that this primitive method was somewhat tricky for all but the most practiced expert. Sometimes light carving with a gouge was employed to heighten the effect, or to create light lines against a dark background. A considerable amount of skill was needed for very fine work because of the cumbersome methods employed. As a result of the modern machine, however, pyrography has become very much easier to master, and is

Below. Pyrography can be put to good use in adding detail to small wooden models, though the simplicity of this example adds to its appeal.

therefore growing rapidly in popularity. Operating the machine is very easy, and you should have learnt the basics after only a little practice.

Using the pyrography machine

Just about the only talent necessary to use the pyrography machine is the ability to draw. The secret is light and even pressure. It is important to begin and end each stroke with the heated point off the wood. If you hesitate during a stroke the heat will cause an unsightly 'blob' on the pattern. The more slowly you move the pencil during a stroke the deeper the burn will be. Heavy pressure should never be used and too much heat will give a fuzzy line. A dull red heat is best for general work. For plain line work, the loop point is most suitable, but for shading you should use a spoon shaped point. To achieve very fine lines you should use the edge of the spoon point. If you want to obtain fine white lines on a burnt background, use a carver's V tool to carve into the white wood beneath.

The best woods

To be able to do pyrography work properly you should choose a suitable timber. Of the woods available, birch, sycamore, holly and lime are recommended. Apart from these, birch ply and veneered boards can be used.

How to make a pyrography picture

Once you have found a suitable board, the first thing you'll need to do is to sand it as smooth as possible using a fine grade glasspaper.

Having made sure that the board is perfectly smooth, you can begin to trace the picture or pattern onto it. First, take a sheet of carbon paper, and lay it—carbon side down—onto your piece of timber. Next, lay a good quality sheet of cartridge paper on top of the carbon paper. The two sheets should be held in place on the wood with the aid of some masking tape. If you intend to draw your picture freehand, begin to sketch it on the cartridge paper in pencil. To make sure that a clear copy appears on your piece of wood choose a pencil with a fairly soft lead to avoid indenting the wood. Should you not feel confident of your ability to draw freehand, you could consider tracing the design. To do this lay the picture you want over the cartridge paper and follow the details in pencil—applying a firm, even pressure. When doing this, it is not necessary to trace in every detail of shading and texture. It is easy to copy the shading straight onto the wood—using the pyrography pencil. Once you have drawn, or traced, the picture you want remove the cartridge and carbon paper from your piece of timber. A clear copy of the picture should be visible on the surface of the wood.

All you need to do now is to follow the lines of the carbon copy. Proceed in the way described earlier in this chapter. Always start and finish each stroke off the wood. Move at an even pace and do not hesitate at mid-stroke.

Having mastered the basic techniques, you can combine pyrography with basic pokerwork to produce some lovely ornaments for your home. The creative satisfaction obtained will make learning the skills involved well worth while.

Wood carvings: designed by nature

Wood carving is an ancient craft, which can be usefully employed to decorate your home. If you look around, you can often find bits of driftwood, and chunks of old tree trunk, lying around on wasteland or beaches. Many of these bits of wood are of an interesting and unusual shape. Using only the basic skills of wood carving, you can, with a little imagination, produce some strikingly original articles with which to decorate your home.

The aim of this kind of wood carving is to exploit and highlight the basic shape of a piece of timber. Many remarkable abstract works can be made by accentuating the contours and knots in pieces of rough timber. This type of work has a very long history—extending at least as far back as the Ancient Britons. It has a number of advantages for the beginner. Only a few simple tools are required. Also, the working of an abstract shape—based on the form of the wood—does not require the same degree of technical skill and training as the carving of more precise works.

Where to find the wood

The timber for this kind of carving can be found almost anywhere. One of the most fruitful hunting grounds are beaches. The more deserted the stretch of coastline the better. Don't go to the popular tourist resorts. All the driftwood will have been removed, along with other debris, to clean up the beaches for the visitors. You'll have more luck if you concentrate on isolated coves and out of the way stretches of coastline.

Look for the larger pieces of timber, rather than small pieces of driftwood. The size of the finished carving will probably be much less than the original piece of wood. The reason for this is explained later in this chapter. You'll need to have your own transport to collect wood from the coast—because of the size and weight of the raw material.

If you don't live within reasonable distance of a suitable stretch of coastline, or deserted beach, there are a number of other places where the right kind of wood can be picked up. Have a look around your locality and take a note of any sites where demolition work is going on. These places often abound with interesting pieces of uprooted tree. Have a word with the site foreman before entering to pick up what you want. You'll need his permission to be on the site in the first place. Also, he'll be able to tell you where some of the more interesting pieces are to be found. Take a spade with you, as you may have to dig the pieces you want out of the mud. For reasons of safety, try not to go on to these sites while work is in progress. After consulting

Right. This striking piece only needed cleaning up and polishing to accentuate the naturally beautiful contours and irregularities of the wood. Note how the outer bark has been stripped away, so that only a little remains to provide a decorative base.

HARRY BUTLER

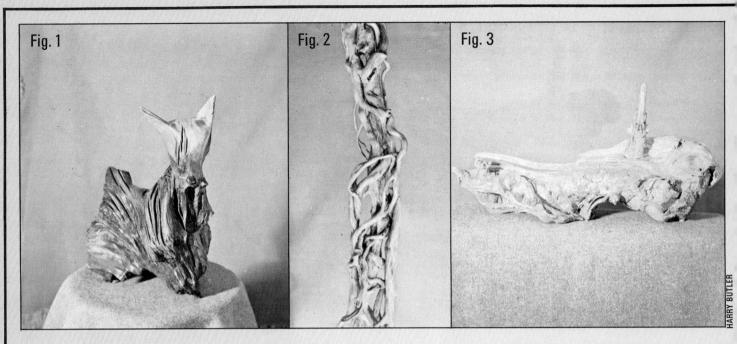

Fig. 1   Fig. 2   Fig. 3

HARRY BUTLER

the site foreman, go to the site and collect what you want while the workers are having a lunch break. This should give you plenty of time to look around.

Another good place to find the right kind of wood is on the banks of rivers and streams. Quite a lot of excellent pieces can be found in these places. Many of them will be half buried in mud, so it's a good idea to take a spade along with you.

Forests, woods—even a small copse—are fertile areas to look for suitable pieces of wood. The roots of trees, long since cut down, are easily found sticking out of the ground. Some spade-work will be necessary to dislodge the root from the earth.

What to look for

When searching for the wood, look for the pieces with more interesting and unusual characteristics. The foundations of some striking carvings can be laid by such things as pieces of well twisted root, or a knotted branch sticking out of a bit of old tree trunk.

The timber you pick up is likely to be in a semi-rotten condition. A lot of the outer surface of the wood will be very soft—due to rotting—and will need to be scraped away with a penknife to get down to the inner 'core' of solid timber. It is for this reason that you should choose the larger pieces of wood. When you find a piece of wood, that you think has possibilities, use a long-bladed penknife to check that the wood is not totally rotten. This is done by driving the knife into the soft outer wood until the blade is stopped by the solid timber beneath. You can assume that the piece is rotten if no solid timber is found by this method.

Some of the best woods for this kind of carving are oak, yew, willow and pine. All have their own special attraction and appeal. For instance, oak roots turns a striking shade of black and grey when semi-rotten. This can look quite attractive in the carving. Another good timber to use is beech—although it's a little harder to come by than the others. The roots of a beech tree are very long indeed, and often

twist and turn in a weirdly attractive way. You'll need to choose a particularly interesting section of beech root—and saw it out. A whole root will be far too long to be of any use.

Drying out the wood

Once you have got the wood home it should be thoroughly washed and rinsed to remove all mud and dirt. Semi-rotten wood that has been lying around for some time is almost certain to be damp—and often quite sodden. Soft 'green' woods are more prone to this than hard woods, and will take several months to dry out properly. A couple of weeks is usually a sufficient drying out period for small pieces of hard wood.

To dry successfully, place the wood in an open shed. Allow as much air as possible to reach the wood—but keep it out of direct sunlight. Never allow wood to dry quickly, because it will invariably split.

Driftwood found on a beach requires special care because it will be saturated with salt from the sea water. The salt crystals in the wood will retain moisture and not only continue the rotting process, but also make it impossible to apply a varnish or wax without an unsightly 'bloom' appearing underneath the coating.

Salt must be leached from wood by immersing the piece in fresh water for as long as possible—a couple of months is not too long for a large piece—with frequent changes of water. After this, the wood should be allowed to dry out slowly by laying damp material such as sacking over it for a week or so, then placing in a well ventilated place until thoroughly dry.

Tools

The tools you'll need for this type of carving will largely depend on the particular shape of timber you are working on. Some pieces are so striking, in themselves, that they require no more than tidying up with a light sanding down before polishing. On the other hand, some pieces need a great deal of shaping before the form of the finished carving emerges.

If you intend to take up this type of carving seriously, you can buy a kit of carving tools. These kits offer a vast array of tools. However,

only a few pieces of equipment are essential when you're just starting. To begin carving you'll need a flat gouge and mallet, penknives of various shapes, and sizes, a number of small riffler files, a range of different grades of glasspaper and a couple of wood carving gouges. All these basic tools can be obtained at your local DIY dealer or artists' equipment shop. On the other hand, you might find a penknife and some glasspaper quite sufficient.

The carving technique

To do this kind of carving you need a certain amount of patience and a fertile imagination. Sometimes a piece of wood will have an obvious and immediate appeal. If you intend your carving to represent a particular subject, beware of being carried away by your own first impressions. The features of the timber that appear to you to have a clear resemblance to the subject in mind, may not be so obviously similar to somebody else. A certain amount of work will be needed to accentuate the relevant features of the carving.

If you are carving an abstract work, close attention to detail will not be as essential.

Whatever the type of carving you intend to make, semi-rotten timber will need to have the rotten layers of wood removed. This can be easily stripped away with an ordinary penknife. By doing this you should reach the inner 'core' of solid timber. Where pieces of wood, which are not affected by rot, are concerned you will have to remove the bark before starting the carving. Use a flat gouge and a mallet for the job. Remove the bark a bit at a time. Hold the gouge hard against the bark and tap the wooden gouge handle lightly with the mallet until the surface of the bark loosens and cracks. Don't hit the gouge too hard, as there is a danger of splintering the wood.

The timber should now be given a thorough sanding down—starting with a coarse grade of glasspaper and finishing off with a very fine grade to remove any rough edges and small splinters. Having done this, give the timber a wipe down with a duster to get rid of any dirt and particles of sand from the glasspaper.

The timber should now be ready for carving. In itself, the carving is quite a straightforward operation. All that is really required is patience and care. Take a carving gouge and—moving with the grain—begin to work the shape of the carving. Remove only a little wood at a time. This will be less tiring than trying to cut away large chunks of timber in one go, and the gouge won't get blunt as quickly. It is important to cut with the grain as the colour and texture of the timber will be brought out much more effectively. Also, if you try to carve against the grain you could easily splinter the wood. For cleaning out and working awkward corners in the carving, use a riffler file of the appropriate size.

Very often, while carving, you will come across a feature in the timber that was not visible in its rough state. This could be a dis-colouration of the wood, or a deformity like a cavity. Many of these unusual features can be very attractive—so much so that you may want to alter the shape of your carving to accentuate this special feature.

Once you have worked the shape of your carving you may want to smooth off some of the rough edges. Give the carving a thorough sanding down with a coarse grade glasspaper. This should be followed by a sanding down with a fine grade glasspaper. Be careful to sand well into any crevices and folds in the carving. Wipe all dirt and particles of glasspaper off the carving with a soft duster.

Finishing

Your carving should now be ready for finishing. This can either be done by polishing, or painting the carving. What method you choose will depend on the nature of the carving. If the grain and texture of the wood are central to the beauty of the carving it will be better to polish it to accentuate these features. On the other hand, if the appeal of your carving depends upon a striking shape, it may be better to paint it.

For polishing you could use a good wax polish. However, for best results you should make your own polish out of a mixture of bees-wax and turpentine. Mix the beeswax and turpentine together, adding turpentine until the mixture is the consistency of syrup. The polish should be liberally applied with a polishing wad. Bring out the shine by rubbing the polish well into the timber with a clean, soft duster.

If you decide it would be a good idea to paint your carving, use a plastic based paint like acrylic. This spreads very evenly, and is easy to apply. To cover your carving successfully use acrylic spray paints. If you wish to use another colour in crevices, and other areas of the carving, it can be brushed on. The advantage of acrylic paint is that it needs no preparation, and is very easy to apply. Its particular advantage, in any creative work, is that it is colour fast.

Mounting

Now that your carving is finished you will want to mount it so that its beauty is shown off to the best possible advantage. There are a number of ways to do this. Probably the most simple is to mount it on an ordinary table covered with green baize. A very effective mounting technique is to place your carving on a large, uncarved piece of wood of the same type as the carving. Alternatively, make the mounting part of the work, and carve it in the same way as the original carving. A really effective mounting technique is to buy a carving screw. This screws into the base of the carving and enables it to rotate on its own axis. Fixing instructions are supplied by the manu-facturer and should be followed closely.

Take a look around your area. You'll almost certainly find many pieces of timber. These could become beautiful decorative carvings.

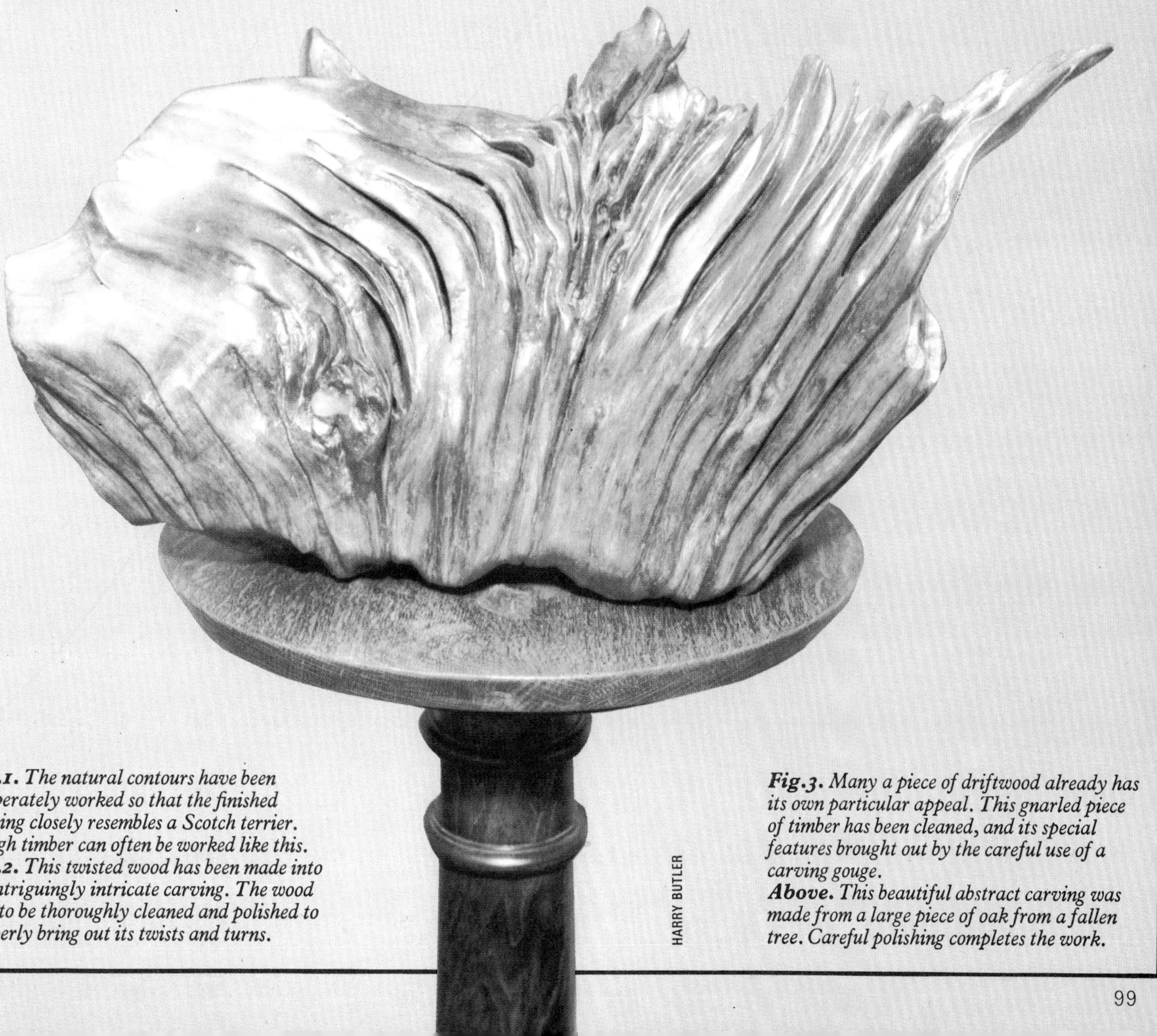

Fig.1. The natural contours have been deliberately worked so that the finished carving closely resembles a Scotch terrier. Rough timber can often be worked like this.
Fig.2. This twisted wood has been made into an intriguingly intricate carving. The wood had to be thoroughly cleaned and polished to properly bring out its twists and turns.

HARRY BUTLER

Fig.3. Many a piece of driftwood already has its own particular appeal. This gnarled piece of timber has been cleaned, and its special features brought out by the careful use of a carving gouge.
Above. This beautiful abstract carving was made from a large piece of oak from a fallen tree. Careful polishing completes the work.

Above. *Papier mâché work was very popular during the Victorian period. This glove box is a fine example of the kind of work produced.*

Decorate with papier mâché

Most people have worked with papier mâché in their schooldays. Since then, it is more than likely that they've completely forgotten about it. However, you can make many useful and decorative objects from papier mâché, and once you have mastered the basic skills your ingenuity and imagination can produce some very rewarding projects. The ability to work with papier mâché will prove a practical and money saving craft.

As long as paper making has existed—2,000 years at least—so has the art of working in papier mâché. The use of papier mâché originated with the Chinese. Not only did they make ornaments and small items of furniture,

they made breast plates and sometimes complete suits of 'armour' as well.

In Britain, articles made from papier mâché enjoyed great popularity in the eighteenth and nineteenth centuries. Between about 1760 and 1812 the most prominent artist working in papier mâché was Henry Clay. Later on papier mâché work was taken over commercially. The most notable manufacturers were Jennens and Betteridge of Birmingham. They became 'Makers to the Queen'.

Over the centuries the basic processes involved in papier mâché work have hardly changed at all. Nowadays however, materials exist that can make your early attempts at papier mâché both more attractive and more resilient. The use of a finishing material like epoxy resin, combined with one of the many synthetic

adhesives available today, will make your finished article extremely tough and hard wearing. If your finished article is finished in epoxy resin it will be protected against damage from acid, water, soil and alcohol stains. Apart from this it will be almost unbreakable. Epoxy resin is absorbed into the paper, and therefore toughens it.

The papier mâché process

Papier mâché is a versatile medium to work in, and you'll find it an ideal material for all sorts of items—provided you are prepared to go to a little trouble to develop its potential. Today's modern materials have speeded up the basic papier mâché process. This means that, after a little bit of practice, you will be limited only by time and imagination in finding useful things to make. A good way of becoming familiar with the basic principles is to make a few simple little things first. Such objects as nut bowls, sweet dishes and ash trays are good for the beginner. Once you have perfected the basic techniques in these small items, you will be able to move on to more ambitious schemes as confidence in your abilities encourages you to experiment more.

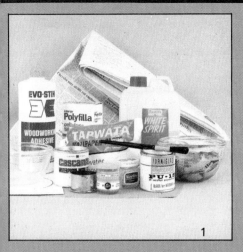

1

2

3

4

5

6

7

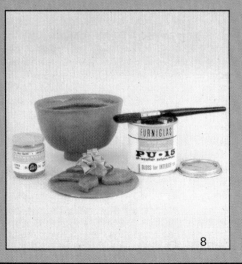

8

9

You don't need a special type of paper for making papier mâché. In fact, old newspapers are the best raw material of all—being thin, absorbent and easily torn. All papers have a grain and can be easily torn into strips if you tear with the grain. Besides newspaper, any unglazed paper—such as wrapping paper, rough sugar paper or tissue paper—can be used to make papier mâché. What paper you use will largely depend on the nature of the article to be made. Shiny and glazed papers are not suitable for papier mâché work. The paper should always be torn—not cut. Torn paper has 'feather' edges, which makes for imperceptible overlaps, whereas cut edges produces sharp ridges.

Glues and pastes

Ordinary wallpaper pastes produce good results when used in papier mâché work. Diluted PVA is excellent if you want to obtain a tough, waterproof, leathery and somewhat pliable result. Ordinary flour paste is the most commonly used adhesive for papier mâché work, and is perfectly adequate for most projects. To make up the paste all you have to do is to take approximately one tea cup full of plain flour. Next, stir in cold water until a thick, creamy paste is obtained. Stir continuously, while adding the water, to prevent lumps forming. Having done this, add boiling water, again stirring continuously until the paste thickens. An alternative to this method is to cook the solution in a tin placed inside a saucepan of water until the paste becomes clear. At this stage add a teaspoon full of powdered alum to improve the adhesive quality of the paste. To prevent fungus or mould developing on the surface of the paste add a half teaspoon full of

Figs. 1 to 9 previous page. 1 shows the basic materials for making the papier mâché bowl. It is best to have all the materials at hand before starting work. 2. Here the shape of the bowl is moulded by shaping the wet paper over a glass bowl. 3. A metal napkin ring is used to shape the base of the bowl. 4. The lid of the bowl is easily made by working the paper over a cut-out cardboard disc. 5. Once the basic form of the bowl, base and lid have been moulded the whole should be given a coating of cellulose filler. After this has dried, the bowl should be given a thorough sanding down with a wet and dry fine grade glasspaper. 6. The 'lip' on the inside of the bowl is made by working the paper over a length of cord. 7. The rose on the lid of the bowl is easily made by carefully crumpling and folding the wet paper until a pleasingly realistic form is produced. The leaves should be made from pulped paper. Once the basic shape has been made, a coating of cellulose filler should be applied. 8. When the bowl has been made, the bowl should be painted in a good quality polyurethane paint. At least two coats should be applied. After the first coat has dried the surface should be given a light sanding down with a fine grade glasspaper before the second coat is applied. 9. The finished job—an attractive and useful bowl. This bowl can be put to good use for storing knick-knacks.

oil of wintergreen. You should now have over a litre of paste. Store it in a refrigerator until you need it. If you wish to make an object with a rigid, even flat surface, a table spoon of powdered waterproof glue should be whisked into the paste after it has been made.

Paper and materials

If you wish to make something that has to be very strong, thin and light—like a lampshade, or a tray—use alternate layers of tissue paper and butter muslin, mull or bandage scrim, instead of just plain newspaper.

Should a very smooth finishing coat be required use a cellulose or plaster filler mixed with diluted PVA adhesive. To finish, rub down once with a piece of wet fine grade glasspaper, and once with a dry piece.

As a modelling material, pulped paper or 'mash' is excellent. You can get this in packs of dehydrated fibrous cellulose. It needs only to be mixed with water to be ready for use. Ready-made pulp, with the adhesive already mixed into it, is also available. You'll find that any kind of paper takes some time and effort to pulp by hand. First it has to be torn up as small as possible. Then it needs to be pounded into a pulpy mass. Making your own pulped paper will be much easier if you have an electric food mixer—as the pulping can then be done fairly rapidly, and an even, lump-free pulp will be the result. If you don't have your own electric food mixer place the shredded paper into a bucket of water. After the paper has been in the water for three or four days pound it thoroughly until a satisfactory pulp is achieved. Such objects as egg cartons and fruit packing trays are good for pulping. Soft toilet paper is an excellent material for finely detailed modelling.

To finish off making the pulp you should boil the pounded paper in the top of a double cooker. The disintegrated paper is then put into a cloth, a bit at a time, and squeezed almost dry. Having done this, mix in the paste until the pulp becomes tacky. You should now boil the pulp for a further period so that the mixture becomes a uniform whole. This second boiling also reduces the moisture content and makes the papier mâché stiffer and more plastic.

Free sculptural forms can be easily fashioned from paper, but you should bear in mind that wet paper work, in any thickness, is very heavy and needs some kind of support. This can take the form of an armature, which remains in the finished piece as a kind of skeleton, or, as a mould on which you form the shape. To make an armature you can use wood strip, dowel or, better still, cheese wire or chicken wire. Polythene sheeting and aluminium foil are useful in papier mâché work as they can be used to line or cover the object, and acts as a very effective separating layer. You can use all manner of cord, string, rope and netting for reinforcing and texturing the papier mâché.

Balloons are a useful raw material for moulds, and can be used to work the shapes of objects such as bowls, hats, masks and lamp shades. When you have finished working the basic shape of the object you should cut and file down any exposed rough edges. Alternatively, the edges should be removed with fine toothed saw, and bound over with a criss-crossed layer

of paper strips—well worked in so that they are almost invisible on the finished object.

Papier mâché can be used as a very effective sound proofing material. For this you should use layers of fruit packing trays, with a slight reinforcing overlay. Apart from providing excellent sound proofing for a play room, music or recording room, this will prove very attractive if done properly.

Tools

You will need very few tools for papier mâché work, providing the metal is still smooth, an old tablespoon serves well for squeezing out excess paste, and also makes a very good modelling tool. Rubbing and smoothing the papier mâché can be done with hands and fingers only. You'll find a pair of rubber gloves useful. When working with some materials they are essential.

Drying

For best results it is important that the object you make is properly dried. Drying ensures that it is well hardened. For effective drying any dry, warm atmosphere will be sufficient. The most effective means of drying papier mâché work is to place it in an oven on *low* heat. You can either dry the finished object until it is perfectly hard, or bake every four layers or so—making sure so that every layer is pasted. Don't model the pulp too thickly at one go. If you follow these brief instructions the object you are making will have a strong internal core which will improve its strength.

Finishing

A papier mâché object can be finished and decorated in a wide variety of methods and materials. This will depend on the use to which the object is to be put, as well as your own personal tastes. Rubbed down cellulose lacquers give a smooth, glossy finish—similar to that on a body of a new car. Household paints and varnishes can all be used on certain objects. If you want a clear coat to protect the decoration beneath from water, use an epoxy or polyester resin. These resins should be applied according to the particular manufacturer's instructions. The degree of preparation and care needed to finish your papier mâché object depends on the particular product you use, as well as the amount of care required to do full justice to any pattern you may choose.

In the eighteenth and nineteenth centuries artists of the calibre of Henry Clay, specialising in papier mâché work, would use about fifteen finishing coats to produce their beautiful products. Nowadays however, technological advance has brought forth many finishing materials which make this extreme care unnecessary to achieve good results.

Papier mâché is still widely used on a commercial scale. Many objects are made of undecorated papier mâché. These include backs for television sets, binders, folders, portfolios as well as stereotype moulds used by printers and picture and mirror frames. Some toys, like dolls and scenery for electric train sets, are still manufactured in papier mâché—although it has been largely replaced by plastic. Finally, hardboard is made by the same process as papier mâché.

Above. Many excellent specimens for brass rubbing can be found in old churches. This one is set into the flagstones of the old floor.

Brass rubbing

Rubbings of monumental brasses not only provide an interesting source of historical research, but are an unusual form of wall decoration too. Rubbings, while embracing an exciting art form, cost very little, and may also afford many hours of pleasure in both the discovery and the copying of a particular or rare brass—or even other items such as embossed Victorian coal-hole covers.

Examples of incised and engraved stone remain from all the great civilizations, but in most cases they show signs of wear and good examples are hard to find. Beautifully cut inscriptions, often combined with figures in low relief, may be found on Egyptian and Babylonian tombs and statues. The Romans were the first to inset bronze letters into stone, and they also engraved sheets of bronze, though these were rarely used on tombs.

Development of monumental brasses

Early mediaeval stone coffins frequently had crosses, and even simple inscriptions, incised into the lid and later still these were further decorated with simple representations of the deceased. Around the beginning of the 13th century these incisions were strengthened by inserting brass or bronze letters and symbols into the stone.

The earliest recorded brass in England is that of Simon de Beauchamp in St Paul's Church, Bedford. Unfortunately this no longer exists and is known only from early records. The earliest surviving British brass is an inscription in Lincoln Minster dated 1272.

Another development in brass memorials consisted of casting large sheets of brass or, strictly, 'latten' (an alloy of copper, zinc and lead), from

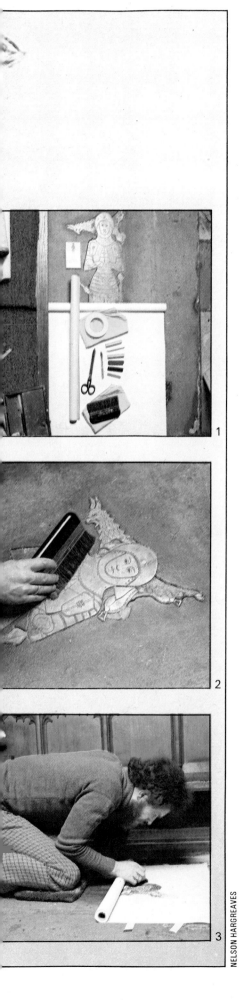

Fig.1. The basic brass rubbing tools— including dusters, wax crayons, paper, and scissors. A wallpapering brush is also useful for cleaning dust from the design.
Fig.2. First, clean the design, using the brush followed by a soft duster.
Fig.3. Having stuck the paper over the design with masking tape, begin to create the rubbing by hard even strokes over the design.
Main photograph. The rubbing begins to emerge. Notice the fine detail that a good brass rubbing will reveal.

a rectangular mould, and then beating them out to the required shape. This was then engraved with intricate designs usually depicting the tomb's occupants, together with an inscription and sometimes a list of subscribers to the memorial. The incisions were sometimes decorated with coloured waxes and enamels, but in most cases these embellishments have long ago worn away. The engraved brass was then set into a stone slab (usually Purbeck marble, which is a high grade limestone, or slate) and held in place with black pitch and metal rivets.

The oldest surviving brass of this type is at Verden near Hanover. The oldest British example is that of Sir John d'Abernoun, dated 1277, at Stoke d'Abernon near Cobham in Surrey. This brass, as are most of the early examples, is deeply engraved and is a fine example of the work of this period.

Brasses became popular because they were not only cheaper and easier to make than the great stone tombs with carved life-size effigies, but a lot harder wearing than stone or alabaster.

Brasses were laid down in Britain primarily between about 1250 and 1650. Although many have suffered the ravages of the Reformation, war, and vandalism, about 8,000 still exist, some in musuems but mostly in churches, large and small, all over the country. They vary enormously from simple letters and symbols to the magnificent examples of engraving produced from 1327 to 1399. These were often canopied with architectural designs done in the finest detail.

Brasses depicted many things, varying from crosses and croziers to fine illustrations of the tomb's occupants, though these were sometimes rather macabre representations of shrouded skeletons. Mostly brasses were erected by and for the clergy, the nobility, and the rich merchants who frequently embellished their tombs with symbols and early trade marks.

Brasses illustrating developments in the history of weapons, costume and heraldry often aid the discovery of the tomb's occupant.

Making a rubbing

Before taking a rubbing you must obtain permission from the vicar or verger of the church, who may ask for a fee. Generally the fee is moderate and there are often reductions for students and young people. Often an agreement has to be signed to the effect that the rubbings will not be used for commercial purposes or profit.

Once permission has been granted, get to the church in good time to find the brass. Some brasses are hidden under carpets or furniture, or may have been relaid in the vestry, in a wall

or roof, or even on the back of a door or organ manual. A guide book may help in the search.

Materials for rubbing are cheap and can be obtained from most art and crafts shops. The paper should be opaque, matt and strong (architects' detail paper is excellent). Coloured papers, including silver and gold, specially prepared for rubbing, are also obtainable. The latter is mostly available in rolls 30 inches (762mm) wide whereas the former is available, with obvious advantages, up to 80 inches (2032mm) wide.

Rubbing wax in the form of specially prepared crayons, such as colorex or Finart sticks, is available in black, white, brown, gold, bronze and silver. The traditional heelball, a compound of beeswax, tallow and colouring, usually black or brown, is available from art shops and cobblers, but the best is prepared specially. Other requisites are masking tape for holding the paper in place, a pair of scissors to cut the paper and tape, two soft dusters, one for cleaning the brass and the other for polishing the finished rubbing, and a soft-bristled nail or clothes brush, also for cleaning the brass.

The brass must first be closely inspected and cleaned with the soft brush and a lint-free duster. Great care should be taken over this, as even a tiny speck of grit can cause a rubbing to tear. Before commencing to rub, a detailed study of the brass should be made. This is in order to establish where the various details are situated and ensure that no important ones are omitted. With complex examples it is well worth making a detailed sketch, but frequently the church will have postcard-photographs for sale which are best used if available.

If the stone around the brass is firm and hard the paper may be rolled out and held in place with pieces of tape. Double-sided Sellotape may be more convenient, but as it is inclined to stain porous stone some churches will not allow it to be used. Should the surrounding masonry be crumbly or badly chipped, then weights may be used. If the brass is situated in a flakey or crumbly wall an assistant will be needed to hold the paper in place. A wooden batten holding the paper along its top edge will be helpful.

Many beginners are disappointed with their first results. Hard, *even* rubbing is the only answer to this. The heelball or crayon should be blunt, since a sharp point would tear the paper, and applied with firm strokes. The rubbing may be done in any direction and oblique, vertical or horizontal movements are all equally acceptable. The important point is that the work must be unhurried and carried out systematically to avoid uneven stretching of the paper. Another point to remember is that heelball becomes very hard when cold, so it is a good idea to soften it slightly by polishing it with a duster until it shines.

It is best to start from the centre of the piece and work outwards, taking care not to go on to the stone round the edges of the metal as this will spoil the outline, One thing to avoid is going off the paper altogether, as this will mark the stonework. Special care should be taken with rivets as these, if not noted before hand, can quite easily tear the paper. If the paper is torn, it can be mended after the rubbing is finished by sticking a piece of paper over the back with a wallpaper paste. Proprietary adhesive tapes may stain the paper.

When the brass has been rubbed evenly all over, and every detail is clearly shown, the rubbing should be first dusted and then polished with a soft clean cloth. The fixing tapes may then be carefully removed and the rubbing rolled up ready for transportation. Out of courtesy, remember to clean up your rubbish before you leave.

Dabbing and rolling

Alternatives to rubbing are dabbing, or dubbing and rolling. A dabbing is made by placing thin paper, such as tissue, over the brass and then dabbing on a mixture of graphite and oline or linseed oil. The graphite and oil are mixed into a paste and then applied with a pad made from a piece of chamois wrapped round cotton-wool. The pad is dipped into the paste and then, to get an even distribution of colour, is worked out on a piece of card. The pad is then applied with even moderate pressure to the surface of the paper. Although the resulting image is grey and the contrast between black and white less distinct than with rubbings, the light-weight paper provides a good impression of the fine detail of the brass. This method is very good for shallow or intricate engraving or where a very uneven surface is encountered such as on incised stone work.

Rolling, another method using tissue paper, is done by applying lino-printing ink by means of a hard rubber roller. This gives a good image with dense colour but is only suitable where the engraving occurs on a flat surface, unfortunately a rare occurence.

Tinted rubbings

As well as using coloured papers and crayons, a good effect for decoration purposes can be achieved by using thin white rag paper together with a white rubbing crayon. This may sound over-subtle, but when a wash of ink, diluted with distilled water, is applied with a soft brush, the wax image rejects the ink while the unwaxed paper accepts it. With a little ingenuity many pleasing effects can be achieved. To stop the paper cockling, when wet, damp the back and lay it onto a large piece of board; then apply brown sticky paper all round the edge. As the ink dries the paper will stretch out perfectly flat.

Other subjects for rubbings

Although monumental brasses are the most popular subjects for rubbings there are many

Below. *The finished brass rubbing. This type of subject is very popular with brass rubbers and makes a beautiful wall decoration. Other designs can be used, however—such as coins and shields.*

others which may give equal pleasure from a decorative if not scholarly point of view. The Victorian and Edwardian eras produced much decorative cast iron ware, particularly in the form of manhole and coal-hole covers. These may be found let into many pavements wherever urban dwellings from these periods still exist. Contemporary builders, though inclined towards long streets, of identical terraced houses, seem to have taken delight in installing coal hole covers with different designs for every few houses.

Other subjects include horse brasses, inscription on bells, slate tomb-stones, embossed paper, leaves, bark and modern relief-patterned plastics. All may be used in many ways to the decorative advantage of a home. The name plates on railway locomotives appeal to some people.

Rubbings as decor

For those who wish to make rubbings purely for decorative purposes, there are many ways in which they might be displayed to advantage. The simplest is to mount the rubbing on to a stouter paper or fine scrim. A modern wallpaper adhesive such as Polycell is suitable for this. Wooden $\frac{1}{2}$in. dowel rods may then be attached to the top and bottom of the picture, and the whole suspended from a wall by means of coloured silk cotton trimming cord. Tassles may also be used as an attractive finishing touch.

Alternatively, the rubbing may be mounted directly on to a wall or on panels set off the wall by means of light battens. Again, wallpaper adhesive is used but it is advisable to use it very sparingly as the rubbing could quite easily wrinkle or tear if it is made too wet. A coat of wallpaper sealer such as Fend is well worth applying as this will enable the picture to be periodically wiped over with a damp cloth.

Another effective use, particularly of dabbings, is to sandwich the picture between two sheets of glass which, when placed in a light box or room divider, can give a most attractive stained and etched glass effect. This is particularly true where coloured inks have been applied to the basic rubbing.

As well as using the rubbings as decorations in themselves, it is possible to use them purely as artwork to be transferred by etching, or simple silk screen process on to glass, fabrics or paper. This will produce an original wallpaper or curtain fabric.

Silk screen printing

Silk screen printing is a craft that is basically very easy to master and yet enables you to produce designs of great complexity. Although this chapter deals primarily with printing on paper, using varying techniques, all kinds of materials can be used.

Below. Silk screen printing is a sophisticated form of stencil printing. With practice, it can be used to produce designs of great subtlety.

Silk screen printing is only one of a number of printing techniques which can be used within the home. Although it is slightly more complex to execute than the other methods, it also lacks the restrictions of simpler methods, thus giving a greater freedom of design and allowing for more intricate and subtle patterns to be worked.

Equipment and materials

You will need a printing frame made out of a high quality timber, measuring approximately 2½in. (63mm) x 1½in. (38mm), which can be purchased from most craft shops. If a large flat surface, on which to print is not available, it is worthwhile to invest in a printing bench. Silk screen printing inks are available in a wide variety of colours from silk screen printing suppliers, and the best applicator for forcing the pigment through the fabric mesh is a squeegee—a wooden handle with a stiff rubber or polythene blade attached. The blade must be kept square and straight by frequent rubbing over a sheet of fine glasspaper.

The best materials for making the screen itself are organdie, bolting silk or nylon, all available from artists' suppliers. Organdie is the cheapest; but nylon is available in several grades of mesh and, while more expensive, can be used more than once and is better for long runs.

There is a wide choice of masking materials, but for masking the edge of the screen—which has to be done at the beginning of the process—gummed brown paper, in rolls 4in. wide, is best. The most common materials for masking the design are shellac flakes and shellac paper. The former should be mixed with equal parts of methylated spirits and is the best masking material. Shellac paper consists of a thin coat of shellac on a backing paper. Gouache or poster paint may be used in conjunction with oil-bound inks and you can even use newsprint to block out the patterns.

Finally you'll need a sheet of glass, a palette knife, an assortment of old spoons for mixing the paint and rags for cleaning the screen.

Fitting the screen

Stretch the fabric over the frame and hold it in place by means of drawing pins or staples. Small pieces of thin cord should be placed between these and the silk for easy removal and to save damage to the material. It is important that the material be stretched drum-tight without any snags and this can only be done if the stretching is done evenly; to this end, the fixing should be carried out in the order shown on page 110. Try to keep the warp and weft running parallel to the frame. The number of pins or staples needed will depend upon the size of frame but they should be spaced ½in. apart.

When using silk or organdie the final tightening is done by moistening the fabric when in position; as it dries, it will stretch tight. Take care, in the first place, not to stretch the material too tight since it may split when moistened.

Masking the design

Once stretched, the screen must be masked round the edges. For this use gum strip. Wet the gum with a sponge and lay it on the underside

Above. *The stencil consists of a screen stretched over a frame, with masking material attached. Complex designs are best cut from a coating of lacquer or shellac.*

Below. *Registering the design on the paper. The first application is registered by careful measurement. All subsequent registration is done with the help of a sheet of acetate.*

Above. *Small quantities of silk screen ink are applied to the masking tape along one side of the screen. The tape acts as a reservoir for the ink during the printing process.*

Below. *A squeegee is the best tool for forcing the ink through the screen. It must be held at an angle of 45 degrees, and dragged firmly across the screen from the reservoir.*

of the screen, masking out all but the area filled by the design. This area of masking not only reduces the frame to the required size, but also acts as a reservoir for the ink.

Making a stencil

If oil-bound inks are being used, gouache or poster paint, applied by brush, may be used to seal the silk. This not only gives a free form of pattern, but has the added advantage of being water soluble. They may therefore be washed off and the screen reused. Shellac flakes dissolved in equal parts of methylated spirit can be applied in the same way as gouache.

If you wish to use either of these two methods of blocking the screen but, at the same time, work from a previously drawn design, first ink in the design on tracing paper with Indian ink and fix the tracing to the underside of the screen with tape. Next, stand or support the frame in such a way that a strong light may be shone through the tracing and the screen. The image should then become faintly apparent, enabling a stencil to be painted. Remember that it is the unpainted areas that will be printed.

A simple stencil may be cut from thin paper (news print will do). This is then fixed to the underside of the screen with several small strips of gum. When the first print is made the ink will serve to hold the stencil in place.

If complex designs are required then lacquer or shellac stencil films, such as 'Profilm', can be used. This consists of a lamination of shellac on paper. The design is transferred to the shellac and then carefully cut out with a scalpel or sharp trimming knife. Only the shellac is cut and the printing area is lifted off and discarded. Once the design is prepared the sheet is placed, with the shellac to the silk, on the underside of the frame. A thin sheet of tissue paper is then placed on the top side of the silk and a gentle heat is applied to this with an iron. This process will fix the shellac to the screen and the backing sheet may then be removed. After gum tape has been stuck round the edges of the stencil, printing may commence.

Registering the screen

The first colour can be registered by careful measurement, but the subsequent colours should first be printed onto a sheet of clear acetate which has been fixed to the base of the frame with tape. This done, a first colour print can be slid underneath the acetate and registration marks set down with masking tape.

Printing

Once the frame is set up, apply a small amount of ink across the right-hand reservoir of masking tape. The squeegee is then placed behind the ink, at an angle of 45° to the table, and dragged to the opposite end of the frame and back again to its starting point. As the squeegee crosses the silk it forces a little ink through any unsealed mesh onto the paper placed below. This squeegee technique will take some getting used to, so practise with different ink qualities and thicknesses before starting to print.

Making photographic stencils

Photographic stencils, though more complex

Above. *The finished product. The colours and design of the print should be chosen to blend with the surrounding decor.*
Below. *This sketch is a rough guide to fitting the screen onto the frame. The screen should be tightened in the order shown, to avoid snags and tears.*

to make than the stencils previously described, do have the advantage of producing a greater degree of subtlety and finesse in the finished print. Half-tones may be easily achieved by means of breaking areas of shade into graduated dots or lines.

Photographic screen manufacture can be extremely sophisticated, needing full darkroom facilities. The process described here needs none of these and is well within the capabilities of most people.

Making a positive

The first task in making a photographic screen is to make a film positive. Take a sheet of translucent, coated polyester film such as 'Kodatrace' or 'Permatrace', and place it over your full-sized design. The film should be the same size as the screen. The design may now be transferred onto the film by means of a photo-opaque paint (Indian ink is not dense enough for this), applied with a fine sable artist's brush. It is important that the paint is evenly applied.

Preparing the screen

Although a dark room is useful it is not essential. All that is required is a light-proof cupboard, or drawer, big enough to hold the screens while they dry. Careful application of black electrical tape and blankets will ensure total exclusion of light.

A solution of gelatine should be melted down in a domestic cooking steamer. One saucepan placed inside another, water-filled saucepan is quite adequate, but ensure that the gelatine is not exposed to direct heat otherwise it will burn and thereby loose its gluey texture.

Apply the gelatine solution, with a soft varnish brush, to the screen fabric. Cover the entire surface evenly.

When the screen is absolutely dry, brush a solution of potassium dichromate or ammonium bichromate over the screen. This must be done quickly, since the screen becomes photo-sensitive as soon as the chemical is applied, and, if possible, work in a cool atmosphere to prolong the drying process. The frame may now be put into dark storage until it is dry; ideally this should take from two to fourteen hours.

The next task is to transfer the positive image onto the screen and thereby produce a negative image. For this three items will be needed: a sheet of glass slightly larger than the screen, a length of rubber hose to wash down the screen and a screen support-board cut to fit inside the screen frame.

Arrange the support-board on some battens and place the screen over it in such a way that the weight of the screen is evenly spread.

Next fix the film positive to the sheet of glass with masking tape and place the whole, paint side down, onto the prepared, light-sensitive screen. These preparations should be carried out in subdued light. When the film positive is correctly positioned the screen may be exposed to light. The length of exposure will depend on light intensity but will be complete when the chemical on the screen turns from a pinky orange colour to deep ginger brown. This will take from about three to twelve minutes.

After exposure to light, the exposed areas will have hardened whereas the unexposed areas, covered by the film positive, will remain soft. All that now remains to be done is to wash away, with warm water, the gelatine and dichromate from the unexposed areas of the screen. When the screen is dry it is ready for use.

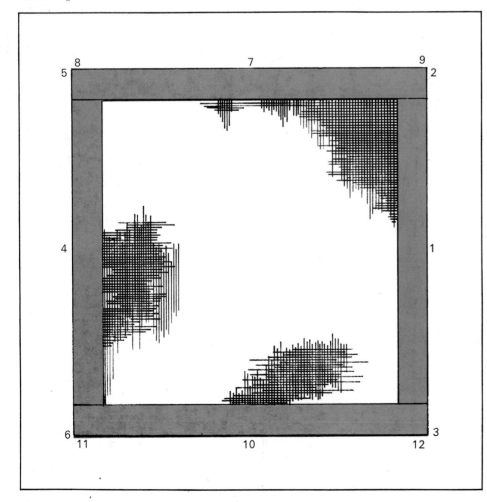

Above. Nail and string pictures can be used to good effect to decorate your home. They can be made to almost any size and shape once the basic technique has been learnt. Also, a nail and string picture can be of a totally abstract design, or made to represent some object.

Nail and string pictures

Making pictures from nails and string is a very simple art to master. Striking abstract pictures can be made in this way, as well as more representational works. Once you have mastered the basic techniques, all that remains is to select suitable colours for the string and the backing board, and beautifully original pictures can be made.

The beauty of nail and string pictures—as a decorative art form—is that they can be made very inexpensively. Also, you do not require the skill and training of the professional artist. Once you have learnt the basic techniques involved you'll be well equipped to make attractive wall designs for your home. All you need is a good imagination and the will to experiment. These qualities will prove particularly valuable when working out the rough pattern for the picture.

The method of making nail and string pictures is very straightforward. In this chapter, simple examples are shown to illustrate the technique. However, there is no reason why nail and string pictures should not be more elaborate. You could use two, or more, strings—running parallel to each other, and forming a double image pattern. Also, you might consider combining the nail and string technique with another art form. Striking designs can be made in this way.

The first step in making nail and string pictures is to consider your choice of the basic materials. These are a backing board, a selection of various types of string and some nails.

The backing board

Your choice of backing board is important. Ideally, it should be made of good quality plywood or blockboard. The best thickness for the board is approximately ½in. (13mm). For the beginner, a panel 2ft x 1ft 6in. (610mm x 460mm) in area is a good size. It doesn't matter if the board is an inch or two larger, or smaller. With this size, you'll be able to work the design without it becoming too intricate—as it would if the board was smaller. Also, the area you'll need to cover will not be too large.

It is not essential that the board be of new wood. As long as the board is not badly damaged—either by old nail holes or scratches and blemishes—an old piece of timber should prove perfectly adequate. In fact, panels from old furniture will have matured and be less likely to warp.

Now that you have chosen a suitable board, the next step is to select the right type of nails to make your picture.

The nails

There are a variety of nails you can use for your picture—both plain and decorative. The best length for the nails is ¾in. (19mm). Also, they should have flat or rounded heads. A head is essential, as it will prevent the string slipping off the nail as you work the pattern. Ordinary panel pins are excellent for nail and string pictures. For that added touch of professionalism you could use decorative brass escutcheon pins in place of ordinary nails. If you decide to use these pins, the ones left over after making the picture could be knocked into the board in clusters so as to complement the design formed by the string.

Having selected the nails for your pictures, you can go on to choosing the type of string you want.

The string

String and cord is available in a wide range of materials, colours and thicknesses. A lot of the string in general use is not suitable, as it is dull and lacks brilliance. Some stationers stock strings in a number of attractive colours, but these tend to be expensive to buy in large quantities. For this reason it is best restricted to small scale work. Probably your best bet would be to visit a gardener's supply shop, or ironmonger. These stock a good variety of coloured strings—usually of the nylon or corraleen type. Many of these strings have a pleasing shine on the surface. This shine can add to the appeal of the picture by reflecting light.

Another excellent material to use is raffia owing to the large choice of colours available. For the more ambitious, sisal cord is a good choice. When dyed, it holds colour well and has an attractive sheen. Also, its hairy texture can produce some very unusual effects. Sisal is only suitable for large scale work—at least the size of a door.

If you have difficulty in finding a sufficient

Fig.1. How to work a circular symmetrical pattern in nail and string.
Fig.2. Here, the method of working a corner section of the pattern is shown. The string is passed from one nail to its opposite number.

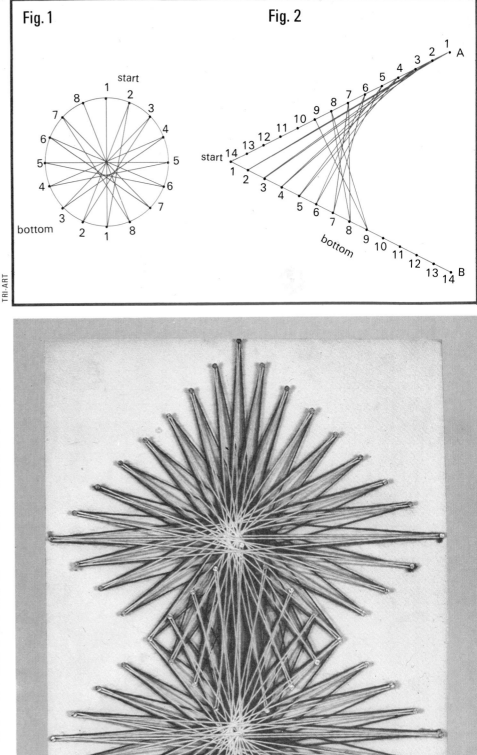

TRI-ART

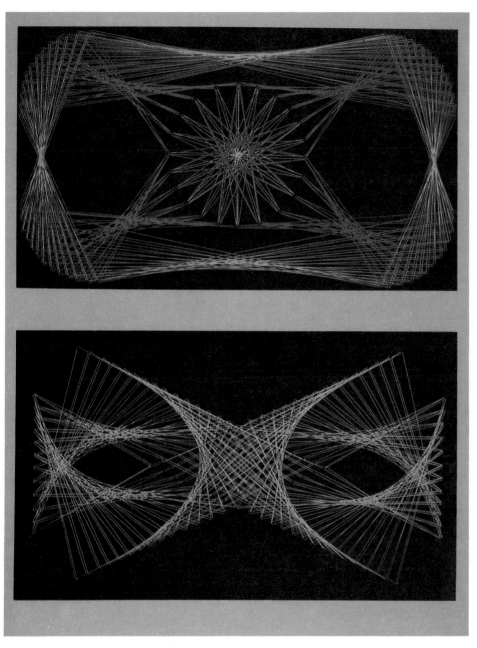

Opposite page. The pattern of this nail and string picture comprises two interlocking diamond shapes.
Above. As can be seen from these two pictures, the design can be in one, two or more colours.

quantity of the right kind of string at a reasonable price, a good alternative is wool. Most wool shops sell odd skeins or balls at a reduced price. The important thing here is to choose colours that contrast well with each other. White wool is very good as it can be used to highlight other colours, and give 'body' to the finished picture.

Whatever kind of string you choose, be sure to get long lengths. The fewer joins there are in any one colour, the better. Make sure that any joins are made at the nail so that they won't show.

Some wool shops stock crochet cotton. This is possibly the best type of 'string' to use. The choice of colours, and range of thicknesses, is excellent. A reel of crochet cotton will supply between 77yds (70.5m) and 150yds (137m), depending on the thickness.

How to make your picture

If you are making your first nail and string picture you could consider buying a kit. These contain all the necessary materials, as well as a planned design. Kits are helpful for learning the basic technique. However, once this has been done you should dispense with the kit. They limit your possibilities, and it is far less satisfying to work to something designed by somebody else than it is to create a picture for yourself.

When you are first learning the basic techniques, concentrate on simple shapes like diamonds, circles and squares. Combine two or more of these shapes—overlapping each other—to create subsidiary designs within the general pattern.

The spacing of the nails is governed by the scale of the picture you wish to make. However, you'll find that, for the most part, a spacing distance of approximately ¾in. (19mm) will prove suitable. If you are working in circles, or squares, space the nails so that you finish with an even number. Where two lines are to cross, this point must be 'picked out' with a single nail.

This is done to retain the correct balance in the finished work. When stringing between two lines of different lengths, make sure that the longer line is an exact multiple of the shorter (e.g. shorter line 10 nails, longer line 20 or 30 nails). This will mean that the string can be taken to more than one nail in the longer line, while being returned to only one nail in the shorter. This method will mean that the design will be balanced when complete.

Before starting on your nail and string picture it is necessary to plan out a design. The first thing to do is to draw a rough sketch on a piece of paper. This can be altered, if necessary, later on, but it will serve as a very good basic guide for the work itself. Or you may prefer to copy an existing pattern from a magazine or book for example. Next draw the pattern more carefully on the unprepared backing board or trace it from the original. After you have marked the positions for the nails—and satisfied yourself that the spacing is correct—pierce the nail positions with the aid of a small bradawl. Once this has been done, the backing board should be given a light sanding down with a fine grade glasspaper. This should remove most of the pencil markings from the previously drawn out pattern.

Once the board has been sanded down, but marks for the nails are still clearly visible, you can move on to choosing the kind of finish you'd like for the board. If you decide to paint the board choose a polyurethane based matt, or eggshell, finish paint. After the paint has been applied, the marks for the nails should still be visible.

Alternatively, you may decide to cover the board with a fabric of some kind. If you wish to do this, use the bradawl to mark the nail holes, after the fabric has been stuck to the board. To fix the fabric to the board use a fabric adhesive such as Copydex. Baize, and coarse weave fabrics like hessian, are excellent materials to cover the backing board.

Now that the backing board has been prepared, the nails can be inserted. They should be hammered in, with a light hammer, and as straight as possible, so that the heads are approximately ¼in. (6mm) above the surface of the board. Once all the nails are firmly in place, all you need to do is to wind the string from one to the other in the way shown in Fig.2.

All that remains now is to mount the finished picture. Fasten two eye-screws to the back of the board and wind a couple of lengths of picture wire between them. The finished work can be hung just like any other picture. Nail and string pictures do not need frames. However, you could consider using a closed-in frame, if only to protect the picture from dust. The front of the picture could be protected by a sheet of non-reflective glass. For larger works this idea will prove impractical, as the cost of the glass would be prohibitive, but the idea could well be applied to smaller pictures.

Siting your picture

Now that the picture is complete, the next problem you'll need to consider is that of finding the best place to put it. Try, as far as possible to put the picture in a position where it will fit in with the general decor. For instance, it would be to add colour and texture in the making of collages and wall murals.

Also, beautiful and original wall designs and table tops can be made by combining nail and string with highly polished pebbles, produced by the method shown in Chapter 6.

If you have a fairly big room, with a plain decor, you could make a large picture to fit in an alcove, or along one wall. This is only a practical idea once you have become practised at the basic technique.

Apart from being displayed alone, the nail and string technique can also be combined with other crafts, often producing striking effects. For example it can be used very successfully

Below. Just about any pattern can be made by using the nail and string technique. Nail and string pictures are never as complicated, or difficult to make, as they appear.

to add colour and texture in the making of collages and wall murals.

Also, beautiful and original wall designs and table tops can be made by combining nail and string with highly polished pebbles, produced by the method shown in Chapter 6.

Once you have mastered the art of making nail and string pictures, you can use the works you produce to add beauty and a touch of originality to your decor.

Engraving
on glass

The art of engraving glass first became widely practised at least as far back as the eighteenth century. Your local museum is more than likely to have some examples of this early work on display. With modern glass engraving tools it should be easy enough to make some splendid and sparkling objects to beautify your home.

Nowadays, there are two different methods of glass engraving—wheel and point work. Wheel engraving is the grinding into the surface of a piece of glass, using small copper discs and an abrasive cutting agent. Point work, on the other hand, depends for its effect upon marking the surface with a point. Early examples of glass

Below. Beautiful decorative panels like the one shown here can be made with the aid of the electric vibro-engraver. Once complete, such panels will bring light and life to the home.

engraving were made using the point work technique.

History of glass engraving

The art of glass engraving reached its peak in the eighteenth century. Without a doubt, the master craftsmen of the art were the Dutch—although, interestingly enough, they preferred to use English glass .Their favourite glass of all was that produced in Newcastle upon Tyne. At about the same time the art of glass engraving began to be taken up by a number of English craftsmen.

Point work engraving

As you can make a distinction between wheel and point work glass engraving, so point work itself can be divided into two styles. Usually, both are combined into any one piece of work.

Although the point is most commonly used to draw lines into the surface of a piece of glass, it can also be used to create thousands of fine dots. These are made by gently striking the surface of the glass with the point. When doing this, you should hold the point like a pencil. Alternatively, you should lightly tap the point into the glass—using a small hammer. Whatever method you choose, the process itself is known as 'stippling'.

In contrast to wheel engraving—which is basically the frosting of the glass—point work relies for its effect on the contrast between light and darkness. A cut might show white against the uncut areas of glass, appearing black.

Glass engraving tools

When you think of engraving glass, the diamond probably springs immediately to mind. For the early glass engravers, this was the only practical method of decorating glass with a point. Today, however, modern technology has stepped in to provide metals of such hardness that glass engraving can be done with a steel point.

About twenty years ago the electric vibro-engraver was introduced. With this, the modern craftsman was equipped with a tool far superior to those used by the artists of two hundred years ago—who produced such superb examples of decorative engraved glass. The principle of glass engraving is the same as it ever was, although much of the effort has been taken over by the modern electric motor.

The best glass to use

Most types of glass can be used for engraving, but some are much better than others. Probably the best type of all is soft lead glass. Of this kind, the most satisfactory to work with is English full lead crystal containing over 30% lead oxide. This type of glass—sometimes known as flint glass—is not only 'gentle' enough for fine work but, due to its clarity and high refractive qualities, will make any engraving work show up more brightly.

Window glass, although it can be used, is not very suitable for engraving. It is extremely hard and will very soon blunt the steel engraving points. The proper name for window glass is soda glass, since this chemical is used in the manufacture. Because of the soda window glass will show a greenish tint when viewed on edge. This also applies to cheap domestic bottles and

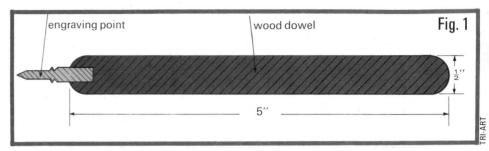

engraving point   wood dowel   Fig. 1

5"   ½"

TRI-ART

Fig.1. It is very important that the engraving point is kept sharp. If it is not, an adequate impression will not be made on the glass. Also, there is a danger that the glass will shatter. A good way of holding the point while it is being sharpened is to fix it into the end of a length of dowel—as shown.

Fig.2. Before the engraving proper can begin, the glass must be firmly fixed over the copy picture. Masking tape is ideal for this. The glass should be laid on a blanket to prevent it being scratched.

Fig.3. The next step is to score the outline of the design—using the point engraving technique.

Fig.4. Shading in the sky is done by wheel

jars, which are not really suitable for engraving.

For continuous work on window glass, such as large panels, a ready mounted diamond point can be obtained for fitting to the electric vibro-engraver.

The glass engraving points

The key to the success of any glass engraving work is the steel point. Unless the tungsten-carbide tip is kept to a needle point sharpness, it will be useless for doing fine work. A slight flatness on a tip will probably bounce off the surface of the glass without leaving a mark. Worse still, such a point could easily chip the glass and shatter it.

By using a green aloxite, the engraving point can be sharpened as you hold it in a piece of dowel rod, as shown in Fig.1. By holding the point in this way, it can be rotated between the fingers whilst moving across the stone at a suitable angle. This angle should be the lowest it can be taken down to, and still wear away the tip. Because the tip is extremely hard, you won't find it an easy job to sharpen. You'll find a

engraving. The wheel should be moved across the glass in even strokes.

Fig.5. Wheel engraving is also used for the grass. A different cutting action is used.

jeweller's eyepiece a useful piece of equipment. One with a $+4$ magnification, or more, will enable you to check the point accurately.

The design

Before beginning your engraving work, it's a good idea to make a detailed drawing of the design you have in mind. As a beginner, you will naturally be tempted to copy someone else's design—but you'll find it very much more satisfying to engrave from a design of your own making. If you are not confident of doing original work successfully, a drawing adapted for engraving will do.

The technique of glass engraving

Very often, it will take a great deal longer to draw out your original design than it will to complete the engraving itself, but the effort will be well worthwhile. A good and carefully prepared drawing will lead to a much improved finished product.

For the beginner, a simple project for practice is that of initialing a tumbler or wine glass. Such

Should this fail to solve the problem, a slight increase in the depth of cut may well be the answer. Remember, however, that this will also mean extra 'hammering' on the glass, which could all too easily result in the glass cracking.

If you do crack the glass, don't immediately assume that it is a result of your own carelessness. Often, glass will crack for no apparent reason. This is unfortunate, but is usually due to the stresses and strains put upon the glass during manufacture, which are only released when the glass is actually pierced. Cracking can even occur some hours after engraving work has been completed. One of the hazards of engraving work is the risk that many hours of patient labour may eventually shatter. Don't let the same thing happen to your enthusiasm, as shattering only occurs in one or two cases in a hundred.

Lines made by the vibro-engraver will be no more than a few thousandths of an inch deep. Because of this, they will easily collect dirt and grease from the hands. An occasional wipe with a patent degreasing solution will soon remove this—making your engraving clean and visible once more.

For solid parts of the design, such as lettering, it is best to just outline the shape first. After the paper pattern has been removed you can proceed to do the in-filling. In order to achieve even finer markings, the engraving point can be used in the sharpening holder. The method will be much the same as the electric vibro-engraver, but of course at a greatly reduced speed. In this way you'll be able to combine the methods of the eighteenth century with the advanced technology of the modern world. It should always be remembered, however, that the vibro-engraver is intended for point work. Wheel engraving should still be done by hand. This is where it is to be done at all, for to rely on frosting large areas of glass to obtain a design is to go against the very nature of the tools and material involved. The best glass engravings rely for their effect on intricate combinations of fine lines.

Providing you possess a sense of balance, as well as a certain amount of artistic flair, you'll be able to create some striking engravings by using only point work. At its best, point engraving is thin and light—the same illusion as glass itself creates.

Above. Simple glass engraving projects are ideal for the beginner. One such is the engraved tumbler shown here.
Right. The tumbler should be held on the knees while engraving takes place. A paper pattern should be fixed inside the glass.

shapes are convenient, since they are cheap and easy to get hold of. Also, it is a simple matter to fix the sample lettering to the inside of the glass. This fixing is best done with a clear adhesive tape, very small strips being all that is necessary or you could use transfers such as Letraset. It is important to make sure that the pattern is level before starting the engraving proper. Once the cut has been started it cannot be removed.

When engraving the glass, the best position to hold the tumbler is cradled on the knees with a black cloth behind it. The purpose of the cloth is to cut any glare from the light. It is for this reason that a piece of black paper should be placed behind the drawn pattern inside the glass. This will prove essential if you intend the pattern to be engraved all round the outside of the glass. Lines showing from the other side of the glass will make it difficult for you to focus properly on those at the front.

In a darkened room, with an adjustable lamp standing on the floor and shining horizontally into the glass, the first cuts can be made. The vibro control on the electric engraver should be adjusted to a very fine setting. Hold the engraver as upright as possible, and as near to a right angle to the glass as is practical. Hold the engraver in the same way as you would hold a ball point pen.

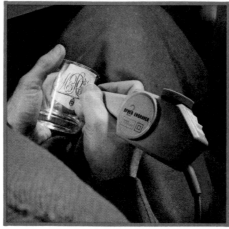

You will eventually come to the stage when the drawing has to be removed, and the details engraved completed freehand. This will apply most to shading. You can do this by gently skating the point across the glass, much as a pencil is used for sketching on paper.

The skills involved in using an electric vibro-engraver are remarkably similar to those needed in driving a car, you go by touch, sound and sight. If, while doing your engraving work, you hear a slight ringing sound or, alternatively, a dull whir, then it is more than likely that your point has become blunt. On the other hand, it may be that the glass you are using is too thin. If this is the case, the point will rebound. This is because thin glass will be slightly flexible. You can overcome this problem by holding the glass firmly while engraving. This will keep the glass rigid.

The finished engraving

There are a number of places where engraved glass can be used to beautify your home. A really ambitious idea is to incorporate engraved glass panels into a partition. This can be used in place of ordinary frosted or clear glass.

You have probably seen glass topped coffee tables many times in the past. Why not extend this idea to include an engraved pattern on the underside of the glass top.

A very simple project would be to engrave drinking glasses with all the names of your family.

When you think about it, you'll find no end of uses that engraved glass can be put to around your home. The technique is straightforward and the equipment inexpensive. Successful glass engraving depends only on your own patience and imagination.

NIGEL MESSETT

These are the inner core of leaves from the African raffia palm, from which the outer skin is removed. It is sold in large hanks by the lb and is quite cheap to buy, but its main disadvantages are that it is of uneven width and lengths and it is not washable. You can sometimes buy it ready dyed in colours.

Alternatively, you can buy synthetic raffia, which is easier to use because it is available in skeins containing a continuous length of about 72ft. It is less bulky and more readily available than natural raffia, and has the additional advantage of being washable and made in a wide range of colours. Its silky sheen is attractive for many projects, although you may prefer the slight 'hairiness' of natural raffia which contributes so much to its texture.

Preparing the raffia

Natural raffia. Tie the bundle tightly at the top with a piece of string and withdraw the strands one by one as you need them. Tighten the string as the bundle becomes smaller.

Pass the strands firmly several times between your thumb and fingers to flatten and straighten them. This will also help to make the pieces supple.

Synthetic raffia. Remove the paper sleeve. If the skein is bound with raffia ties, leave on the one which is made from a short piece and is simply wound round and tied. Undo the other tie, which is made from the two ends of the skein, leave the end which comes from the inside of the skein free and wind the end which is on the outside round the skein and tie off. Use the free end for working—this can be pulled out quite easily without untidying the whole skein.

If the skein is bound with rubber bands, leave these on and tighten them up as the work progresses. Work from the end of raffia which comes from inside the skein.

Use it opened out to its full width (about $\frac{3}{4}$in.) by drawing it between your thumb and first finger before you start work. It may close up a little afterwards, but it will look much more attractive and you will be able to prevent it from twisting.

Plaited raffia

With this method, several strands are plaited together and then the length is coiled into the required shape—usually round or oval—and stitched together. Small baskets can also be made from plaiting, although here a piece of cane should be inserted during the sewing to give strength. Either natural or synthetic raffia can be used. Some practice at even plaiting is essential before you start actually to make anything.

The plaiting is worked with three strands in the technique used for braiding or plaiting hair. The width, or thickness, of the plait is determined by the number of lengths of raffia used in each strand, and here you will have to experiment since it will vary, depending on the raffia and the tightness of your plaiting.

Raffia work

Raffia has long been a popular material for small, decorative items like mats for the table and floor, lampshades and baskets of all types. These can quickly and cheaply be made at home, using simple, age-old techniques. The finished articles have a natural texture which fits well with all decors.

Plaiting, winding on card or cane foundations, and coiling with cane are just some of the methods of working raffia, and the only tools you need are a needle and pair of scissors. Raffia work is pleasant, non-taxing occupation and, once you get into a rhythm, it is the sort of thing you can do while chatting or watching television. Some of the simpler projects are also ideal for children.

The raffia

Traditionally, of course, only natural raffia, in the form of straw-coloured strands, was used.

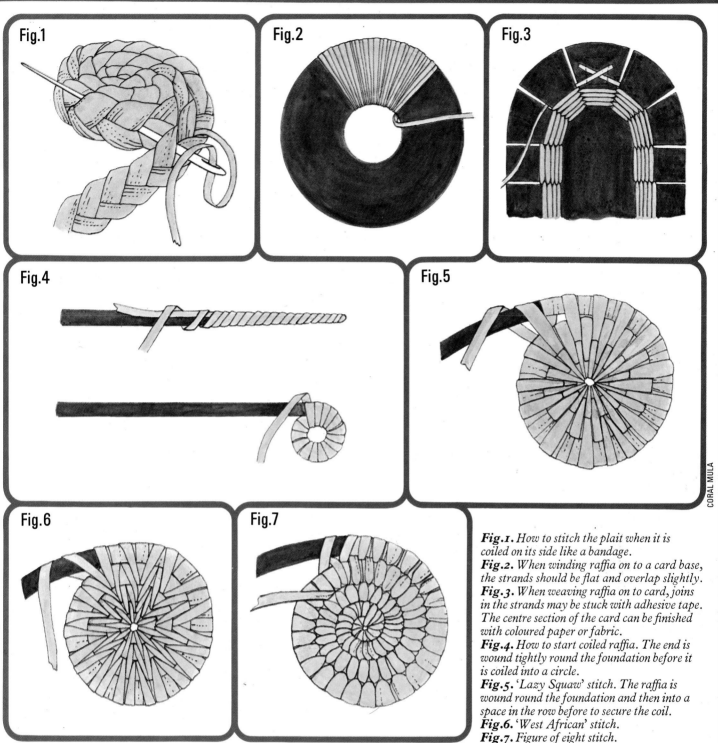

Fig.1. How to stitch the plait when it is coiled on its side like a bandage.

Fig.2. When winding raffia on to a card base, the strands should be flat and overlap slightly.

Fig.3. When weaving raffia on to card, joins in the strands may be stuck with adhesive tape. The centre section of the card can be finished with coloured paper or fabric.

Fig.4. How to start coiled raffia. The end is wound tightly round the foundation before it is coiled into a circle.

Fig.5. 'Lazy Squaw' stitch. The raffia is wound round the foundation and then into a space in the row before to secure the coil.

Fig.6. 'West African' stitch.

Fig.7. Figure of eight stitch.

To start, take a number of pieces of raffia and place them alongside each other with their ends uneven. The ends are left uneven so that you can add pieces without the joins coming in the same place.

Knot the ends of a piece of string, about 12in. long, and loop it over the middle of the raffia, passing the other end of the string through the loop and pull through tightly. Bring all the pieces of raffia together so that they hang with their ends down from the string. Put the string on a hook.

Divide the raffia into three equal sections, judging by feel, rather than number if you are using natural raffia. Start plaiting in the normal way, keeping the plait as compact and flat as

possible. Take each strand across the others almost horizontally, rather than at a sharp angle, and use your thumb to flatten the plait after every move.

To add a strand, place the new piece by the side of the old one and start plaiting it the usual way. Any protruding ends can be trimmed off later.

As the plait lengthens, you may find it easier to unloop it from the hook and tie it further down and re-hook it.

The length of the plait needed depends on its thickness and the method of coiling (see below). As a rough guide, however, for a round mat with 6in. diameter, you will need 3-4oz raffia, making it into a ½in. wide plait, 15ft long, if

the plait is coiled on its side or 9ft long if it is coiled edge to edge.

The same amount of raffia will make an oval mat about 8in. long. For this, turn down the end of the plait 2½in. to make a double thickness and start winding round this.

Sewing up. The plait may be coiled flat and sewn edge to edge as for the rag rugs, or it may be coiled on its side, rather like a bandage. This second method is very neat, and gives a thicker table mat for hot dishes. In either case, use a piece of raffia and a blunt needle for the sewing.

To make a neat, tapered finish, discard pieces on the outside of the plait gradually until only two or three are left in each strand. Cut off the protruding strands, and darn in those which remain in the plait. Press the finished mats with a wet cloth and fairly hot iron.

Baskets. To give the baskets stiffness, a single length of No. 6 centre cane is placed between the plaits as it is coiled up. Soak the cane in water for a few minutes to make it pliable and start coiling the plaits, placing the cane over the join on the side which will come inside the finished basket. Take the stitching over the cane.

Work the base of the basket as for a mat first, then turn up the sides, holding the plait at the angle you require. Stitch firmly, holding the cane tautly. If you have to join on a new piece of cane, taper the ends of each for about 1 in. and overlap them by this amount.

Winding and weaving

Raffia can also be wound or woven on to card or cane shapes, which remain inside the article when it is finished. The shapes can be bought **very cheaply from handicraft shops or else you can make your own, quite simply, thus giving the article an original touch.**

The shapes for winding are normally solid, with a cut-out section in the middle for the raffia to pass through. For weaving, the shapes are divided into wedges with slits (in a similar way to cutting a round cake) of which there should be an uneven number for the raffia to pass over and under.

Winding

The success of winding depends on the raffia being wound so that the strands lie evenly side by side, and for this you may find that synthetic raffia is easier to use. On a mat, where the raffia is taken over the outside of the card and through the centre hole, take care that the strands radiate evenly from the hole on the right side of the mat, but slant on the wrong side.

To join on new strands, tie the ends together with a reef knot on the wrong side near the hole, and tuck the ends under. The knot can be hammered flat, if necessary. To finish off, thread the end into a blunt-pointed needle or bodkin and pass under the winding on the wrong side. Cut off and tuck the end inside.

Weaving

Start at the centre hole of the mat and secure the end of the raffia on the wrong side with the adhesive tape. Take the raffia over the first section, under the second, over the third and so on, pulling it quite taut so that the strand lies round the edge of the centre hole, but without distorting the shape. Continue adding rows, pushing them well together.

To join on a new strand, take the end of the old piece on the wrong side of one of the sections, and cut off level with the slit. Take the end of the new piece through the slit, cross over the old piece and stick the ends down with adhesive tape (Fig.3).

To finish off and cover the edges of the card, cut a few strands of raffia and place round the edge, and stitch on with oversewing, placing each stitch level with the sections. Darn the ends of the strands into the weaving.

Cane frames

Baskets can also be made from cane frames on to which the raffia is wound or woven. The raffia is wound over the sections for the sides and base separately, and then the pieces are stitched or nailed together.

Coiled raffia

With this method, the raffia is wrapped round a piece of cane to give body, and the whole thing coiled into the required shape in the same process. String, cord or strands of raffia may be used instead of cane, if you prefer. Neither the string nor the cane should be less than $\frac{1}{8}$ in. diameter.

If you are using cane, soak it in water to make it pliable, and shave the end to a point.

Place the end of the raffia over the end of the cane or string for about 1 in., then work back over this length, wrapping the raffia round (Fig.4). Coil this into as small a circle as possible, and secure with one or two stitches.

Pass the raffia over the cane and through the hole in the middle of the ring. Wrap round the cane completely, so that the cane is coiling round the ring, and pass the raffia through the whole again. Continue round, working stitches like this and always wrapping the raffia round the cane completely before passing through the middle hole. Overlap the raffia slightly, but do not cover the previous wrap completely. This is known as 'Lazy Squaw' stitch (Fig. 5).

For the second round, wrap the raffia round the cane as before but pass it through the

Below. *Raffia, coiled over strands of cane in the 'Lazy Squaw' stitch may be formed into baskets of different shapes. A flower pot of similar size, can act as a guide to the shape.*

spaces which were made by wrapping it round the cane only.

As you progress, you will have to make more stitches in order to cover the cane completely. This can be done by working two stitches, separated by a wrap, in one space evenly round the coil.

West African stitch. This is similar to Lazy Squaw stitch but in the second row the raffia is taken over the cane into the space of the previous row, wrapped completely round the cane, then taken into the same space as before, thus forming a V. In the following row, the stitches are worked into the opening of the V (Fig.6).

Figure-of-eight stitch. Here the raffia should be brought up through the centre of the coil from underneath, under and round the cane, down behind the edge of the coil and up through the centre again, forming a figure-of-eight. In the second row, the figure-of-eight is worked round the cane and the first row, thus making a very firm fabric.

To join on a new length of raffia, place the end of the old piece and the beginning of the new piece alongside the cane. Wrap the new piece over them, then continue working in the usual way. Trim off any projecting ends when a few stitches have been worked.

To make a basket, start off like a mat and make the base to the required diameter. To form the sides, place the cane on top of the last row and work the raffia over it, held in this position. For upright sides, place the cane exactly over the previous row or for slanting sides place on the cane so that it sticks out slightly.